Still Standing

A mother's raw journey from the shadows of loss to the dawning of hope

Denny Meek

First published by Ultimate World Publishing 2020
Copyright © 2020 Denny Meek

ISBN
Paperback - 978-1-925884-89-0
Ebook - 978-1-925884-90-6

Denny Meek has asserted her right under the Copyright, Designs and Patents Act 1988 to be identified as the author of this work. The information in this book is based on the author's experiences and opinions. The publisher specifically disclaims responsibility for any adverse consequences, which may result from use of the information contained herein. Permission to use information has been sought by the author. Any breaches will be rectified in further editions of the book.

All rights reserved. No part of this publication may be reproduced, stored in or introduced into a retrieval system, or transmitted in any form, or by any means (electronic, mechanical, photocopying, recording or otherwise) without the prior written permission of the author. Any person who does any unauthorised act in relation to this publication may be liable to criminal prosecution and civil claims for damages. Enquiries should be made through the publisher.

Cover design: Ultimate World Publishing
Layout and typesetting: Ultimate World Publishing
Editor: Marinda Wilkinson

Ultimate World Publishing
Diamond Creek,
Victoria Australia 3089
www.writeabook.com.au

EARLY PRAISE FOR

Still Standing

When studying psychology at Macquarie University as young adults, Denny and I spent countless hours discussing theories of human behaviour. It seemed there was an explanation for everything. Those discussions have continued over the years since but the quest for answers has often just raised more questions – especially in a life like Denny's.

This is a brutally honest and candid account of a life lived to the limits of emotional endurance and a mother's unrelenting search for answers. The descriptions are raw and the pain behind them is palpable, but this is no 'why me' story.

It's the journey of a mother navigating her way through a well-meaning but often disjointed health care system programmed to standardise the human experience. It reveals the extent to which 'mother blame', in the absence of definitive science, continued to provide a convenient fallback position as a general assumption. It explores the impacts of family violence, and challenges traditional patriarchal notions of parenting.

It's also a story of a family, a mother's loving tribute to her four beautiful and unique children – because they were, and are, here and their stories need to be heard.

Recommended reading for those contemplating a career in human care, especially mental health, it joins the dots between theory and real life, and offers hope for change for those working to make a difference.

Jane Alison Day, BA Psychology

If the universe can make decisions, it could not have chosen more wisely when selecting Denny to become an educator of grief. A book like this requires great personal strength, courage and insight, and in writing it, Denny confirms she possesses these in abundance. Dragged unwillingly and repeatedly through the Valley of Death, Denny's story is both heartbreaking and hopeful. It paints an uncompromising image of the often chaotic indifference of life, yet gives hope to all of us, not only those affected by grief, that despite the darkest of days there is always the potential for life and love. This is a masterful work, and is deserving of its place alongside other literary giants on the topic. With authority and clarity, Denny has composed a powerful lens for looking at the bigger picture of life, and death, for everyone; particularly those who have to stop, and learn to put one foot after the other again.

Nathaniel Buchanan, former History Head, Qld Education Dept

During weekly sessions as Allie's private psychologist, I had the absolute privilege of sharing her journey with Anorexia Nervosa for a brief time in her adolescence. Allie always struck me as kind and warm and despite struggling at the time, her love and affection for her family was always evident.

There are not many good books out there on these subjects from the lived experience but this one is top of my list right now. It will be an honour to share it in future lectures.

Denny's story will not only touch you as a parent, it will inspire you to want to be better. Her strength, humbleness, openness and courage is on every page. You will finish this book and immediately want to read it again.

Dr Peta Stapleton (nee Hartmann)
Clinical and Health Psychologist, Associate Professor Bond University

Still Standing should be compulsory reading for everyone working or intending to work in health and human services. It is impossible to put down once you start. Writing with vivid intelligence, courage and compassion Denny Meek documents her life at 'the edge of the world where the dragons are' through some of the most painful human experiences: the death of a baby, domestic violence, anorexia and teen suicide. Through her relentless interrogation of self and society, Denny challenges powerful myths about mother and woman blaming while sharing hard earned lessons on how to live with 'big questions unanswered'. Professionals will benefit from the insights Denny offers into what is actually helpful during the darkest times and beyond, from a voice rarely heard: the woman, partner and mother.

Wendy Bowles, Professor of Social Work and Human Services
Acting Head, School of Humanities and Social Sciences, Charles Sturt University

Denny does the impossible in so many ways. For those who have never been close to understanding the immensity of grief and loss, she helps you understand her journey. She is able to write for you about a capacity to love in the face of death. Her journey is of grief and loss of several children regardless of the length of days they lived. She then provides an insight into the added complexity of loss by suicide where nothing makes sense nor provides reassurance for a mother's grief.

Denny tells you about her journey by weaving together five strands of her life, which include the challenges of infant loss, domestic violence, mothering a daughter with an intense eating disorder and the suicide of her two young adult children. Many books have been written about each of these, describing the experiences that form part of the emotional journey with and through distress and grief. This book offers an understanding of all of these experiences in one person's life and is a tribute to an exceptional journey. It is exceptional in describing the immensity of the emotional impact. It is exceptional in showing the demands on human capacity to continue to somehow feel and function. Finally it is also exceptional as it describes a road rarely travelled amid the overwhelming desire to lose oneself and withdraw from others and the world. The one thing Denny could control was the timing of her return.

So much of life and living revolves around being oblivious to our frail and fragile states of being. The privileged ones, who have not experienced deep grief and loss, can invest in hope and aspiration. However they may lose sight of, and access to, a profound sense of life priorities and the raw value of each of us. This book will take you there without needing to experience loss yourself. It will also remind you of grief lessons forgotten and buried, and the wisdom of the many steps necessary to take on as impressive a journey as Denny's.

Alan Richardson, Psychologist,
Educator and Clinical Psychotherapy Supervisor

Contents

Early Praise for *Still Standing* iii
Dedication ix
Introduction xi
Prologue 5
CHAPTER 1: The Colour Blue 7
CHAPTER 2: Cradle to the Grave 39
CHAPTER 3: Breaking the Silence 51
CHAPTER 4: Mama Bear Solo 77
CHAPTER 5: Pursuit of Perfection 95
CHAPTER 6: A Withdrawal 123
CHAPTER 7: Beauty and The Beast 151
CHAPTER 8: Reflections from the Valley 183
CHAPTER 9: Private Ryan 203
CHAPTER 10: Catapulting out of the Valley 209
Appendix A 221
Appendix B 223
Bibliography 225
Acknowledgements 231

Dedicated to:

Simon
Joseph
Allie
& Ash

Introduction

Whosoever survives a test,
whatever it may be,
must tell the story.
That is his duty.
Eliezer Wiesel
WWII Concentration Camp Survivor

*I*n this memoir are intense life stories I've wanted to tell for a long time.

From the Valley of Grief, I became a recluse, and in sharing from that exiled state, I hope bereaved parents find a place where their losses are honoured.

In situations of powerlessness, I continued journalling. In sharing my excerpts, I hope the disenfranchised find a safe space of understanding and validation.

Journalling through a challenging life has been my key coping mechanism. Available to me 24/7, I've written to communicate with my self: to help me process experiences, to see my ideas reflected on a page, to recognise behaviour patterns in myself and others, to clarify thoughts and revise conclusions, to advise and encourage myself. From the depths of new insights, my journal supplies a hard drive to hold inner dialogues between conflicting voices striving for clarity, to hoard precious memories I was scared of forgetting, to file dreams where my children have communicated with me. It's become a type of portal where I could speak to them, maintaining our humour, caring and love, while gradually establishing aspects of a new relationship. Journalling for me has been more than containing grief in words. In a death-denying world, the loss of my children has prompted me to speak my truth in whatever language I could find.

In his book *Full Dark, No Stars*, Stephen King says bad writing 'arises from a stubborn refusal to tell stories about what people actually do' and that he has no patience with writers who hold onto ideals that humans are either all good or all bad, or that things work out well in the end.

I like this. It frees me to show my story as it happened, rather than caretaking a simpler picture, nurturing cherished assumptions that cushion our everyday lives: that children who've died were angels who 'didn't need to stay'; that perpetrators of domestic violence are character-flawed fiends; that women in violent relationships are weak; that people end their lives because of mental illness; that Anorexia Nervosa is caused by domineering mothers; that the loss of a baby isn't as painful as the loss of a grown child; that God is good; that there's a 'good reason' for everything; that meaning in life is to be found, if you only look; that life is about lessons, and the more painful the 'lesson', the more important the learning.

It's freeing to not bear this responsibility. To not have to work with, around, uphold, or even disprove commonly held notions, but to leave my story with readers to make sense of themselves. To present it all as it was. To not have to safeguard impressions, but to unveil puzzling paradoxical truths, and let them speak for themselves: *Life is confusing.*

Working on this book has given me a purpose. Belief systems toppled to the bottom of my grief pit, ushering me into a 'dark night of the soul' – a time without meaning. This period wasn't about appearing 'strong', even to myself, or of choosing beliefs I'd have preferred to embrace, but of making meaning for my Self. A blessed morsel of stubbornness kept me plodding with determination to express my complaints to the world. *I will have my say.* Articulating my journey impelled me to process from those depths; I had to push harder, further. The book became my mission, lighting my step, pulling me forward. Have I found 'meaning' in my losses? No. Has book-writing been 'cathartic'? No. But constant pushing does birth a significance for me.

My story includes a spiritual journey in which I began life as a Christian. In my late 30s, I also became a professional Reader of the Tarot. For five years, in many different environments, I read for the public – in my home, in theirs, at Sunday markets in Bellingen, the Gold

Coast, at expos, festivals, Tarot parties, on a psychic phone line and as the in-house Reader at a Medieval Theatre Restaurant. When Readers/Readings are referred to here, they're differentiated with a capital 'R'. My beliefs have continued to evolve since then, and as always, I have no need to convince anyone – including myself – of any particular viewpoint, but would continue to encourage others to trust their inner knowing, to accept what resonates with them.

In real life, themes don't inhabit neat chapters as they do here, but cross each other messily. Some chapters overlap in time, so note the dates and strap yourselves in for the ride!

For the men with whom I had my relationships, who featured in my life as my intimate partners, I retain a kind of loving. There's much that can't be conveyed in a book. *Life is complex.*

My personal reply to the mother-blaming social attitudes I encountered around Anorexia Nervosa lies in continuing to learn to love myself through it all, and despite it all, the cultural reply to which lies in addressing these attitudes more openly. I hope relaying our story helps.

Suicide is another issue our culture struggles with. In sharing our story, I take a risk: that when lives are viewed through the suicide lens, the mind is looking for answers, and the existence we spent as everyday interactive people will be missed. Each day of that invaluable life is seen in reverse, back through the lens of that death, rather than forward from the moment of their birth. Significance is attached where there was none, normal behaviours pathologised, strengths of character overlooked, so great is our need to understand. Just as an anorexia sufferer looks in the mirror and sees a distorted image of what's there, so our perception is coloured when looking back through the suicide lens. It doesn't show us what we're looking for; it shows us what we're looking at – there are no answers, no absolutes – but it allows onlookers safety, with opportunities to scrutinise others' lives from a distance, and to shift or shore up the walls of their assumptive worlds.

Lens aside, I've needed to write about my children – because they were here; because for however long it is, a life on this planet counts; and because every human life, with all its stories, is amazing, colourful, precious, and sacred, and deserves to be honoured.

21 January 2003

It was just after 3am when the knocking woke me.

I'd been in bed for only two hours. *Must be Simon – can't find his key so he's knocking.*

There are voices, more than one – male voices – and they're not whispering. *Must be some of Simon's mates looking for him.*

Through bleary eyes I see a torch shining through the window. Are they uniforms I'm seeing through the leadlight? Ashley's sitting up. He's been woken by all the knocking.

I flick on a light and approach the entrance. It's the police. *Might have the wrong address.*

I open the door of my life to its major turn and surrender control – if I ever had it – into the hands of fate.

'Mrs Meek?' asks the police officer with the torch.

'Yes,' my obligatory response. At any other time I would've said, 'No. It's *Ms*.' But three police officers are not knocking on my door at this hour to play gender games. I move my little pawn in cooperation with the great Chessboard and vacantly watch formalities tumble out his mouth.

I think he tells me he's a senior constable. He asks if it's alright if they come in. The absence of alarm in his voice, I greatly appreciate. He sees my 10-year-old son sitting upright on the lounge and asks if there's somewhere we can go for a chat.

I lead the procession up the stairs through the dark house, again very grateful for the lack of urgency in this messenger's manner. It's giving me a moment in between, of breathing my last few breaths of the life I came to gently love, before I must say goodbye to it. As yet I don't know why, and that ignorance is bliss. Thank you God for the angels you send to look after us in these most shocking moments of our lives.

Upstairs, the senior constable doesn't sit on the couch next to me. He sits up on the arm. He's the 'teller', and we're all in position.

'You're Simon's mother?' he checks.

'Yes.' Again, I'm grateful for the extra second, for it is the last second of my old life.

'I'm afraid we have some bad news.' He opens wide the heavy door and escorts me straight through it. 'Simon passed away last night.'

'NO! NO! NO! NO! NO!' I'm shaking my head. 'NO! NO... No... No... No...' My hand holds my forehead. I'm falling through the moment. My eyes shut. My head wants to shake it away. **'NO!'**

A shallow breath ushers itself into my body. I lift my face.
'How?' I look at the senior constable.
'He gassed himself in his car.'
'Oh my God! Oh my God! Oh god! *Ugh!*' I've involuntarily grabbed the constable's hand, clutching it tightly. '*Oh, God...*'

Another breath in of my new life.
I ease my eyes open, inhaling shock. Moments pass. *Stunned.*
Where was Simon? Quick to comfort, they carry me into details. '...mouth of the river', 'edge of the sea', 'peaceful place'... I hear only splinters... 'a few trees...', moon 'still quite full'. My eyes stare ahead, my disbelieving mind conjuring a place I don't know... some dark riverbank with small lonely oak trees, Simon's empty car parked on the side, a long way from anywhere, no person around, no sounds, a sad desolate setting.

Who found him? 'A young couple noticed his car on their way out of the car park. They flagged down a council worker in a passing truck and asked him to ring an ambulance...' I spend minutes in between trying to get my mind to absorb minutiae, the only one ringing, *Simon passed away last night*. Thankfully the officers don't talk, but wait for my next question.

How does the mind even keep functioning? It is surreal. *Simon has died*. Eighteen years and his life finished. Dead. *Surreal!*

The sober young officer standing doesn't speak. The young female officer in the armchair opposite adds an occasional detail. 'Simon looked very peaceful,' she tells me. *Did he?* 'Yes, he looked asleep in the moonlight.'

A closeness settles over the room. The senior officer gently follows procedure. 'Had Simon been depressed, had anything been troubling him lately?' He hadn't been *in* a depression I tell them, but he'd suffered a blow when his Charger crashed two-and-a-half weeks earlier. I knew that was hard for him, but I would not have expected this.

Is there someone they can call to come and be with me? No thanks, there's no-one I want with me right now; no-one would know how to share this with me.

Later they ask again. I scan the obvious choices and again tell them no. 'You might be alright on your own just now,' the constable tells me, 'but later when you start to feel a bit differently, it'd be better if you had someone with you.'

I succumb to the logic and surrender my poor sister's phone number.

Four am. The female officer rings, and delivers the news. My sister's desperate '*NO!*' echoes through the mobile.

This is just the beginning...

Half an hour later, I sit down next to Ash, my arm around his child's body.

'Sweetheart? You see how the police are here?' He nods. 'Do you know why? Did you hear us?' He shakes his head no. 'They brought some very bad news Ash. It's very bad news, okay? It's Simon, sweetheart... Simon's died.' Ashley's face begins to crumple into a cry, as though in a dream, and falls on my chest. His innocent sobs soon fade into faint sniffles. I sit and hold him for a while, both of us quiet...

I realise I must go and tell Allie. I walk halfway up the hall, turning on lights as I go. I don't want to wake her into this new life. I want to let her sleep peacefully in our old life, where she still has her big brother, of the Hansel-and-Gretel duo. She hears me coming and taps her touch-lamp.

I sit on the side of the bed; Allie's propped up on one elbow, looking at me. 'It's bad news, Allie.'

'Is it Dad?' A little frown furrows her brow.

I shake my head.

'Is it to do with Simon's car?' the little frown deepens.

Fifteen years is all she got with him.

'Simon died.'

'No he didn't,' Allie tells me. She shakes her head at me, pupils dilated. 'No he didn't... No he didn't... No he didn't...'

'He gassed himself in his car.'

'No he didn't.'

I look away, trying to absorb what I just said.

We are motionless, dazed.

After a moment, Allie asks, 'Does this mean we're not going camping?'

'I think it'll take a while for us to realise all this means for us,' I quietly reply.

'The police are here… Do you want me to bring Ashley up?'

Yes.

I go and get Ash and walk him up to Allie's room, my arm around his shoulders.

We sit together on the edge of Allie's bed, huddled against the moment.

The three of us stare, glass-eyed, in stunned silence.

Tasmania, 1983

The silence breaks.

Two pairs of curious eyes fixed on me as my little Austin puttered through the township, its main street stretching 700 metres from one end to the other. I'd never been here before, and the locals knew it.

At 22, the world at my feet, I'd expected to return to Sydney, the prospect of another degree or prestigious job, lively social life, all ahead for me in Australia's largest city.

Instead, life was bustling me along in the opposite direction, doors flying open, to the remote quiet of outback Tasmania.

Here in St Mary's, population 600, I was to start work with the young unemployed at a Community Youth Support centre, in a project that'd been closed for three months.

My first few days saw only two participants: a French boy named Olivier and a hippie from the hills named Peter. By the end of my first week, the pair had gone roo-spotlighting together, and one had accidentally shot the other in the foot. Peter went to hospital and Olivier went into hiding.

This certainly was an adventure. *I could die here and no-one would know.*

But I'd been brought to this island for a reason: to meet my husband, to conceive my first child.

The day the hippie strolled into CYSS, I rolled my eyes inwardly. *I'm gonna have to work with all sorts in here, aren't I?!* It was when we said hello – there was a prolonged timeless moment, a hiccup on the continuum – and this is the one I've looked back on all my life. It's *this* moment, right here, like others, I've wondered about: *Was it meant? Was there really a choice?* I didn't believe in love at first sight, yet I fell despite myself. The term 'soulmate' wasn't in use, past lives were a concept used in India, yet I'd never felt more met before in my life.

An intelligent man, Pete had grown up in Melbourne. He now lived simply in a cabin on a hillside, no electricity, no running water. Psychically sensitive, he felt closer to God in nature, the fewer material distractions, the better. The bush provided an uncomplicated refuge among the elements, birds and animals, and the peace he sought to renew his energies. He read his bible at night by kerosene lantern, his German shepherd curled at his feet. No TV, he preferred to sit and ponder his own thoughts, gazing through flames in his pot-belly stove.

For months, I fought a losing battle. Despite Olivier's insistence that *he* should be the one to win my heart – because he had 'a nicer car' than Pete – I surrendered to the pull that was greater than me. I didn't just follow my heart; I followed my soul.

Just out of St Marys, Pete and I were gifted five acres on a Christian community – and there's another one of those moments. *What if we'd settled in our beloved Tassie and lived on that land?*

I took the hippie to my hometown instead, back to 'the north island' as Tasmanians called the mainland, and we were married.

After our wedding, living on a diet of Violet Crumbles and watermelon, we watched my belly grow.

We were sure we saw a foot push against the skin of your outside world several times the other day. It seemed you'd changed positions. Sure enough, at the doctor's the next day, your back was down the opposite side. You used to get the hiccups too! And I'd hope that you'd be born with your dad's eyes.

CHAPTER 1

The Colour Blue

*You made all the delicate inner parts of my body
and knit me together in my mother's womb...
You saw me before I was born.
Every day of my life was recorded in your book.
Every moment was laid out before a single day had passed.*
Psalm 139:13, 16, New Living Translation Bible

March 1986

'Cover that baby up!' Dr Betty's instruction is urgent.
His mass of long black hair is wet. His first cry is yet to pierce the air.

'We've got him under the lamp!' A nurse's voice.

'Weight 7lb1oz!'

'See if he'll take a drink,' Dr Betty suggests.

Covered in vernix, the soft little body's swiftly wrapped and handed to me. At the breast, his mouth doesn't suck. The warm new bundle lies flaccid in my arms, eyes closed. I want to drink in every feature, but Dr Betty's taking no chances.

Another moment and our new son is whisked out of the labour ward.

Under the brighter lights of the nursery, Dr Betty takes a closer look. The sleepy baby's a dusky colour, his chest drawing in slightly as he breathes. The stethoscope checks heart and breathing – both are a bit fast. The paediatrician is called, checks him over and injects intramuscular antibiotic. He's X-rayed, swabbed everywhere, tested for infection. A nasogastric tube inserted through his nose, taped across his cheek, will feed him in the humidicrib.

In those first few days of our son's life, we didn't know what was happening. The symptoms weren't adding up. My pregnancy neared its end with a slow leak in the membranes at 36 weeks, and again at 37½ weeks accompanied by a fever. It confused the medicos, threw them off track. They were looking for a possible intra-uterine infection: our baby could be born with septicaemia, pneumonia, brain damaged, or dead. He was induced 2½ weeks early and monitored.

Next morning, a sister pushes the trolley into my room, nametag: 'My name is JOSEPH'.

'Here he is!' Smiling, she passes the tiny baby to me. He relaxes into the snuggle. My love is powerful, instant. Pete and I get in close for our first cuddle, brushing Joseph's soft cheeks. Smiling, we identify his features: his eyes big and dark, eyebrows widely arched, Pete's olive skin, slender hands and fingers held in square fists, broad shoulders, a long body, and masses of thick black curly hair. He's so good-looking! Joseph just blinks – three of us in this heavenly bubble.

My dear Dr Betty attended twice daily, conferring at every change with the paediatrician. Joseph was feeding well, feeding poorly, breathing fast, breathing more normally, heart rate often high. 'Some babies just take a little longer to get used to being in the world.' I noticed his hands and feet were sometimes bluey-grey. She was concerned about pneumonia and instructed staff that 'he's not to get cold', stirring a disquiet in me.

My parents bring Simon, now 18 months, who looks big propped up on my bed beside his baby brother. What a buzz: we can refer to our sons as 'the boys'!

It's ironic how Life directs people onto your path, brings you a step closer to experiences, fascinating how we're inexplicably drawn to understand them. In the nursery, feeding their babies, a new mother talks constantly about the stillborn son she'd had the year before – of her reaction on finding out he was dead, of his birth, his burial arrangements. I'm intrigued: I feel deep compassion, but also unsettled to hear how she went to the mortuary and asked to see him, holding him, sobbing, 'Oh my baby, my baby.' Her new son's now asleep in her arms. *Why is it so nice that your new baby looks like his dead brother? Why are you talking so much about your baby's death last year?* The idea that women who'd lost babies would be plied with, 'Go home and have another one' was ridiculous to me. But I'd wonder ahead if her new baby had brought balm to her grief.

It relieves me to hear a doctor say they 'always listen to a mother's worry'. I mentioned Joseph's jaundice on Day Four, his bilirubin level tested high, and he was treated with phototherapy in the humidicrib. On Day Five, I mentioned his visibly fast breathing; another X-ray revealed fluid in his lung. 'The *infection*!' Dr Betty was relieved, mostly. The paediatrician diagnosed pneumonia and started him on antibiotics.

On Day Six, I had to go home – without Joseph. He needed to stay in the humidicrib for now.

Entering the kitchen door, no big tummy, no baby in my arms, a moment's eye contact with my mum, and the emptiness erupted; I sobbed buckets.

The following afternoon, the maternity sister phoned. 'The doctor wants the paediatrician to have a look at Joseph's latest X-ray. You might like to drop your next bottle up to coincide with his visit? He can answer your questions.'

4:30pm: the elevator door dings and lets me out to the familiar smells and cool air of maternity.

Dr Cherry, the paediatrician from Tweed Heads, gives me his full attention, pulling up Joseph's X-ray on the light box.

'This mottling in his lung hasn't cleared up.' He replaces the X-ray. 'Today's X-ray shows the fluid's all over *both* lungs.' Through the dark film, white streaks cloud Joseph's lungs.

'The pneumonia's worse?'

'I'm not sure it's pneumonia – he's not responding to the antibiotics. His breathing's almost twice what it should be...'

This sounds dreadful! What's happening?!

In his humidicrib, Joseph's wearing only a nappy. Dr Cherry checks the tiny body with his stethoscope. 'Heart rate's 168... better if it was 120.' He feels his abdomen. 'Liver's up too.'

Oh GOD! I no longer hear other words. My heart rate has soared. My head's scattered. *PETE!!*

Back in the office, Dr Cherry looks squarely at me.

'Right, he'll have to go straight to Brisbane.' Two hours away.

NO! My hand hits my chest.

'I *think* Joseph might've been born with an abnormal heart structure,' his gentle, direct manner helps. 'In Brisbane they can do tests, and they're equipped to deal with problems they find.'

'How soon?'

He checks with a nurse. 'The ambulance leaves in half an hour.'

Shocked, adrenalin pumps, my mouth dry. Unseeing, I scour the noticeboard in front of me. *Not sure it's pneumonia… his liver's up… straight to Brisbane…*

I turn to a nurse. 'Would you please ring my parents.'

Joseph, due for a feed, begins to snuffle around. Dr Cherry's given him injections to help his heart pump more efficiently, and to help him start to wee out the fluid in his lungs, now suspected congestion from his heart not working properly. To allay possible stomach upset on the trip, he tells the nurses to give Joseph a half-feed. A sister hands me a small blue esky, an ice brick, and three bottles of my now-labelled expressed breast milk.

'If Joseph does have a heart abnormality,' I ask Dr Cherry, 'will he be alright?'

'Depends.' Grabbing paper and pen, he draws hearts, chambers and vessels. For a moment, my world seems weirdly back-to-front. 'Some of these conditions are *very* rare. Sometimes it can be a hole between the chambers. Or a problem with a main vessel. If it's *this* one' – pointing to a diagram – 'they'll put him on heart medication to help him out for a while. But I don't *think* it's that.'

I really hope you're wrong! 'Which other one could it be?'

'Most of these can't be helped just with medication.'

'What do they do?'

'Open-heart surgery.' Eyeball to eyeball.

'On a *baby*?!'

'Yes.'

Oh I hope you're a bad doctor! Hope you don't know what you're talking about! Hope you're prone to exaggeration! No-one here's mentioned hearts to me this week. Unfortunately his integrity and conviction leave me in no doubt.

'The little ones do quite well. They recover quite quickly. And Joseph's a good colour.'

'Can they do something about *any* structure?'

'Almost – unless he has a chamber missing.' He sketches the picture. 'If one of his four chambers is missing, there won't be much they can do for him.'

'He'd *die*?'

'Yes.'

Staff buzz around preparing for our trip, while I search Joseph's tiny body for clues of what lies ahead. His broad square shoulders, thick hair, square clenched fists: I see strength in these features, exuding the aura of a fighter. I take heart.

Late this sunny Sunday afternoon, out the bottom door to emergency, the ambulance is backed up to the waiting bay doors. I haven't been in an ambulance. Donna, the maternity nurse, helps load Joseph's humidicrib. My parents have brought me a bag – and Simon. I quickly cuddle Sime, and hug my parents goodbye. *I don't wanna do this.*

The driver starts the engine. 'Fast trip, or normal speed, Donna?'

'Normal, thanks Roy.'

No siren, no speed – just those urgent flashing lights.

A whole two hours away... time to process...

On the outskirts of town, the driver wants to chat. My stomach clenches, my eyes glass over. I can't speak across the lump in my throat... I stare out the passenger window, Dr Cherry's drawings filling my head. Stretching away from the roadside, like lifetimes merging together at the end, perfectly straight rows of green sugarcane rise, no water leaking from one row to the next, no stalk growing out of place. At this trip's end, no such order awaits. A fate already spreads out before me in the tiny heart that will change my life, where some chamber leaks from one to the next, some vessel grows out of place. *Joseph might die!* I don't wanna think about it. *They might be wrong...* It's too late for denial to stop this unfolding.

Every now and then along the freeway, I turn back to Donna, glimpsing Joseph's dark hair in the crib. 'How is he?' *Will he die before we get there?* My real question.

'He's good... just having a little sleep.'

I feel my eyes protruding like unseeing glass. 'How's his breathing?'

'Good,' *she doesn't want to tell me,* 'better than before we left'.

And Joseph's a good colour, I make Dr Cherry's voice repeat in my head.

I know God allows some people to go through terrible things... but this is me...

I shut my eyes. *As long as it's not the missing chamber.*

Too soon along the freeway, the driver turns around. 'The Mater, Donna?'

'Yes, Roy.'

Too big... too urban... too anonymous...

'Is that the Stanley Street exit, or Vulture Street, Donna?'

The furthest away – please...

'Stanley Street exit.'

My stomach constricts, my abdomen cramps as 'STANLEY STREET EXIT' burns itself into my memory forever.

We arrive at the back of the large hospital when Pete pulls up in our XB Falcon. I need his hug, his familiar feel, his comfort. We follow staff as they rush Joseph's humidicrib through the passageways.

Striding down a corridor of the Mater Children's Hospital, I'm disembodied – one of those mothers whose baby had to be taken to a large city hospital. Into the darkened children's ward, passing large windowed rooms, small children pop up from their beds to watch. Toddlers on the other side of the glass, attached by tubes to drip-stands at their sides. Three and four-year-olds, large newly stitched scars right across the top of their small shaven heads. Each step we take pulls us further inside this other world of seriously sick babies, alarm bells screaming. *Where in this scene do we belong?! What's in store for us? Don't think! Breathe deep. Look straight ahead.*

Joseph's humidicrib is wheeled into a square well-lit room, monitors, sockets, leads, medical equipment packed around its walls.

Donna turns to us. 'All the best!' ...and the only person who knew our names leaves the big Brisbane hospital.

Staff in white uniforms wheel equipment around Joseph's humidicrib, turning on monitors, connecting wires... a sense of battening down the hatches.

It's three hours since Joseph's half-feed. He's started snuffling around, whimpering, his mouth turning towards the hand that accidentally brushes his cheek. I head into the booth as a young blonde sister sticks round white pads onto Joseph's torso.

'He's due for a feed –' I begin.

'This is *mum*, is it?' she glances at me.

'Yes.'

'Gee he's grumpy, isn't he!' She fastens another 'happy face' to his soft new skin. 'A grumpy bub!'

'He's just hungry,' I plead uncertainly on Joseph's behalf. 'Could he have his feed soon?'

'We have to do some tests first. Just take your bottles to the nurse – she'll put them in the fridge for you.'

'When would he – his feed –' I step out of her way.

'When we finish our testing... Maybe... an hour?'

Joseph's dummy is pushed aside as he starts to cry.

Pete and I are asked to remain outside the testing room. Before long, the young nurse pierces Joseph's skin with a needle – the first of several tonight. The scream Joseph releases somehow sounds like the beginning.

Our backs against a far wall, Pete and I stand by, and through the booth's large window, watch Joseph scream through hours of continual testing. Our baby is held flat, turned over, prodded, pierced with needles, X-rayed, swabbed, turned again by the three young expressionless staff. No comfort is given – no dummy, no back patting, no reassuring tones. In Joseph's voice, we hear the distress that resonates with an awareness of his helplessness, and ours too. When he draws breath at the end of each scream, we hear he's not going to stop, that his screaming's going to go on and on and on. I imagine staff have to disconnect themselves to carry out their work, but it's not their feelings I care about. It looks like Joseph's been abducted by aliens, and is being scientifically investigated in their high-tech brightly lit booth.

'Where's *mum* staying?' a nurse asks us. Joseph and I have become nameless: 'mum' with-a-small-m, and 'bub'. Accommodation is the last thought on our minds.

We're ushered to a unit where we can stay overnight. Returning twenty minutes later, Joseph's cries echo up the corridor. He's been turned onto his tummy, now screaming so hard, limbs so taut above his clamped umbilical cord, he looks to be almost physically crawling. He is eight days old.

Screaming on his back now, little arms clenching and flailing, I see the young nurse use her thumb from underneath his chin to force it upwards, trying to shut his mouth. She wants to take a reading from one of the monitors; apparently Joseph's crying is distracting. My mouth drops open in disbelief.

I step closer to the booth. When she notices me, she gives Joseph's back a couple of token pats, stretching away from him, as though avoiding connection, her face blank.

Through the window of a dimly lit room facing the nurses' station, a mother gently rocking her sleepy toddler beckons me. I pop my head around her door.

'Don't watch!' she whispers.

'They're *torturing* him! That nurse was forcing his mouth shut – trying to stop him from crying!'

'I know,' the mother replies, 'it's not convenient to their testing when they cry... But there's nothing you can do. They have to do these things. It's best you go away somewhere else. Don't put yourself through it. *Don't watch!*'

She seems familiar with the system. I don't want to abandon Joseph, but I have to acknowledge her logic.

Pete and I accept this. We go for a walk, and never do watch Joseph being tested again.

More than three hours after our arrival, we return to the ward. The testing's finished. Our baby's finally being given his feed. An older nurse holds a large syringe attached to Joseph's nasogastric tube. The mixture's very white – not the cream colour of breast milk. 'What's he having?' I ask.

'Nan (*formula*),' she smiles.

'He's on breast milk. He has three bottles of expressed milk in the milk-room fridge.' *Is there some medical reason for this?*

She checks Joseph's chart, her smile fading. 'Oh... so he is... *"EBM"*... Well, he'll have it next time.'

Where are we?? No-one matters here!!

Pete and I watch our son like stunned zombies. A different baby now, he's no longer 'a good colour'. Lying on his back, he pants, eyes closed, breathless, pale, dark head on the side, unmoving, oblivious to his surroundings. His hands, wrists, and feet look like grey pin cushions. Even to us, Joseph *looks* very sick now.

Before we leave, we talk to the young doctor with the ice-coloured eyes. 'Seems to be a problem with his heart,' he says.

'Do you know what it is?'

'Not exactly. We're sending him to Chermside, north of Brisbane, tomorrow morning. Ambulance leaves at 6:30.'

7:00am: We pull up at another hospital on Brisbane's north side. It's 15 hours since Pete and I thought our baby had pneumonia and that we'd soon be bringing him home. We escort staff and humidicrib inside big glass sliding doors. We know no-one's name, no-one knows ours, no-one's explaining much. After this 'test', we assume we'll return to the Mater.

On the ground floor, we trail Joseph's humidicrib into a long warm nursery. An array of sockets line walls behind humidicribs and cots. Babies of different ages lie in metal-framed beds with high sides, amongst six cots in a row under bright colourful curtains. Sun beams through large windows onto a forest of twirling mobiles hanging from the ceiling. This is the cardiac nursery of the Prince Charles Hospital. We'll soon discover that its ten beds hold the sickest heart babies in all of Queensland and northern NSW.

The sister in charge behind the desk, an older woman with short grey hair and glasses, barks loudly at staff who've brought Joseph from the Mater. *'DON'T* show me your PAPERS! I'm not signing any papers till I've had a look at this baby! Right? The papers can wait! The baby comes FIRST!'

The words would comfort me, if the tone didn't terrify me. It's Sister Margaret Morris who's marched very smartly into our lives this morning. With a bark only a little worse than her bite, we're about to learn how highly she prioritises her patients and their families.

She introduces us to Cardiologist Dr Andrew Galbraith, who opens the side of Joseph's humidicrib with gentle hands. 'We'll take Joseph in for an echocardiogram – like a depth-sounder that scans his heart – giving us a better picture of what's going on.' His voice is tender, his eyes soft as he gazes over our baby. Before placing his stethoscope on Joseph, he rubs it on his own shirt to warm it first. *Thank you, God: a humane doctor.*

While Joseph's in Echo, we're advised to book a nearby motel.

Later, Dr Galbraith asks us into his private office, where laminated posters display pictures of the heart and varying abnormalities.

'We think Joseph was born with a very rare formation – here,' he says, pointing. 'Only 1% of babies born with heart abnormalities have this structure – and it's complicated. It's called *Total Anomalous Pulmonary Venous Drainage* (TAPVD). All four veins coming back from the lungs are going to the wrong side of the heart and mixing with the used blood.'

Pete and I listen closely, trying to breathe steadily, intent on every word. Joseph had done fine in utero while my heart-lung system was oxygenating his blood across the placenta for him, but as soon as he was born and his own heart-lung system kicked in, he started to circulate used and oxygenated blood – together – around his body.

'Cyanosis' – the blue colouring in Joseph's lips, hands and feet – is caused by the poorly oxygenated blood circulating around his body, the oxygen not properly reaching those outer peripheries. About a quarter of babies born with heart abnormalities have the rarer structures resulting in this blue colouring. Joseph is a 'Blue Baby'.

'We can correct TAPVD with open-heart surgery,' Dr Galbraith continues, 'and if he gets through that, we expect he'll be okay. Some other more common heart conditions need further surgery as the child grows. We expect to correct Joseph's problem now and that'll be it.'

'There's also a small vessel babies have before they're born near the top of the heart that closes off at birth. Joseph's didn't.' The doctor points again. 'This is *Patent Ductus Arteriosus,* a little more common, not as serious as TAPVD, but we'll need to correct it. For now, it's actually a small help to Joseph to have that vessel open, so we'll give him something to keep it open till surgery.'

'You're sure this is what he has?' Pete nods to the TAPVD diagram.

'As sure as we can be. We'll need your permission to do a cardiac catheterisation to confirm it. There's a slight risk with the catheterisation, but if he doesn't come through that, he almost surely would not have made it through surgery.'

It suddenly strikes me as ludicrous that the cardiologist's sitting chatting calmly about these life-and-death issues. I feel a scream rising in my throat. *This is bullshit! You don't know what you're talking about! You're making this up!* I feel I'm about to lose control, to shriek, or laugh out loud. This would later be described to me as *hysteria*.

'I was worried he might have a missing chamber...'

'No, he has all his chambers.'

Thank God!

'How many babies are born with his condition?'

'One in 20,000.' A statistic we will *never* forget.

'I took a few drugs when I was younger,' Pete tells the doctor. 'Could that've caused Joseph's heart problems?'

'No. Its cause is unknown, but we *do* know it's not caused by things like that. It's just something in you two as a couple.'

'Our other son's heart is fine.'

'Yes,' Dr Galbraith nods. *Serious congenital heart disease is not all that common.*

'Will any other children we have be alright?'

'They *will* have an increased risk of being born with a heart abnormality – four times greater – than the rest of the population.'

'When will Joseph need the surgery?'

'By the end of the week.'

'Is this the only way to fix it?' Pete has the presence of mind to continue asking what I don't.

'Yes. They've been correcting this condition successfully with open-heart surgery for five years now. It's the only way to correct it.'

'Will he make it?'

'There *is* a high risk, maybe a 30% chance, he won't come through.' Pete and I exchange glances. 'But if he doesn't have the surgery, he will most certainly die.'

His words, bare, chilling, slice the air like a scalpel.

Pete will sign our permission this afternoon.

'How long will the surgery take?'

'Around four hours – if all goes as we expect.'

'When will you do it?'

'We'll try to fit him in – in the next few days.'

Pete heads out for a ciggie. I sit beside the humidicrib.

This is impossible, Joey... Look at you. You're perfect! How could you be so 'deformed' on the inside?? 'DIE' by the end of the week?? I search his striking features. The urge to flight impels my body to run to the motel, to stay there till it's over. *...IMPOSSIBLE!!*

From the inside of this new world, I finally give in to the tears... freely audibly weeping.

Reflection from 11 March 2012

I didn't understand what I felt in that moment. The courage it'd take just to face the open-heart surgery – even if things did go well – was more than I could imagine, let alone actually muster.

How hard can emotions be? When fear is involved, they can get tricky. 'Grieving for a baby,' I remember learning, 'can be complicated. They're too small to express harder emotions at inside yourself, because they're defenceless.' Add to that, a very sick one. In that moment, it was dangerous for me to love my dear little son, my love flowing normally as it would if he was well, and not maybe about to die.

Sister Morris is watching from her bench. 'Would you like to speak to the social worker?'

I look down, covering my crying mouth. *I don't know.*

Sister Morris seems sure of how this place runs – as reliably as a bypass machine.

I relent, and Sister Morris makes us an appointment with Bridget.

From her small office on the eighth floor, in her thick Irish brogue, Bridget explains. 'Parents handle this situation differently. Smoking more, wanting to run – they're normal early reactions for parents whose babies are diagnosed with life-threatening conditions. You might be frightened of getting too close to Joseph because he's very sick – and if he dies, you *will* get hurt.'

'Some parents run,' Bridget continues. 'Bit by bit, they'll start to show an interest in caring for it themselves, because afterwards it looks like it might survive, and be safe for them to love again.' I don't want Joseph to feel – or be – abandoned. *I don't want to miss out on him* either.

'Some parents don't take the risk at all, and only let their heart go when they're finally driving home with their baby, down Rode Road.' The way Bridget says 'down Rode Road' sounds profound, like *It's all over – you made it.*

'You haven't been expecting a baby with anything wrong with it,' Bridget continues. 'You need to grieve the normal baby you were expecting – the one you have all this love to give – and get to know the new baby you *did* have, the one with the heart abnormality.' This sounds sad to me. 'Because if Joseph dies, and you haven't loved him freely, you'd probably live with regrets for a long time. If you've loved *him* and he dies, it'll be a little easier for you.' Something inside me is shifting…

'And either way, whether he's to die or live, Joseph deserves to be loved by his parents now. You're his mother, and of all the people praying for him, and all the medical people here helping him – which he does need – he came from your body just over a week ago, and it's *your* love he needs.'

The fear clutching at me lets go.

'Do you cuddle Joseph?' Bridget asks.

'In a humidicrib?'

'The nurses will help. There's a long plastic tube beside each crib that connects to an oxygen outlet on the wall, with a plastic funnel at the other end; you drape that over your shoulder and when you hold your baby, the funnel blows oxygen directly in his face.'

Excited to be close to him – no longer feeling redundant, but supported as involved parents – I can't wait to cuddle our baby.

From then on, it doesn't matter how many tubes, drips, wires or equipment clutter our son's tiny body, we don't see it. Bridget has helped our love flow to him unimpeded. Already Joseph has enlarged our capacity to love.

I'd been expecting a perfect baby. I got a different 'perfect baby'. *Thank you, Bridget.*

That afternoon, Joseph's catheterisation confirms Dr Galbraith's diagnosis.

Wednesday morning: Sister Morris asks if we might want Joseph christened before surgery. Dedication – our equivalent – what we had for Simon, is what we decide for Joseph. She gives him a quick sponge bath, dresses him in a white christening gown, brushes up his curls, leaves his feet bare, takes photos. It all feels so urgent.

The local Baptist pastor speaks with Pete and me in the parents' room. 'Will you trust God whatever the outcome?' *Yes!* 'No,' Steven says, 'you need to think about it. If Joseph comes through surgery, you'll be *very* grateful, and feel that your prayers have been answered.' Yes! 'But if he doesn't come through surgery, will you still trust that God's answered your prayers? That he has the best interests of all of you in hand?'

That sometimes God says 'No' is another consideration for us – its stakes unthinkable. Steven reminds us of the Abraham of our bible being asked to hand his son over to God. 'In a way, you're being asked to show that much trust.' This is harder than we were expecting when we phoned Steven – much more of a 'test' than we'd realised; a quantum leap in faith.

After a prayer, Pete and I confirm: Yes.

Steven comes into the nursery, and washes his hands with the antiseptic soap. Placing one hand into the humidicrib, he rests it on our ill baby, and prays with sincerity. It's sobering, but the prayers comfort me.

Within a few short minutes, Joseph's dedication is done.

Reflection from 19 March 2012
How I've mourned the uncomplicatedness of my Christian faith back then – and the trusting young woman who faced that situation so bravely. How I've wanted to return to my naïve conviction that in every moment, I was upheld by a God who loved me dearly...

For two hours on Wednesday afternoon, Joseph goes downhill. His temperature's dropping, his body a grey colour. His heart rate high, his breathing sometimes three times faster than normal, he's pulling in the top of his trachea, in his neck, and around his chest and ribs, right in to breathe, nostrils flaring, panting to pull air in any way he can, even through his skin. *Such* a look of desperation. His dark eyes roll in his head, the whites of his eyes grey, his little brow furrowed in a worried expression babies sometimes get when they're desperately ill. Frothing at the mouth this afternoon, Joseph's in severe heart failure, the accumulation of heart fluid exuding into his lungs, now oozing out his mouth. It's exhausting sitting beside the crib watching him, battling the intruding panic. But I'm not going anywhere else.

Pete's just gone for a ciggie, returning sooner than expected. 'Someone's here to see you.' A familiar face peeks around the door: the minister from my parents' church in Murwillumbah, who'd visited us in the local hospital when Joseph was born. We'd told my parents we didn't want anyone else here, but as soon as I see Brian I charge at him for a hug.

He comes and sits with us beside the humidicrib. Joseph's breathless, grey, incredibly sick. It's hard for Brian to watch. Before long, he turns to me. 'Do you have to stay here?'

'No. But I *am* staying. I'm not leaving him.' This unusual display of assertiveness helps me feel clearer, stronger.

We don't sit for long.

Right on 3pm, the phone rings. 'JOSEPH MEEK TO MAIN THEATRE,' Sister announces.

The moment's relief reminds us that this could also bring the end for Joseph.

Sister Morris attaches a portable oxygen tank under Joseph's humidicrib, tucks his charts under her arm, bustling out of the nursery, Pete and I keeping pace either side. Rushing through the children's ward to the elevator, she slides the crib between visitors waiting for the lift, and hits the button. Seconds stretch forever – curious eyes peering at the crib – before doors open. 'EVERYBODY OUT!' Sister Morris bellows at those inside.

In an instant, she's pulled the humidicrib inside.

'How far can we come?'

'This far.' She hits the button; the lift doors shut.

Joseph is *gone*.

Pete and I look squarely into each other's eyes. *Was that IT???*

We head to the motel, where we phone our families, requesting prayers. Family phone others. Across several thousand kilometres along Australia's east coast, from Townsville in Queensland to St Mary's in Tasmania, the prayer chain flows quickly like great vessels into arteries, then capillaries, until over a thousand earnest hearts are pumping out one fervent plea, each beseeching the same request.

After the last call, we're on our knees, Brian kneeling with us, praying the most ardent prayers of our lives.

Four hours is a long time to wonder what's happening with your severely ill baby.

Is a machine breathing for him yet? Is his heart holding out??

In the main theatre of the Prince Charles Hospital, a team of 15 specialists and their assistants, masked and gloved, capped and gowned, led by Dr

Greg Stafford, watch closely as the tiny patient is lifted from humidicrib to operating table. An oxygen mask is placed over Joseph's nose and mouth; he's soon anaesthetised. A breathing tube is passed down his windpipe to his lungs; the ventilator begins to breathe for him. Monitors display his heart and breathing rates.

Through his right groin, a small tube will carry pacing wires through a main vessel to his heart.

Dr Stafford makes an incision down Joseph's fine chest.

A whirring bone saw cuts open his baby breastbone (sternum). The retractor winds apart his delicate ribcage to expose directly underneath his tiny heart, no bigger than a walnut, racing at twice normal speed.

The large silver bypass machine now redirects the blood from Joseph's heart. Controlled with full attention by the perfusionist and his assistant, bypass lines will remove the carbon dioxide from Joseph's blood, oxygenate it, and pump it back through his body. His body temperature will be lowered by cooling his blood as it flows through this machine.

The small duct near the top of Joseph's heart that should've closed at birth is cut and tied off. *PATENT DUCTUS ARTERIOSUS* is corrected.

The next most critical phase requires Joseph to go into circulatory arrest. With bypass, no blood's been pumping through his heart; from this point, no blood will pump around the rest of his body either. To avoid damage to his brain and other organs, Joseph's body is further cooled into a deeply chilled state.

Two hours and six minutes after the lift doors closed to us on the ground floor, the main vessel from Joseph's heart is clamped shut. A flat line on the monitor registers no heartbeat. His baby body is almost totally drained of blood. No breathing on his own, no heartbeat in his heart, his brain activity all but ceased, and now no blood in his body. For the next 17 minutes, his blood will be held in the PVC circuit lines of the bypass machine. No visible or measurable difference now exists between Joseph's state and a dead person.

Through microscopes over the cold baby body, an exact and vital incision towards the back of Joseph's tiny heart is made.

For a moment I lift my head. After we've been praying for some time in our motel room, an unyielding serenity starts to flood my chest.

A different flow will now begin in Joseph's heart.

TOTAL ANOMALOUS PULMONARY VENOUS DRAINAGE has been corrected.

Sections of Joseph's heart are stitched together again, his blood warmed through bypass, pumping throughout his body, rewarming it. His heart accepts the blood through its new structure – and spontaneously begins to beat.

In the left side of his heart, a valve that hasn't had to function at full capacity before, the mitral valve baulks a little at the new flow.

At the motel, a clear strong peace is permeating right through me. I feel uplifted. Assured, relieved in my spirit, I'm certain Joseph will come through. I've felt knowingness before, but not of this magnitude. *Does the hysteria want me again? Am I sensing the surgery outcome? Or is this what it feels like to be prayed for by a thousand people at once?*

When Joseph's body temperature is almost normal again, bypass is discontinued. His heart takes over circulation on its own. His mighty little mitral valve steps up to the plate, functioning normally.

Joseph's heart is repositioned in his chest, his ribcage wired together again in three places down his tiny sternum, the outside of his chest stitched up with absorbable thread.

In our motel, four hours have come and gone since Joseph went to theatre.

Taut minutes stretch…

7:26pm: our phone finally rings.

'Mrs Meek?'

'Yes.'

A pause… 'Would you like to come to the post-operative ward now? We've got Joseph here.'

Alive – or dead??

'Is he okay?'

The forever-awaited reply arrives… 'Yes he is.'

Oh God, oh God!

I turn to Pete and Brian: 'He *MADE* it!!!'

~

All being well, a patient's stay in post-op would normally last two to three days before returning to the general ward. We're about to discover that for some patients, the post-operative period sometimes brings complications. Until Joseph's second day post-op, I'd had no *real* idea that anything could be as life-threatening as the surgery. I thought we'd passed the test and were on the downhill run.

Today, small amounts of blood appear at the top of Joseph's ventilator tube. It's coming from inside him. Today, he's started bleeding from the nose and mouth. Curtains drawn around his bed, Pete and I are asked to wait outside. As they'll be a while, a nurse suggests we go for a cuppa.

Dr Stafford, Joseph's surgeon, is called: an X-ray shows Joseph's left lung has partially collapsed. He's developed an internal bleeding problem occasionally seen in this situation called *Disseminated Intravascular Coagulopathy* (DIC), a bit like haemophilia: he now won't stop bleeding. This isn't good when you're trying to heal a wound to the heart – or in any intensive care situation. People die with DIC. As a non-medico, I've come to gauge the seriousness of things we're not expecting by how the doctors deliver their assessments. If they're happy, I'm happy. If they're serious or concerned, my day whirls into a spiral of worry.

I'm falling. Already spent from the surgery, I have no energy to go through more. 'God pulled him through before,' my parents remind me by phone, 'He obviously wants Joseph alive'. No words come. This is dire *– and yes, there is cause for worry.*

My energy flagging, I return to post-op. Joseph is to receive a blood transfusion with frozen plasma and platelets, the clotting agents in blood. I sit by his bed and watch the everyday substance from an everyday person, doing what these specialists can't do, flowing through a line into my son's tiny body. I think about the stranger's obliviousness to how this vital gift would be used, moved by the hope the simple but crucial substance carries for Joseph. I'm so grateful to this stranger for hopefully saving my baby's life today, I vow I'll pass this gesture forward and donate my own blood in the future.

By night-time, Pete and I return to the motel. We're exhausted. Each time I wake through the night, I phone post-op to check on Joseph.

Morning comes and the first phone call finds our baby still going. The bleeding's eased; he's 'much improved' on yesterday. Our dark-haired little fighter with the broad shoulders and determined fists is still holding his own.

Day Three after surgery and Joseph continues recovering from the DIC. Dr Galbraith tells us we're lucky; sometimes the plasma-platelet transfusion doesn't work. The paediatrician leaves post-op shaking his head, 'Joseph's 100% on yesterday.'

Saturday afternoon: The thud is loud. It lands on my upper arm.
I look at my husband. *Surely that was it.*
Another thud. *OW! Don't look at him!*
Another punch, and another, and another, and another.
'Stop!' I hear my yell carry outside our curtained room. '*STOP!*' *Will they ask us to leave the motel?*

Pete and I didn't fight very often. I could count on one hand the number of times my husband was violent with me...

This afternoon, my parents had brought Simon for a visit. We took him to see Joseph, had a little play with Sime, and when they left, the gruelling road stretching out endlessly before us — of nursing Joseph back to health, with that far-off day our lives might return to normal — overwhelmed us. Simon had just left — and Pete and I both fell.

In our room, we started to snap at each other. Pete standing over me, I spat it out. 'Hit me then, Pete! We both know you want to.' I didn't think he *would*.

It's three days since Joseph's surgery, fourteen days since I gave birth.

Chatting in the nursery, Sister Morris lets me see her notice my damage-coloured bruises, elbow to shoulder. 'He's taking it out on you.' I nod. We exchange a long wordless look. *'It's 100% inexcusable.'* — 'Yes it is, and you'll notice I'm not covering it up for him. But please don't say any more... "extreme circumstances"... I'll shelve it for later... let it pass for today...'

That night, we're back by Joseph's post-op bed. As we have every other day, we continue helping him to recover. I'm *shocked*, dreadfully sorry for Joseph on the ventilator, for having this happen with his parents. Amidst the urgent beepings of post-op, we stroke the little bare stretch of skin on his lower leg, tell him we love him, and push forward to tomorrow.

Day Four post-op: The results from Joseph's transfusions are good: his DIC has eased. A main line comes out from his groin today, transferred to his foot. His condition looks less critical now.

Every milestone Joseph reaches on this journey carries a huge celebration, representing so much worry and hope on our part, so much healing effort on his. Each achievement after surgery – opening his eyes, moving his limbs, coming off a drip, coming off the ventilator, establishing good blood pressure, having a system declared 'stable', losing the urinary catheter, going into nappies, starting physio, coming off physio, increases in the amounts of EBM he can tolerate, taking milk from a bottle, losing the nasogastric tube, finally (hopefully) taking the breast, having him lastly declared 'out of heart failure', and further into the distance than we can see, the biggest achievement of all – taking him home – all these milestones, spanning our long weeks at Prince Charles, become the measures by which Joseph's recovery is gauged, our current lives governed, and our deeper emotions ruled.

Fifteen days old: In this light, it's just *lovely* when Joseph's umbilical cord falls off today!

Day Six post-op: Joseph's recovered enough to return to the nursery.

Three weeks old: bathing Joseph myself – for the first time.

Three-and-a-half weeks: transferring him from humidicrib to cot, dressed in a checked cowboy shirt, his soft blue bunny in the corner.

From the motel, I'm moved to the nurses' quarters on the hospital grounds, where Sister Morris has arranged breastfeeding mothers to stay. Pete heads back to Murwillumbah.

Dr Stafford drops in to check on Joseph. 'I'm very pleased with his progress,' he smiles. 'He's no longer in heart failure. Surgery's been a fantastic success. Healthy normal life.'

Couldn't be better!

Yes it could... After a feed, Joey's looking up into my face as I'm talking to him. The dear little expression begins to break over his face, a look of recognition in his dark round eyes beaming *not quite* directly into mine. The loveliest most precious of rewards: he *smiles* his newest smile at me – despite all he's endured.

Gradually Joseph's established back on to full-time breastfeeding. No more medications, his latest X-ray *CLEAR*.

WOO-HOOOO!

One month old: Pete's parked our XB at the hospital doors, the bassinette strapped into the back seat. *Oh God!* That *feeling*, heading 'down Rode Road', that moment Bridget described... As we drive, I'm checking the back seat, making sure it's real. He looks *beautiful* travelling in our family car. *We're taking Joseph home!*

Two hours later, Pete carries the bassinette inside and sits it on the dining room table. Mum, Dad, Pete and I stand around staring into it, our smiles softly admiring, deeply awed. His little cry sounds *divine* filling the house. It's miraculous to see Joseph sleeping and feeding like a normal baby, as though he'd never suffered such trauma.

We're so happy with our new son, we feel almost invincible. We break our own rule, and take Joseph to bed with us – tiny and way too cute sleeping between us in our big bed.

Five weeks old: we take him to church. We need to formally thank the congregation for their prayers. A traditional flock, they break *their* rule and clap the little baby they'd embraced so fervently into their hearts.

After the service, a parishioner approaches Mum. 'We've got a claim on that baby.' Twenty-six years earlier, Fred and Rene had to make the trip to Brisbane, oxygen tent in the back of their car, to transport their son – another blue baby with suspected *congenital heart*. Nothing could be done for their little Ronald. He died at 10 days. Fred and Rene consented to an autopsy, specifying to doctors, 'If it'll help other heart babies of the future'. Their story deeply touches me. I'll take Joseph to visit them on their dairy farm soon.

Pete and I have decided to move from Melbourne, to be near Prince Charles Hospital. After church, and a blissful week together, Pete heads south to bring our belongings.

Simon frequently props himself up in the corner of the lounge, arms outstretched, asking to nurse 'Jophess'. Simon's the one now helping me bath the baby, handing me his washer, cotton balls, towel. He doesn't think much of his little brother's crying, but seems to understand. All I see from Simon towards 'Jophess' is immense love. He gives Jophess kisses on the forehead, pulling back to look adoringly at him. I don't know how Simon knows when he's so little himself how to be a big brother, but this sort of love seems innate in him. Simon's depth stuns me.

The front door opens to a young mother looking as tired as I feel. Mikhali, born less than 24hrs after Joseph, and his mum, are a welcome sight. I babble Joseph's journey out to Kerry as we let the babies kick together on the floor. Born the same weight, a noticeable size difference shows my son's energies have been demanded elsewhere: *survival*. He'll catch up soon.

Joseph's next appointment isn't for another fortnight, so I question when I *think* I see signs of heart failure reappearing. I count his breathing. It's continually a bit fast now. Consultations with our GP, paediatrician and X-rays, reveal Joseph *is* in heart failure again. 'He might've come off his medications too soon,' Dr Cherry suggests. Sister Morris has taught us to draw up and administer medications ourselves, should our babies need to go home on them. Thankfully, I can look after my son myself, at home.

Joseph's condition doesn't improve. Ten days later, he's waking every hour crying, sometimes vomiting. Mum takes him in the mornings so I can get two hours' sleep before she goes to work. Joseph and I are both exhausted.

Just past seven weeks: back at Prince Charles for an early appointment. This time it's different. I'm teary, I don't know why. *We might have to go through it all again...*

Over the following days, Joseph's symptoms wax and wane. Dr Galbraith has spent two hours with him in Echo, emerging drained. 'Sometimes the pulmonary veins (coming back from the lungs) can become blocked with scar tissue,' he explains, 'but I've checked his veins and they all seem clear'. He'll take Joseph in for catheterisation. Further surgery looks likely at some stage.

Almost two months old: I don the white gown, wash my hands with pink hibiclens, and turn to open the side of Joseph's humidicrib. I don't believe it: he looks *terrible!* An awful colour, he's panting quickly, desperately, nostrils flaring, extremely uncomfortable. *What's happened??*

Today's nursing sister is new. 'Joseph looks dreadful!' I blurt. She comes to check. 'He doesn't look too good, does he?' She doesn't make any calls. I don't think she's dealt with an urgency like this. 'Could you please ask Dr Galbraith to start his rounds at our end this morning?'

The wait is excruciating. Joseph's struggling terribly. He can't get enough oxygen. That anxious look's furrowing his brow again: *Mum, Mum, help me!*

After an eternity, Dr Galbraith arrives. 'Could you please check Joseph first?' Dr Galbraith examines him, then makes a phone call.

'We're going to take him up to post-op, to give him some help with his breathing.' The cardiologist's presence always reassures me. He mentions a possible *obstruction*; he'll need to do the catheterisation. He's got his finger on the pulse.

I just wanted Joseph out of that distress. I hadn't thought of what 'intubating him' would mean.

In post-op, lying totally still, he's now fully sedated, eyes closed, not looking around anymore, not even flickering. I can't communicate directly with him. Tears escape my eyes. Edgy, I have no patience.

By day's end: slight progress. 'He's improved a little throughout the day,' Dr Galbraith observes. 'See you outside catheter theatre in the morning – about 6:30.'

～

2.10am: The phone in the corridor is ringing. I've not slept well – tossing, turning, waking, drifting. It's exhausting having a sick child and I'm usually out like a light. Still fully breastfeeding, the trauma of what's gone on in the last two months takes its toll. But this night, my sleep's been restless. I don't know what keeps waking me.

Three mothers are staying in the nurses' quarters. Only one of us doing night feeds this week.

The ringing continues. *Vicki must already be at the nursery.*

Heading up the hall, I remember I've left a message for Pete to phone me back. Logic hasn't woken up to the time.

'Hello!' My loving tone expects long-distance pips, my husband's voice.

'Mrs Meek, would you come up to post-op immediately,' the nurse shoots words down the phone. 'Joseph's deteriorating rapidly.'

My stomach grabs. 'Is it serious?'

'Yes it is.'

If I wanted to be dramatic, I could say, 'And the rest is a blur'. But that's not true. Without being dramatic, the events of this night remain the most vividly remembered of my life.

I drop the phone and run to my room, fighting the Sister's words. *You've got the wrong baby, Sister. I know which way mine's going – it's not downhill! You've phoned the wrong mother!* Denial's soft landing is meant for such moments.

Shaking, I yank on my skirt, bra that won't hook, fumble my shirt, not reacting fast enough. *Shit!* Every hurried movement seemed to slow, like in a nightmare. *Hang on Joey, Mummy's coming.*

Many hundreds of times have I remembered since: bolting down the corridor, the sound of that poor young mother's feet sprinting along old corrugated carpet, pushing through the front doors of the nurses' quarters, bursting into the still dark night. Calling security escort – not an option. Bounding up the path, taking the concrete steps two at a time, rushing across the lawn, I look up to the lights of the post-op wing. *Please God – Please don't let him die! Please don't let him die!* I'll never forget how my pleas, out under the quiet stars, seemed to fade into the dark, unheard. My mouth dry from anxiety as I run, desperation tightens around my body, my prayers bouncing back at me from a metre above my head. No time to get a prayer chain going now. Everyone's asleep – *everyone* – blissfully ignorant, clueless of this moment. As alone as the last of my species, I beg into the air, racing through the hospital doors, up around the stairwell onto the second floor, begging, frantic, *Please don't let him die!* Running, begging, pleading as I run, *God, PLEASE!* Even in these moments, my prayers feel powerless in the face of whatever I'm running towards.

Outside the post-op door, I don't ring the bell. I break the rule and walk straight in.

'His mother's here,' a voice says.

A dozen staff crowd around the end of Joseph's bed, many arms folded across chests, watching intently whatever's happening on Joseph's brightly lit bed. More hurried steps further into that shock, I round the corner to see for myself...

The surgical registrar on the other side of the bed is pounding *very* quickly on Joseph's chest, his baby body lifting up and down under the pressure.

I look to the screen monitoring Joseph's heart rate: a flatline. Although not loud, its single monotone, in the absence of beeps, deafens my memory of that sight.

How many splits of a second did it take in that slow-moving nightmare to realise they were performing a resuscitation attempt on Joseph? In some moments now, it still shocks me.

Next to the registrar on the other side of the bed, Dr Galbraith's here – at this hour, 2.25am. This is *so* very serious. Around the other side of the bed, their attention is fixed on Joseph. After a moment, Dr Galbraith looks up at me, dry-mouthed. 'His heart just *stopped*!' His voice cracks on the last word.

I stand in close beside Charles the paediatrician, his fingers on Joseph's wrist, monitoring his pulse.

The CPR pounding under the bright light is strong, fast and urgent.

The heart monitor remains the same. No peaks, no troughs. Only a straight flat white line, and that one single tone, splitting the screen horizontally in half, drawing the line between life and death.

Joseph doesn't look physically distressed, or uncomfortable. He appears calm amidst the critical attempt by these skilled professionals to save his life. As soon as I see him, the look of utter peace about Joseph in the centre of all this fuss takes me by surprise.

Dr Galbraith looks up at me. 'I think we should stop now.'

No! 'How long have you been going?'

'About five or ten minutes.'

I look down at Joseph. He could not be dead as soon as I walk in here! He could not be *dead*!

'Isn't there anything more you can do for him?'

'We could try for another five minutes if you like.'

'Yes!' Of course!

The cardiac massage is resumed.

Soon, from the heart monitor, I hear a beep, and jerk my head to look. A heartbeat!! Joseph's heart *beat!!* There it is – a peak and trough – travelling across the screen!

Charles is the only one who glances at the screen. He doesn't take the same hope I do. I seem to be the only one to whom it means anything. I look back to see the lone heartbeat leaving. No more of those beautiful peaks and troughs. Only one. The single monotone returns, as the heartbeat visits the screen temporarily, then departs.

I'm painfully aware of the seconds ticking by as the pounding on Joseph's chest continues. 'I guess it's brain damage by now?' Such a thing isn't possible in that beautiful little head of thick black hair. No-one answers. 'Charles?'

'Joseph's on a ventilator. His blood's being oxygenated, which reduces the risk of damage.'

Thank you.

Scalpel in hand, Dr Galbraith's tried to find an artery in Joseph's groin, but his vessels have collapsed. He moves closer to me, pupils dilated; gentle but serious, 'I think we should ***stop***.'

I bore hard into his eyes, thoughts racing each other across my mind.

You're not God! You're an imperfect human being! Do you realise what you're saying? There MUST be doctors in the world who know more than you do about this. In America they're doing heart transplants on babies. Surely someone over there knows what to do here... I glance back at Joseph as the moment stretches. What else could be done? *...How do I get someone here from America right now? At 2.40 in the morning...* We stare intently into each other's eyes. The second stretches as a different light falls over the cardiologist's face. He's looking into me like the human being God has placed in charge of my baby. *You're the one. You're Joseph's doctor – here, right now, to make this decision...*

I break my stare into the doctor's soul to look back at Joseph. For an unreal moment, everything is calm – as though all along, Joseph and I both knew this was the moment he was going to die.

He lies on the sheepskin.

Very still.

'Alright then,' I concede.
'But would you just take his tubes out? I really want a cuddle.'

Charles obliges and starts carefully pulling up the 'happy faces' from Joseph's unmoving body.

The crowd slowly disperses.

Prince Charles Hospital
Baby Joseph Meek
Post-Operative Ward. 28.4.86
Death occurred at 2:40 hrs
Mother notified and present

~

I have never come close to death before.

There was no difference. Between Joseph hours before, sedated and ventilated, and in the moments after his death, there was no difference.

When the surgical registrar doing the cardiac massage, removed his hands, Joseph's skin was white from the pressure of the doctor's fingers, but the colour gradually returned. I could see bruises around his little body, needle marks in his arm. He'd had a rough time that night.

Dr Galbraith leant across to me, looked in my eyes, and shook his head. 'I am *very* disappointed.'

'I know. I'm sorry about that.' Glancing back at Joseph: 'Poor little baby.'

'Yes,' Dr Galbraith looked at him with me, sadness in his voice.

Surveying the scene, something drew my gaze. My eyes sprung open. Joseph's chest was still rising and falling.

He's still breathing! 'Ugh!'

Dr Galbraith saw me notice the ventilator. '... *Oh...* the ventilator,' I mumbled.

'Turn the ventilator off,' he told Charles.

With the flick of a switch, Joseph's lungs released their air for good, his chest falling for the last time.

Now there was no movement. Just a limp little body.

It was my first glimpse of 'deathly still'. Through a descending fog, I stared hard at it. *This is what my son looks like dead.* I had a feeling I needed to spend as much time with it as I could.

While I was phoning Pete, they removed the equipment from Joseph's body, and wrapped him in baby blankets.

I slid into an armchair, holding Joseph. 'I'd like to be alone.'
The nurse drew the curtains and left.

I stroke Joseph's face, his hair, I kiss his forehead, his soft cheeks. I hold him up next to me and hug him. He's not moving, not breathing. I try to take in what this means – our dear little black-haired boy, his dark eyes never to open again, his dark lashes never to blink again, little rosebud mouth that will never again tell me what this life's been like for him, his slender baby fingers now fixed into fists – losing their grasp on life tonight in his valiant struggle to stay with us. I hold him close, kissing his dear little cooling face, hearing my whimpering gasps as my tears fall.

A nurse pokes her head around the curtain. Do I have family or anyone local they could call? 'My parents are staying at the nearby motel. Would you ask them to come please?'

Dr Galbraith returns and sits with me. Thoughts surface of Fred and Rene's unselfishness from the church, from which we've benefited. I know I must pass this forward. 'You'll want to do an autopsy,' I bring it up to spare Dr Galbraith having to.

'Yes – if that's alright.' He needs to understand why this has happened so that heart babies of the future can live. Now I see how hard it was for Fred and Rene to give this permission. I look down, stroking Joseph's cheek.

'They mustn't touch his face.' I outline Joseph's soft black curls with my index finger. 'Or his head... And they must wait till my husband has seen him.'

It seems minutes before the curtains part again and my parents' faces appear. Mum would later say the tears on my face, my dead baby in my arms, was the saddest thing she'd ever seen. She said I looked fragile, like a little girl holding a doll, that she'd knelt down and tried to cuddle us both.

Dad's holding Simon, only 20 months old, in nappies, his eyes taking up half his face. I want to hold Simon too, but my thoughts and movements are slowing from shock. I'm so glad to see him. It's such a relief to look at his face and see that I'm still a mother.

'Joey's died, Sime,' I show him. 'See, sweetie?' I move Joseph towards Simon so he'll see the word I just used means a person doesn't move anymore (*ever*) and it looks like this. I kiss Joseph to show Simon it's still okay. 'See Sime?' Simon's eyes are the same as his brother's; it comforts me to look into them. 'Joseph's not coming home with us, Sime. We have to say goodbye to him.' As I lift Joseph to him, Dad brings Simon close; Simon bends down and gives Joseph a kiss on his forehead as he'd done countless times at home.

Mum notices Dr Galbraith look away from this. When she looks back, the doctor's eyes are brimming with tears.

Dad leans across quietly to me. 'Would you like me to say a prayer?'
'Yes.' I'm so glad he suggested it; even the thought of it is comforting. Dad asks in his soothing prayerful voice for God to look after Joseph till we all meet again. The thought of not seeing Joseph for the rest of my life breaks through the numbness and I start to cry. He's only a baby. I'm only 25. It'll be so *long* before I see him again.

Simon wants to get down and look around. Dad leaves to take him back to the motel; Mum stays with me.

A staff member asks if I have baby clothes for Joseph. I give her my room key and tell her where to find the bassinette with Joseph's 'going home' clothes.

Cradling him, I look over his body. 'I was so proud of his hair!' A tear trickles. 'I won't be able to call them "my boys" anymore.' Some part of me senses I won't be leaving Joseph in the ground, but will be carrying this loss through the rest of my life. 'I'm young to have this happen.'

Staff moves us to a more private post-op room. With one hand, I've arranged baby clothes on the bed, carefully placing Joseph next to them.

I slowly begin to lift his little arm. Even asleep, people still have some tension in their limbs, but this is different now; this is dead. My eyes watch my hands pull Joseph's limp arms through his clothes, pull the top over his dark curly head that refuses to wake up, no tightness stretching into sleeves, no objecting from his limbs. Having to lift his body more to dress him, having to lift my awareness through the shock, from the impossibility that he's dead, I make myself feel what this means. I dress him in all his clothes, right down to his knitted bootees, from legs that don't retract, over feet that lie totally still, but *Joseph's dead* will be impossible for a long time to come.

Two hours have passed since he's been lying in my arms. The sister says she'll have to call for a mortuary attendant to come and pick him up; they don't like to leave it too long.

'Where's he going?'

'To the mortuary.'

'Where's that?'

'Down on the basement level.'

'Could I take him there myself?'

The sister hesitates. 'I guess you could. We'll have to go soon, before people start to wake up.'

Perhaps Sister Morris has taught me my rights.

The three of us – Post-Op Sister, Mum, and me – set off quietly through corridors, stairwells and floors of the Prince Charles Hospital, Mum and the sister walking either side of me. Wrapped in a bunny rug, looking beautiful in his going-home clothes, I carry Joseph, stroking his face, his hair, watching him intently the whole way.

Between pure white walls, we begin the last walk down the long corridor to the mortuary, silent except for the echo of our footsteps on the concrete floor, and the faint hum of mass refrigeration somewhere nearby.

I've continued trying to orchestrate an active role in this surreal night, like you might try directing a nightmare while you're having it – had been handed my baby from the sheepskin of his post-op bed, had dressed him myself, had carried him down through hospital floors and corridors myself – and hope that perhaps *I* could be the one to now lay him to rest in his new freezing cradle. I would know exactly where he was then. And in this act I could still be his mother – to the very last.

I postpone what's coming as much as I can, squeezing out every last second of my life with Joseph, mothering him to this last moment. I do *NOT* want to part with him. Looking down at his lifeless little face as we walk, stroking his baby soft cheek that doesn't respond, tracing the curls of his jet black hair, of which I've been so proud, I don't take my eyes off him.

At the end of the corridor, we arrive at a big silver door, mortuary attendant standing outside. The man looks so plain to be receiving my baby, no post-op professional air about him, no protective gown to prevent the passing of germs to Joseph. It's no longer necessary. We're at the other end of this process, and it no longer matters.

'Could I put him in there?' I ask the mortuary man.

'No,' attendant and Sister answer in unison, without a thought.

'Could I see where he's going?'

'No, love,' the post-op sister replies, 'it'd be too hard for you'. They seem certain. It seems procedure.

This is the end of the line.

I ready myself to hand Joseph over, giving him my last kisses, telling him in my mind, *I love you Joey, Mummy loves you*, inching closer to the attendant. The moment slows down, begins to freeze, the realisation overcoming my mum that this is it – she won't be seeing Joseph again. As my baby's received into the attendant's arms, an uncontrolled death wail breaks its bonds and releases itself from deep inside Mum's chest, followed by loud sobbing into the air, into her hands, and into the Sister's shoulder.

Mum sobs this moment out for all of us.

CHAPTER 2

Cradle to the Grave

*A mind that is stretched by a new experience
can never go back to its old dimensions*
Marcel Proust

May 1986

On my knees, I'm peering intently into red earth. The freshly dug little grave is where Joseph's small white coffin will come to rest. Around us, other babies are buried who, for their own reasons, have died at the beginning of life. The baby boy of a woman I'd attended Sunday School with as a child is right nearby. I half-turn to look up. At our request, only immediate family and Joseph's godparents are graveside after the funeral. Now clustered behind me, I stare long and hard from face to face, trying to take it in, trying to make it all real.

It doesn't work. It stays surreal.

∼

In the months after Joseph's death, I was somewhere else. My body lived in my parents' house with Simon, while Pete was in Melbourne. I'd asked for a separation for these few months, as Pete was only able to express his grief as anger, and direct it at me, and there was no space amidst it for my own grieving. With the outside world, I remained the polite person I'd always been, while simultaneously being vacuumed into an inner world I'd never been to before.

Almost immediately, I became hypersensitive. Terms like 'defect', 'deformity', 'malformation' offended me deeply. *How can a heart that's given so much be referred to as 'defective'?!* I've always explained Joseph's condition as a congenital heart *abnormality* (the 'A' in TAPVD stands for Anomalous, which means abnormality). It's important to me that people understand. I can't bear that his little smiling face couldn't speak for itself.

For many weeks, a smell lingered in my senses of the disinfectant they'd washed Joseph's body in after he'd died. I smelt it in everything, even the flowers people sent. *What right do flowers have to live anyway? Why take life from my baby and give it to them? I don't want them, I want him.*

Initially I cried, but in the following months, tears hid themselves. I kept expecting the grief to hit me, to suddenly come out all in one go. *Is this shock? Is it denial?* I understood these defence mechanisms from the intellect, but from the inside of the experience, they were totally unrecognisable...

May 1986

Something's numbing me. Sad thoughts and tears expose my heart – frozen – with only its outer layer, its pericardium, feeling sadness. We go for drives in the countryside where cows graze in green paddocks, creeks ripple over rocks, purple mountains darken against afternoon skies... yet this beauty cannot lift me, cannot permeate my eyes' corneas and penetrate the thick fog behind them. I may as well be looking at a blank wall. Where are these feelings that register Death??

Other than immense love for Simon and Joseph, I couldn't seem to feel. This worried me. A lot of things worried me. The whole episode tipped me upside down – starting with the assumption I didn't know I'd made that *children outlive their parents*, and the dawning that our little family would never be whole again. I didn't feel any of this consciously. For a long time, I was mostly just numb, empty and truly irritable.

A sharp vulnerability separated me from people's good intentions. Never had I been so sensitive to unasked-for advice. 'Now dear, *don't* go to the cemetery too often. Joseph's *not* out there, he's in heaven with God.' *Of course: how did you know that's why I go? ...A baby doesn't belong in the ground anyway – especially at the beginning of winter.* 'Have another baby.' *Indeed: replace him – like a broken toy.* People's spiritual explanations as to why Joseph had died were as far-fetched. 'Perhaps it was better he died than stay and live a life of pain.' *You don't understand Joseph's condition. A repaired TAPVD doesn't pan out as 'a life of pain'.* 'Maybe God wasn't going to let another baby into Denny and Peter's marriage until they sorted their problems out.' *So it was our fault. How much stress are you allowed in your marriage before God starts knocking off your children? Wouldn't He know the death of a child is the greatest stress a marriage can suffer?* 'Perhaps God knew Denny had as much on her plate as she could handle and this was His way of sparing her more.' *So it was my fault. I was so weak, my baby had to die to 'spare' me exerting myself. You think living with your child's death is easier than worrying about their life? You'll never know how mistaken you are.* I didn't like it when people said it was God's will that Joseph died. Allowing such a thing wasn't part of my concept of *God*.

I began to miss all the days I wasn't having with Joseph, and all the priceless moments I'd shared him with others who wouldn't spend their lifetime aching for him. People now seemed fascinated with him, using terms of endearment only I'd used in his life, pretending a closeness with him they hadn't had. 'The whole town's waiting for Denny to fall apart,' Mum's work colleague told her several weeks after the funeral. Being closely watched felt like others were clawing at pieces of my grief for my breastfed baby. I began to retreat into the 'grief cocoon', to preserve the little I'd had of him, to keep these real parts of him alive and in a safe place.

Inside that cocoon, every second of Joseph's life was relived, every moment mourned in countless ways. Dark-haired babies, passing ambulances, infants crying in public each triggered Joseph's pain for me. It began to puncture me, pulling me into the hurt he'd endured, long after the innocent triggers had passed. Each time I'd let Joseph cry, hadn't burped him enough, hadn't talked to him – so he'd *know* he was loved – every missed opportunity haunted me with a feral longing for him, a stabbing guilt for having taken his days for granted. I worried I wasn't as good a mother as I'd let everyone tell me I was. I felt guilty having enquired so much about his medical details – as though I was escaping into my mind from being a 'proper' mother, because I was scared and needed to understand – when it wasn't my understanding of his medical condition, but only my love, Joseph needed. I tortured myself for having spent his pregnancy not ready for another baby, wondering if that'd somehow caused his heart abnormality. I glanced back countless times through following years, re-wondering.

Down in Melbourne, Pete resented people telling him the pain was worse for me. Not all fathers got involved at the Prince Charles Hospital, as Pete had. He rode the roller-coaster, then carried Joseph's body out of the church in his white baby coffin. Pete was grieving deeply and didn't believe it was worse for the mother when a baby dies.

Over the phone, tension was ever-present with Pete. Every time we spoke, we argued. We didn't want to fight; we wanted to be close and comfort each other, to share our grief. I'd want to forget about it when I got off the phone, but it'd sap my energy anyway.

My grief got physical. Insomnia, headaches, a constant lump in the throat now accompanied my days. Terribly tired, I had a shaking inside. Mum said she watched me eat everything she put in front of me, which sustained them all, yet I lost weight. Frequently drained, I had less patience with Simon, which made it all worse. I felt not here... a vacant shell... an echo of a dead baby's mother.

'There's something wrong with me,' I spilt my worry to Dr Betty. 'I'm not crying – I don't think I'm grieving.'

At Joseph's funeral, I'd turned to see Dr Betty's face so awash with tears, I didn't recognise her. *'He was a- beautiful- baby!'* her words choked out as she hugged me. In her surgery weeks later, her tone is practical. 'Of *course* you're grieving! Grief isn't just crying. You think of your baby, don't you? You look at his photos? You feel sad? You wish he was still here? There's a lot more to grieving than just tears, you know!' Dr Betty *did* know, but it would be a long time before I saw it for myself.

I got tired of mulling everything over in my mind. The idea of 'healing' had changed for me. After Joseph's surgery, he no longer had TAPVD. He appeared to have been healed, then suddenly died. Did that count? *Every extra day you have with someone you love 'counts' very much.* But was it *healing*? After Joseph's death, the word 'healing' would never mean 'cured' or 'Total' again.

Inside I was angry at abortion, angry at suicide – angry at choices that seemed to take life for granted and throw it away. *I wanted my baby! I didn't have a choice whether he lived or died.*

It was jarring to hear the woman next door yell at her children, swearing with impatience for trivial incidents. *I didn't swear at my children. Why does she get to keep hers?*

Although reincarnation wasn't a mainstream idea then, there was no way my mind could even glimpse Joseph being born to another set of parents on the other side of the world, he and they oblivious to the pain I was in, and would be in for a long time.

Psychologically, it was gruelling. The irritability was constant, overwhelming. It felt like things would never improve, that I'd be in this awful black space forever. From here, I could see that all human pain wasn't on the same continuum, and that you couldn't show people this level of pain who hadn't experienced it. It stripped the superficial layers from whatever I looked at, revealing an intuitive 'seeing' that I sensed came with the depth of pain.

'Little darling,' my dad said to me two weeks after the funeral, 'it's a lovely world, and you're going to be alright, you'll see – you'll be happy again soon.'

'Dad, I hate this world! My baby's died – in the ground – and I wish I was with him. I don't wanna be here. I wanna be with Joseph. Simon's the only reason I'm still here. But this is *not* a lovely world!' It was the first of several monologues I'd launch at Dad through the years where he wouldn't know what to say. I've watched others sometimes put my dad – a former Methodist minister – on the mat, to unknowingly represent God, to apologise on His behalf and on behalf of religion in general.

I hadn't been a rebellious teenager, but living with my parents again now, grieving the death of my child, parenting issues were in my face. My parents hadn't been reminded often that the raising of their children was finished, and that although I needed their help at this time, I was an adult, and Simon was my child to rear. It took a bit of rehearsal for me to form those words aloud too. I couldn't be close to them, which made me feel like an unruly adolescent ingrate.

Socially, mothers were cautious with their babies around me. One mother found out I'd just lost mine, and mid-conversation, physically turned her back on me, her body between me and her baby. *Yes: grief might equal insanity. I might suddenly cry hysterically. Or go crazy. I might try to grab your ugly baby and run off with it.*

Kerry wasn't afraid. She'd known Joseph. She'd brought a growing Mikhali to Joseph's funeral and offered me a nurse afterwards. I chose one of Joseph's outfits to give to Mikhali.

Many cards and letters showed people's caring. It comforted me to reply with stories about Joseph, especially to the women's bible study group I'd attended in Melbourne throughout the pregnancy.

One letter from a well-meaning mum offered hollow comfort: now that she'd had a baby son of her own, she *'understood'* what I was going through. She only had to *'imagine'* losing him to know how I felt. It was lovely to receive these letters, I really did appreciate them, but this sentiment did not comfort me. The mother *could* not understand, or even *begin* to imagine.

Another month on and people's awkwardness about my loss had a couple of them physically cross the road when they saw me coming.

Grief hadn't been spoken about openly in Australian society for very long at this time and social attitudes towards grief played themselves out in my dreams. *I'm carrying Joseph around in my arms, dead. When I pass by people, I try to hide his face, hide his head under his bunny rug before they see him, so they won't know he's dead. (As per Dr Betty's first instruction, I 'cover that baby up!') Fortunately, I'm able to keep Joseph's deadness hidden from them.*

I had dreams that Joseph had died in other ways. *I'd been having a shower with Joseph and put him down for only a moment. I look to see him face down in the drain grate, his striking crown from that dear little black head of hair facing up. He's not moving. In a split second, he's drowned in the bottom of the shower.*

I went to the cemetery often and sat by Joseph's grave. I feared losing memories of him... *I miss your warm little body, your baby soft limbs, your amazing hair, your big dark eyes, your little round mouth, your endearing smile, how light you were to pick up and cuddle...* I put my hand on the green grass above where his coffin was laid. *How far down are you? What state is your dear little body in now?* A mother's mind goes there. *I didn't have you for long enough, Joseph. I know anything short of eternity with you isn't long enough, but it was such a short time. And the more time passes since then, the shorter the time I had with you seems... until I sometimes wonder if you were here at all.*

I looked at all I had left – my clothes, a few material possessions (not much!)... *I'd give everything I have for just one more day with you – even on the ventilator and paralysed. If you were warm and alive and could hear me whisper I love you in your baby ear...* I would've given EVERYTHING.

In the baby section at the cemetery, one mother has lost three babies. I look up to the sky. *Being 'given the strength' to handle this is not enough, God – losing Joseph is way too much to ask. One child is too many. How could someone be asked to go through this three times??!!!* I don't fear this happening to me again – I know it won't – but it's a torturous thought that it did happen to this poor woman *three times*. I can't fathom it. I can't even fathom losing Joseph.

About the only individual I trusted was Simon. He didn't react to me the way others did, didn't harbour private opinions of me, pretend to understand me, or give me advice. Had he been an insecure child, it might've been different, and although I did tire of his normal demands, his grounded interest in playing with whatever he was given, in his uncomplicated childlike way, meant I could manage his straight-forward company and be myself with him.

At playgroup before Joseph's birth, I'd clicked with another Christian mother who had a son the same age as Simon, named 'Joseph'. In relating minimally to others after baby Joseph's death, this friendship provided soothing support. Simon and the other Joseph played well together while Christine and I drank tea and talked. Christine *listened*.

My cheek against the little boys' cheeks, and the warmth of Simon's active healthy body, was comforting. Warmth itself – amidst flashes of baby Joseph's forehead like ice – came to represent life to me. I was intensely aware of how easy it would be to lose Simon, who looked smaller again without the real baby around. A flash of Simon's little body still and ice-cold too intruded my mind; I shook it off. I didn't mean to be preoccupied with Joseph's death. *I wish I could just enjoy Simon's life; he should be enough to distract me from my grief.* A new depth had surfaced in my appreciation of what a beautiful child Simon was, what a cooperative, lovely, gentle little boy. I felt deeply for his sensitivity and worried about being too harsh on him, about squashing him. I began writing notes to myself on the sort of parent I wanted to be – a habit I've continued throughout my parenting years, whatever was going on – reinforcing to myself the different ways I wanted to show my children they were loved.

As for his developing grasp of Joseph's death, Simon would come into my bedroom every morning and go straight to Joseph's cradle. The morning after Joseph died, I started to cry. 'Joey's not there, Sime. Joey died.' Simon wasn't content to lift the top bunny rug to find Joseph. He lifted the next rug. 'Bubba!' Then the sheets one at a time, 'Bubba! Bubba!', the little pillow, the mattress. Despite the heartbreaking cry Simon would have after seeing Joseph cold and unmoving at the funeral director's, he'd repeat this ritual at times over the months, his big dark eyes searching through layers of his toddler awareness for his little brother. Sometimes I'd watch Simon through the day for signs of recognition that Joseph had 'died', or to see if he sensed my grief. One afternoon he tapped me on the leg from behind. I turned around: he'd tipped a silver bowl upside-down on his head to make me laugh — which it did! Other than that, Simon would be in the moment of his play, eating, drinking his bottle, listening intently as he was read children's stories. Except for peeling through Joseph's cradle, I had no idea what he'd absorbed. I imagined having 'the boys' at home in a normal routine, how Simon and Joseph's relationship would develop — an imagining that continues today. At this time, I was going through the motions physically to look after Simon, and although at times his tears were close to the surface, I was relieved of the added security our living with Mum and Dad provided him.

I believed Joseph wasn't in a physical body anymore, that he was with God, but I didn't know how old he was, and I couldn't stop worrying about him — sometimes frantically.

June 1986

God, does Joseph still need me? Who tells him he's precious and loved, that everything's okay, that he doesn't have to fear the future? Does he know he's not going to have a major change of caregivers again? He needed my love to get through surgery; does he still need it now? Does he understand what he sees around him? Or does he feel bewildered? What if he wants to know things but can't talk yet to ask? Does he ever feel lonely?

I generally believed Joseph was happier with God, but in moments these motherly worries pierced me with desperate panic.

The religious pressure to come through victorious probably came as much from me as from others. I assumed it was weak faith that I didn't want to live on earth without Joseph. At the shame of not 'coping properly', my self-esteem suffered. I feared criticism for these feelings no-one understood. Several people told me I was 'too analytical', 'too intense'. *Ouch.* Helpless to defend myself, I pulled the fragile me – the *real* me – further inside.

Where was I with God in all of this? It ran deep and took its time, like a slow-moving underground river. I felt like a pawn, sometimes like a square on the board. Feeling closer to Joseph at church, I started attending twice on Sundays, looking for answers. I knew the rules about not questioning God, but I asked anyway.

July 1986

It's like You've taken advantage of my commitment, knowing I have no choice but to learn, develop and grow from all this. Sometimes it seems You'd have to be sadistic to allow such suffering, especially if You love us 'more than we can know'. You've said You won't let anyone go through more than they can handle, but how much is that? Why do some people lose everyone close to them? Why do some have nervous breakdowns? Why do some get suicidal? WHY did you let Joseph die?

Others I'd meet had lost their belief in God when their child died. But despite burning questions with no simple answers – despite feeling so low, tired, worried, anxious, irritable, angry, frustrated, and that I could *not* stretch myself any further – my Christian belief didn't come into question. I was relieved to have one less shattered foundation to sort out.

'Why do people talk *at* you and think they understand?' I asked the counsellor. 'Everyone's telling me how I'm feeling, not feeling, should or shouldn't be feeling, what I should be doing, not doing. I just want them to shut-up and listen!' Decades later, I'd read that people who didn't get sick in their grief were those who were allowed to grieve, who had someone to just listen. The social worker agreed to try and play this role, admitting after two sessions that he was finding it hard not to advise me. He did something for which I've always been grateful. 'Keep a *Feelings* diary,' he suggested. 'Write down *whatever* you're feeling. In your writing, don't censor anything or edit. Just go wherever your feelings might take you.' Like gas in labour, this unchecked honesty sometimes scraped the top off the pain, bringing moments of relief; at other times it seemed to only heighten feelings. Overall it began to teach me a value of my emotions, and get me in touch with a level of myself I hadn't connected with so directly before. *I want to be a full human, not just a good one,* I decided. Diary writing didn't answer my big questions, didn't lessen my irritation, didn't resolve the pain, but it did give my grief some expression, helped clarify the turmoil of that inner world, gave it some structure, and has been an invaluable practice through the decades. In the feelings diary that became my journal, there are now well over two million words.

Throughout the months, I came to regard Joseph as an angel who didn't have to stay – although that meant I wasn't good enough to go too. Some things I'd believed before his death would change in my grief. I'd heard sermons preached on 'original sin' – that all people are sinful, that even before a baby's taken its first breath, the baby's sinful. I no longer accepted this. I felt sure the pastors who'd preached these words would've felt – and interpreted scriptures – differently had they experienced what I had.

I wondered why we get so upset at death, why it consumes us, why it's so hard for us to accept, and why if we get less than 'three score years and ten' for a lifetime, we feel ripped off. *How did we come by that expectation?* I didn't get an answer to that, and decided that for some people, two months *is* a whole lifetime.

In the first weeks after Joseph's death, I'd think that if he'd just come back to life, everything could go back to how it was: his return would fix things. Not only would I not feel this permanent unbearable sadness, but *I* could go back to how I'd been. But after months without him, while I didn't understand the processes of what the loss was doing to me, I realised his coming back wouldn't return things to normal. Joseph's dying had taken with it my innocence about life, a naivety that couldn't be restored. The things I'd seen from that depth, and how it affected me, were real and couldn't be erased. I was changed.

Over time I concluded that a nervous breakdown is a way of coping; you're still alive and can recover. Having spent months wanting to die too, I saw that for some, even suicide is 'a way of coping'.

I decided after several months that it was God's hand that we were able to bring Joseph home for those few weeks, that that's why I was able to nurse him at home for that last week. I realised too that even if God Himself gave me His reason/s why Joseph had died, nothing would change. It wouldn't take my grief away, wouldn't make it all okay inside me, wouldn't wipe out what I'd seen and felt since. Having THE reason/s wouldn't satisfy my thirst to understand life, nor quell the permanent ache of separation in my heart. *What 'reasons' could address questions asked from the depth of such ferocious pain anyway??* I'd still miss my baby, still be stuck in this human existence without him, having to work my own way through it. There'd be no shortcuts. My grief wasn't responding to logic, so I suspected that when it matters, human beings couldn't understand, or contain in our minds, God's whys anyway.

My mother-in-law, who'd flown up from Melbourne for Joseph's funeral, sent me grief writings. Distributed by *The Compassionate Friends*, it supported parents who'd lost a child, and was the only literature I'd found that handled the subject respectfully, with a depth of understanding. They didn't suggest parents should be over their grief in a certain time or should experience anything in particular. Parents wrote beautiful poetry and letters, sensitively expressing grief for their child who'd died, reflecting where I was. I devoured the material.

Two parents in the town who'd lost a baby, one to cot death, the other stillborn, sought me out. We had a discussion with several other bereaved parents from the Gold Coast, two representing SIDS (Sudden Infant Death Syndrome), about starting a local grief support group. A group wasn't formalised from our meeting – the dynamics didn't sync up at the time – but I saw a lot about my situation in meeting the other parents. I saw that a stillbirth is the ultimate paradox – life and death in the one event – and that it was a loss largely unacknowledged by our society. I saw that I was fortunate to have had Joseph for two months, to have known him and had a relationship with him. Through the years I would feel lucky next to other mothers I'd meet, that Joseph lived long enough and pain-free enough to learn to smile.

> *A smile happens in a flash, but its memory can last a lifetime*
> **Bertrand Russell**

After four months, I decided I was ready to reconcile with Pete. We reunited on Simon's second birthday.

That night, I fell pregnant with our third child.

CHAPTER 3

Breaking the Silence

For even as love crowns you, so shall he crucify you
Kahlil Gibran, 'The Prophet'

afternoon, 6 September 1986

Moving our belongings into the chalet from my car, tension is mounting. As soon as my comment, whatever it is, passes through the air, I feel it: I'm at risk. I turn to walk back up the steps again, and Pete snaps. I hear him dashing up behind me.

In an instant, his hands are on my shoulders. He grabs me by the back of the arm and neck. Pushing my head forward, he marches me to the XB, spins me around and hurls me backwards over the bonnet. My back arching, he grasps my neck with both hands as months of anger tighten around my throat. His brow knits into a slight frown. He picks up my head, making a movement to ram it back into the bonnet. Two inches from my face, his dark eyes burn into mine. 'I feel like KILLING you sometimes!' the whites of his eyes now glowing.

I close my eyes, look at him again, but don't want to look. Tightening his stranglehold around my throat, he picks my head up several times, wanting to smash it hard back into the bonnet, barely stopping himself. I don't remember what other words he utters into my reddening face.

His hands close off my windpipe. I can no longer breathe. I can feel my face heating up. Under his fingers, he'd feel my heart trying to pump blood faster through the now constricted vessels in my neck. *Let me breathe!* Where were my hands? *How long have I got?* Seven to fourteen seconds is all it takes for the average man to strangle the average woman. *Is this it? It can't be! Not on this sunny afternoon?* I start to struggle. *No! Not after surviving Joseph's death! Not here! Not now!*

Simon, aged two years and one week, is hovering around my lower legs.

Another moment and Pete jerks my body upright, whirls me around, and rams my head down at the neck. Marching me forcefully down the lane to my car, he shoves me into the driver's seat and slams the door. 'Now FUCK OFF!' he yells. Through the passenger window, I see the top of Simon's blonde head bobbing on the other side of the car. He's whimpering, trying to get in.

I open my door, start to get out, not looking in Pete's face. 'I'm just going to put Simon in.'

'No you're NOT! You've deprived me of him for long enough! He's staying with ME!' He picks up a now-crying Simon, and heads towards the chalet.

If I leave, Simon will be safer. If I try to wangle Simon's safety, it'll get worse. It's me Pete's angry at. He won't negotiate.

Panting, shaking with adrenalin, I start the car. Trying to reverse out calmly, my heart pounding, I'm hardly able to see the world I'm driving in. The shock is dreadful. I cry a little, but not much. I can't believe what's just unfolded – and that I'm driving away from Simon.

My neck hurts. Eventually I check it in the mirror. Red throttle marks around my throat, some raised welts, a small bleeding nick on one side from Pete's fingernail.

I drive straight to the police station.

It's a Saturday afternoon.

No-one's there.

I went shopping with my mum recently. At a counter in a women's clothing store was a box of white ribbons, bracelets and badges. White Ribbon Day, held in late November, has been part of Australia's campaign to stop violence against women. My mum bought a ribbon – not because she's ever been on the receiving end of it, but because I have.

Domestic violence was the reason I became a single mother, the reason my children grew up without a dad in their home. Human relationships are complex, marriages the hardest to keep together under the easiest circumstances. I didn't get to discover other reasons mine might've ended. Domestic violence was It.

To tell of the violence is to tell only part of the story. Leaving out his good qualities is to lie by omission. Then you wouldn't understand why I and so many women stay. When violent partners are painted only black, DV continues to be misunderstood. Their respectable qualities don't excuse their violent behaviour, but to a listening ear, may help explain our efforts. We hold the mantle for growth, the hope for change – in these, the men we love. My husband was a deep soul, significantly wounded as a child by the violence in his parents' marriage. I've sometimes wondered if the love we felt the moment we met *had* to be so deep, so profound, to bring three special children to the planet. And my subsequent partner for three years was a charming man with valuable qualities I wanted in a mate, whose love for my children was genuine. Violent men can be very likeable.

After the strangling episode, I went ahead with a DVO against my husband. At court, they asked if I'd like to wait in a side room beforehand, in case I felt scared seeing Pete. We'd lost Joseph less than five months earlier. I didn't wait in the side room.

In court, Pete was asked if he objected to the DVO. He tried to specify his terms, which made him look like a control freak, with which the magistrate had no patience. The DVO was granted in minutes.

April 1990

Simon still remembers the fighting that led to our separation at Kingscliff, when Allie was only four weeks old. He wasn't yet three.

By the final episode, Simon was five and didn't see anything. He heard Pete shouting at me, 'If you want an argument, I'll give you a fucking argument!' He didn't see Pete pick me up and throw me against the door, or the bleeding cut to my lower arm from falling onto the door hinge. It was 11:30pm. The shouting woke Simon. He started crying from his bedroom.

In our new house, four hours south of Pete, the marriage had now ended.

Simon chats with me on the couch. 'When Dad used to visit, you used to talk to each other all the time. Dad used to tell us (*Simon and Allie*) to go and play. And I'd feel left out – like we weren't that important.' *Good articulating for a five-year-old.*

journal 2 April 1990

Pete and I had a love for each other that not everybody has, so deep, of such quality, it was like fairytale love. If other people getting divorced feel this way, I don't know how they go through with it, where they get their strength from and how so many could be doing it. In some ways, this feels as devastating as Joseph's death. Divorce is horrible – the next worse thing to death; harder in one way – Pete's still here and I have to *force* myself to stay away.

Simon was grieving his dad, sobbing at night, 'I want Dad, I miss Dad.' I'd wanted to stop the violence perpetrated through the generations.

There's enough violence in the world; not my precious little boy too! I see what a monstrous task it is for Pete to change deeply ingrained attitudes; they're just a part of him. But I'm changing, and succeeding. I'm giving away the security I've always had, daring to allow the boat to be rocked. It's hard, but change is possible, if you have the courage, the help (for me, James-the-counsellor), and the motivation to see it through.

When I left my marriage and started counselling with James, I learned details about domestic violence – about the 'violence cycle', and that while I must always consider my safety first, the worst thing was to *not* defend myself, or stand up for myself in some way – however menial – in the moment of abuse. I learned that it's very hard for a person to stop their violent behaviour, that much hard work and commitment is required of them to change. I learned too that at the first instance of violence in a relationship – *leave.*

I'd left my marriage because I wanted a second chance at the ideal: a loving husband and happy children/family.

Next time I'd choose with my heart *and* my head.

Rob was an intelligent man, a trained high school teacher, who'd articulate his fascination with nature. He saw humour in life, and was musical, plucking his acoustic guitar of a morning, wandering around the room, sometimes singing. I liked the free spirit. He owned his home, worked his own business, and did his own thinking – an individual. His parents weren't divorced and there'd been no violence in their marriage.

Three months into the relationship, a shocking discovery: Rob had been violent with his previous partner.

'You *know* I would've wanted to know that!' My look is direct. 'I left my marriage because of that! Why didn't you *tell* me?' He shrugs.

But it was too late. He'd said when we met that he'd been categorised 'sterile' by two different specialists, several years apart.

I'd thrown away my pills.

Within two-and-a-half months of meeting, I was pregnant.

Rob's place was given a makeover to accommodate a new family – a big adjustment for him. When the baby was three weeks old, we moved in.

Although I'd already experienced his surprising verbal abuse during the pregnancy, the first time he laid harsh hands on me, our baby was six weeks old.

letter, April 1992

Dear Rob,

...I wish love could overcome these things. I wish your love for me could make you calm towards me, and loving. I wish it enabled you to take some blame instead of levelling it all at me, and saying all those nasty things to me. I wish my love for you made me worthy of your respect. I can't help feeling you don't love me much when you treat me like that...

letter, April 1992

Dear Denny,

...If I could only turn back the hands of time and approach last night with a clear rational head instead of the emotive, crude, cheap and irrational one I had. I feel bad inside... terrible for doing that to you....

It only gets worse as I try and face all the things I've done. When I grabbed your arm Denny, I squeezed it hard, because I was trying to hurt you...

You did a wonderful thing in coming to see me at lunch... it brings me such joy to see my 'family' like that. I don't know how I can put it all in jeopardy with such 'brat-ish' behaviour. I want to be the 'patriarch' in our union... I'm sure it would be the most rewarding thing I could achieve in my lifetime. When I'm on my own I feel that life is hollow and that there's something missing...

It was an arm squeeze. The baby's only six weeks old.
But the spoken assault was not so infrequent.

letter, 18 June 1992

Dear Rob,

In case you're interested, I feel very strongly about the verbal abuse you've heaped on me these last few days. TOTALLY *unacceptable.*

I gave myself six months to see if there'd be any changes, but if this is all it's going to be, I won't even stay six months. The good bits do not compensate for, nor excuse, the bad. I cannot pull your weight for you.

letter, 19 June 1992

Dear Denny,

In case you're interested I too feel that I have to stop my verbal abuse. I know it's impossible to have a healthy relationship when that goes down. My family means everything to me. Hopefully we'll talk when I come home and I can apologise.

As genial as he was, behind the scenes Rob became domineering.

July 1992

He's been at the pub. In his absence, a friend who's working for him asks to borrow his van, to pick up building supplies in the morning, so he can continue working. It's a practical suggestion; I agree. Rob apparently decides it's time to assert his authority – or is it just one of those times a man's temper 'gets the better of him' and the woman wears it? Is it the beers? I've tried to make the right decision. I shrug at his anger at me lending his friend the van. He doesn't like me shrugging.

I'm leaning against the kitchen sink. He storms across the room, grabs my upper arms, yanks me to his side of the room, starts shaking me, yelling that I'm not to shrug at him. He shakes me harder and harder, so violently it rips my clothes apart, neck to knee. My new winter sweatshirt goes straight to the ragbag.

> *At the first instance of violence, you leave.*
> *You don't put up with it till it gets worse; you leave.*

So I did. Ash was four months old. I got a little unit down by the sea for me and the kids. I'd continue working on the relationship from a secure distance, staying with Rob when it was safe, escaping to shelter when it wasn't.

I discovered my feelings about DV had shifted. Leaving my marriage to the man I loved, I'd taken a strong stand against DV. I begrudged it trying to intrude into my life again. Rob's violence was 'wasting' my divorce. I seemed less *capable* of putting up with any more. I resented Rob holding the monopoly over Anger – he being the only one allowed to express it. As it was in my marriage, the threat of his temper began to control my days.

letter, September 1992

Dear Denny,

I know I was a shit last night. My mood swings can occur so quickly now. All I can say is that I'm aware of my temperament problems and shortness and I'd love to be able to get it out of me. I wish I could show more self-constraint and just learn when to shut up. Anyway, you were right in leaving last night. You assessed the situation well and I respect you for that. I've got to stop screwing up and interrupting the flow of Simon and Allie's lives. That of course goes for you too.

Please think positive.

letter, 26 November 1992

Dear Denny,

...I've wasted 12 months of your life... and Simon and Allie's... by being the person I've been... I haven't been seeing things the way I should've. My eyes and my heart have been receiving a distorted image or view... Today, I've seen it all a little more clearly...

...I've let the most petty insignificant occurrences blind my perception of the real you. I've managed to turn the most innocuous remark into a reason for World War III. I've even gone looking for reactions from you that I could use to justify my own petty, immature feelings of being 'let down' by you....

...We humans can really fuck up whenever any pressures are put on us. It's so easy to lose track of reality and the really important things that make this relatively short life on planet earth. You seem to have a better handle on it than what I do... Possibly Joseph's death tuned you in a lot more to it...

I haven't listened to your dad's tapes yet but already I feel positive. I feel like I've come out of a mist this morning... There were the usual tears for my impending loss... but there's also something else... it's a feeling of knowing that *I* have to get my anger under control... it's almost as if I can't wait to get some guidance. It's something I have to do by myself... but no matter how hard it's going to be... it's going to be worth it... The love in your notes tells me that. I've just got to see it all clearly... Keep the mist away and live in the sunshine. Let me become the man I was when we first met and let you be the person whom you are… Twelve months of anger and resentment is such a waste…

From the inside of a violent relationship, the apologies are profuse and come from his depths. They're *real*. He's humbled by his violent outburst, and genuinely doesn't want to lose you. The REMORSE is heartfelt.

It's not so black-and-white for you. You have a child with this person. Father absence is a thing. It was Simon, aged seven, who'd asked bedside when Ashley was born if he and Allie could start calling Rob 'Dad'…

You want to believe in a second chance. You haven't been into your own future yet and seen if this works or not. Life relies on hope for the future, acceptance of flaws, forgiveness…

But there's no balance between the REMORSE space and the abusive one. These splinters don't connect and negotiate with each other.

He buys into the BUY-BACK phase, working hard, pouring heart and soul into pursuing you again. Perhaps less consciously, he wants to see all his cleverness at controlling you…

It's amazing the lengths we go to, to not feel our powerlessness.

You work it all out, make sure your agreements are met – this is your best negotiating time – it *will* work out now.

And into the HONEYMOON phase you go. Both relieved to have not broken up, you're closer than ever, riding a high. *This* is how it feels to make a relationship work!

Even if you're alert to not assuming responsibility for his anger, you don't see that his good behaviour at this time perpetuates the cycle.

Merrily, for now, you get on with life.

Eventually the little things start. Minor things, really – and why rock the boat that's taken so much effort to stabilise? Everyone has to do *some* overlooking, *some* compromising. No-one's perfect, including you. The timing has to be right to communicate.

Before you know it, tension is BUILDING UP. You're not keeping track of his intimidation; your energy's going into placating the space between you, but your resentment about that's on the rise.

It peaks. Something always makes it peak. You could stand up to him, but he won't be told what to do by *you*, you *mother figure*! He STANDS OVER you.

And there you have it. EXPLOSION. Violent outburst. Abuse, injury, outside maybe, inside definitely, almost always worse than before. Shock, Anger, a Split.

But he can't stay in that heightened state of righteous anger forever. You leave and stay somewhere else. Time passes while he calms down; you lick your wounds and reflect a little more. He feels bad, you start to miss each other, except this time it'll be different.

Yet facing the *real* end of it, you start to grieve. Could I have done something differently? He undoubtedly could, but was I too quick to leave? Of course, he'll tell you that you were, he'd tell you anything if he thought it'd weaken your resolve. But *was* I? Is *this* the episode that could've turned the whole relationship around?

Why is this your decision? Why is the relationship yours to maintain? Why is it your fault if it fails?

Your doubts and questions undermine you – as they're meant to.

A perfectionist is not a good match with an abuser. The abuser, on the hunt to control, plays on your self-doubts to put you down ('gaslighting'), with which your perfectionist's harsh critic readily concurs.

And so the violence cycle repeats.

HONEYMOON, BUILD UP, STAND OVER, EXPLOSION, REMORSE, BUY-BACK; repeat.

Violence and abuse in my life made me someone I didn't want to be. Not only in the relationship, in standing up to him and fighting back, but in myself. It put me on the back foot, having to defend myself at almost every turn. This was not my idea of 'love'.

In my marriage, I decided that if determination alone could stand up to brute strength, I had it in the bag; I discovered it couldn't. James told us that aside from their natural physical inequality, he accepts that a man and woman might be 50% each responsible for pushing each other to anger – but that a person tipping their anger over into violence is 100% their responsibility. Their arms don't flail out uncontrolled at random passers-by. They have full control over who they show their violence towards.

5 March 1993

After a relatively low-key argument, it escalates quickly. Rob and I are both on our feet. I'm holding Ashley. Rob yanks my hair hard, shoving me against the wall with a verbal assault. 'You fucking mole!' He's grabbing me by the neck and jaw, pushing me around – 'I'm holding the baby!' (is he blind?) – he pulls my hair hard again, shouting abuse, 'You're a piece of shit – don't forget that – you're a fucking piece of shit!' He leaves marks all around my neck. Gouges where he's seized me with his fingernails – another on my thumb – scratch marks over my body. He tries to shut me in the bedroom, roaring, 'Don't *dare* say another word!' He spits full in my face, then leaves. A handful of my hair comes out afterwards.

mid-March 1993

COURT ORDER SERVED: ADVO

A 'complaint against the defendant' was heard in court.

Rob was now legally prohibited from 'assaulting, threatening, molesting or harassing' me.

1 April 1993

We'd already seen two counsellors I'd arranged for us.

We started attending a Domestic Violence group at Lifeline, Broadbeach, every Thursday afternoon for two months.

Rob attended the Perpetrators group. I attended the Survivors group. We learnt about the violence cycle, anger, self-esteem, and DV-related issues.

18 June 1993

'You're a fucking piece of shit, Denny. No wonder your husband left you!' (*He didn't.*) 'You're nothing but a fucking useless piece of shit.' 'Bitch!' 'Dickhead!' etc. – all yelled at me with Simon standing between us.

I was living with DV in the era in which the law, and the law's attitudes, towards it changed.

Back in Melbourne **1985**: Pete – my husband – won't let me up, I'm struggling, he's got me pinned by the wrists, raised voice, leaves welts, bruises.

The following day, when he's at work, I phone the police. I'd just seen a program: women can take out a court order against their violent partners.

'Could you tell me about the new domestic violence court order?' I ask the officer.

'Nuh. Never heard of it.'

'My husband was violent with me yesterday... What do you normally do in these situations?'

'Oh... we don't really like to get involved in domestic disputes, luv.'

Forward to the Gold Coast eight years later, **1993**: with new partner Rob – he comes home very drunk, vomits, flips out at my plans to go away the next day – gives me a temporary fat lip, a cut, 'Fucking piece of shit', 'Bitch', etc.

I phone the police.

'When did this happen?'

'The night before last.'

'Who did you speak to about it then?'

'No-one.'

'You mean this is the first time you've reported it?'

'Yes.'

'Why?! You shouldn't wait overnight – you should've called us immediately!'

Even with greater social awareness and 'support', I felt dreadful contacting the police – guilty, like we should be handling our marriage dynamics ourselves, that bringing the police into our relationship was my call, and therefore my fault. *How does all this become a woman's responsibility?*

I felt shamed by both reactions, as though whichever way *I* was handling it was the wrong way.

I was afraid each time the police were involved – phoning them, going to the station, to court for a DVO. I was terrified that taking *any* action would incur the wrath from which I needed protection, which had to be provided by outsiders to our relationship. Because he'd see it as me gaining power over him, I was terrified it'd unleash greater fury than before. The fact that it didn't (at the time) showed they *knew* their violence against me was wrong, that their bullying game had been called by an external adjudicator – the law. Violence is illegal. They'd got caught.

But the law couldn't legislate against my fear, against the internal dynamics of our relationship, against the uneven power balance, against the patriarchy, chauvinism, sexism, misogyny, or the daily effects of his intimidation – only against the physical manifestation of all these cultural attitudes, together with each man's personal issues – in their abuse towards me.

journal 19 May 1993

I want a more normal life for my children. I want them to feel greatly loved no matter what. I want them to feel totally accepted, so that they can accept themselves. I want them to feel, and be, confident, to feel confident socially with others. I don't want my children feeling like I do.

I'm glad of my unit. It's safe here; and it's *my* place.

I've felt like such a prisoner at his place. I don't know how I *ever* stood the pressure!!! You don't realise you're losing your sense of freedom until you feel your freedom again. Other feelings crowd in, distract you, take all you have to cope with; you lose what's important to you.

Amidst coming and going from our little beachside unit, I'd communicate through letters to Rob my reflections on where I was at, about the relationship.

24 May 1993

...My sister said to me during the week that she could see a change in you last weekend. You weren't constantly trying to put shit on me to get a reaction, you were taking things a little more seriously instead of having to joke off about everything, and you were behaving more respectfully towards me...

...But your violence is *unacceptable*...

...I love you and would stay with you – if the relationship was a satisfying one for me, AND for ALL *THREE* of my children...

...You need to do some communicating with me. It's the only way this could work...

21 June 1993

Can't believe the day I've just had. Must be one of the worst I've had with him. Not a moment's peace from start to finish. Where does he get the energy??? I was so exhausted by dinnertime, I was nearly collapsing, but he was still fighting, as strong as ever.

I can't believe I'm still here, sinking in this quagmire. These dear little children. They're so precious. They show him so much respect. And this is my adult life. For all of us, it goes by so quickly. What am I still doing here??

I gave myself six months and I probably didn't expect it over before then. I was psyched up to give it a go, but it no longer makes sense to stay.

He pushed me again twice. Spent much time trying to build a case for me being a slut. Made up much derogatory 'conversations' between supposed college lovers about me.

One in four Australian women is subjected to Domestic Violence.[1]

22 June 1993

Another unbelievable start to the day. *'Cheap little gutter snipe'* he called me, while sitting at the table having breakfast with the children. 'Why don't you go for a drive and contemplate some telegraph poles – like you did before.' He can't resist using my vulnerabilities against me. I'm always sorry for confiding in him.

July 1993

I had to get us away. In the mid-year school break, I packed us up in my little Sigma, and took the children for a holiday to Canberra. They hadn't seen snow before.

On a lonely road behind Mount Kosciusko, the darkness descended. Travelling further into the night, I hoped our car would hold out, because we weren't passing any other cars at all, and it wasn't a great place to break down.

Simon had had a vomiting bug in Canberra, which we assumed was a 24-hour one. We'd pushed on with our trip. Around a particularly windy stretch, Ashley suddenly manifested the bug up his oesophagus and down his front. As fast as I could, I pulled over roadside in the dark. Within 15 seconds, Simon was out of the car vomiting in unison with Ashley. Then Allie was out, joining in, in sympathy.

The image: a cold lonely road from snow white to pitch black, no car had passed us for two hours, my three children all vomiting outside the car at the same time... Why would I *cry?* The chilly Kosciusko night echoes instead with sounds of a mother reaching her limit: spilling out into the darkness, while her children retch, a loud maniacal cackle, as she's tipped over the edge...

At the domestic violence Lifeline group, we're encouraged to record violent incidents, to get a clearer picture. The facilitator of the women's group suggests we get to recognise their 'tactics'.

May–July 1993

Some of his terms of endearment for me:
'Fucking Parasite'
'Fucking Sponge'
'Fucking Dumb Bat'
'Fucking Lazy Bitch'
'Bee-in-your-bonnet'
'Thin-skinned'
'Nose-out-of-joint'
'Hole!'
'Dickhead'
'Fucking Selfish Bitch'
'Puerile!'
'Immature!'
'Piece of shit'
'The most useless person I've ever had'
'Fucking Useless Piece of Shit!' (it used to be 'You *talk* shit'... now we've progressed...)
Tells me he's only with me because it saves him going out and looking for sex.
Wears me down: tells me on a daily basis how bad I am, that I'm nothing but a piece of shit, that I'm a bitch, a slut, that I'm fucked. 'Why don't you go and finish your dinner outside with the other dogs!'
Blame, blame, blame.
Diverting focus away from his bad behaviours, onto me.
Turning positive things I do into negatives.

journal 19 May 1993

Am I basically insecure? Is unhappiness familiar territory to me? Do I make up things to be unhappy about? Do I look to have him fill my needs all the time, rather than either giving to him, or else filling my own emotional needs? Is it biochemical? Or something that needs to be sorted out and just appears exaggerated at times? Everybody feels overwhelmed sometimes. Do I feel it more often? Or in a more exaggerated, or more intense, way? Will I ever naturally be able to feel contented in a routine stable life, without some change to cope with or some problem to work on?

> *The torturer scores a victory over his victim when the latter,*
> *in the grip of doubt, begins to torture himself.*
> **Elie Wiesel**

I thought because of what I'd learned about DV, I could manage this situation. If it got physical, it was black-and-white: the boundary had been crossed and I could take action – leave. But the damage of the verbal abuse, which I had not lived with before, was far more insidious. Like a cancer below the surface, the continual belittling, the degradation, the pointed humiliation, the often tailor-made abuse – not just once, and not when it was just us, but sometimes in front of others, usually and indifferently in front of the children – would silently snake a shady path through my self-esteem, until finally I didn't even realise I was feeling like the 'fucking useless piece of shit' I was constantly being told I was. You hold your own, you refuse to call yourself a victim, stuffing your responses in the moment, telling yourself it doesn't affect you, but it does, and it's actually that it's so subtle, you just don't realise it.

Neither did I see that I still had to grieve my ideal: the husband and children, a family life. I hadn't worked that want through yet, hadn't convinced myself it wasn't going to happen for me and my children. This was my last chance. My children wouldn't be calling another man, 'Dad'. Cherishing that ideal continued to put me – us – at risk.

I'd been reared a Christian, to believe the best about others, to look for it, to hold hope for everybody. This hope dies hard. 'Do unto others.' *Would I want my children taken from me?* 'Respect others', 'give them a hearing', 'believe they'll come good'. Working through my ideals, my questions, with integrity was not straightforward from the inside of the relationship.

It wasn't just the rearing of my children on my own I was baulking at either. I hadn't been socialised to be an independent woman. I'd had no modelling for emotional or psychological autonomy from another half, and didn't automatically know how to face a life on my own, complete in myself without a man. I would've told myself I could do these things easily, but actually *doing* them involved psychological and emotional skills, unsupported by my culture at the time, that I didn't yet have. And since I was unwilling for my children and I to continue living with violence, I had to be part of a generation of mothers who pushed through unacceptable relationship issues, to take the rearing all on our own shoulders, who'd finally be supported legally with DVOs, and financially with a Single Parent payment to enable a choice.

We did produce more rounded young men. We contributed softer young males to the world who'd begin the shift from 'macho' to 'metrosexual', encouraging them to open doors to more of their sensitive selves. I am so proud of this generation of stay-at-home dads, reaching deep inside themselves to learn new gender roles and rear their children in gentler ways.

Between each violent episode, life continues as usual, tension often present. I wash, cook, take care of the baby, he goes to work, the children go to school. DV hides itself in normality, without favourites, across every social/economic strata of society.

To reassure himself of his control over me in our everyday life, Rob *minimises – denies* if he can – his abusive behaviour, victimising himself, while blaming me, *maximising* anything he can 'get' me on.

After a while, sections of the violence cycle begin to drop out.

27 November 1993
Rob hardly bothers with the Buy-Back now, skips the Honeymoon and gets straight into business, hasn't gone through the Remorse phase for a while. 'I called you a slut and I'm not sorry.' 'So I called you a fucking idiot and told you to shut up. If you can't take that, you're as weak as piss.' His affection fades. He doesn't cuddle me after sex anymore, turns his back instead – no word, no kiss, no brief embrace.

Gradually the dynamics of the violence cycle weaken the foundation of the relationship.

When I have the energy, my concerns creep in.

I can dance with Anger however I like – his, mine – it's all my unspoken responsibility.

He has control. My resentment grows.

Most women will leave between five and seven times before they're able to leave permanently, each time becoming stronger and more confident.[2]

journal 22 September 1993

I had one of those dreams last night. It was so scary, it permeated my whole being. The feeling is still with me today.

I was in the Sigma, Simon and Allie in the front. Allie was next to the window, and we were in that little side street that runs up beside the police station. There was another car blocking us. We couldn't turn around, and while we were waiting to get past, a man was trying to steal a red car behind us. Trying to break the front window to get in, he was becoming more and more desperate... Suddenly, his mate got out of the car, because too many people around were witnessing what they were doing. He held a gun with both hands at arm's length, and shot the driver of the car that was blocking ours.

I said to the kids, 'Put your heads down'. I nudged our car into reverse and started to coast backwards very slowly. But I knew I wasn't going to get out of it. I knew we were next. I could see Allie's pretty little head with pigtails down just below window level. I worried she'd be first, or even me.

I woke up sweating.

This is what makes the dream feel like one of *those* 'dreams': Tonight when Rob and I were in serious discussion, he was worked up the whole time, and said, 'You can understand why men go and shoot their wife and kids!' These words after last night's dream...

Would he allow his thousands of resentments to push him that far? I'm meant to wonder.

The violence from each of my partners was different. Each was being directed by inner core beliefs that they should be in charge of me, that I should do as they said. Pete wasn't verbally abusive. Even his rarer physical violence was from a different place – almost as though driven by volatile biochemistry. It was explosive, it was terrifying. But he was a spiritual man. Right through our marriage, he loved me and I knew it.

Rob's violence rose suddenly too. More predictable, it was way more frequent. His verbal assault far exceeded his physical abuse; it was shocking. 'Don't kid yourself I love you!' he'd jeer. 'I've only got you here because it's the only way I can live with Ashley.' *He no longer looks at himself, doesn't seem to know how.*

'Explanations are not excuses.' – **©Denny Meek**

I'd learned THE worst feeling in the world was to let a string of abusive comments go by, or a violent incident, and do nothing to stand up for myself. When you're being attacked, it's a fine line between asserting yourself and attacking back, and I didn't always return respect for abuse. Sometimes I let myself fight like a normal person. It's tough to interface, especially when your attacker speaks no other language, although such venom doesn't flow readily from my mouth. Self-protection in the home was something I *had* to learn, followed by standing up for myself, and eventually fighting back. I hated living like this; I didn't like fighting, and didn't like being the person I had to become. It was an empty existence to me. I was staying because this *was* our second chance, many days being faced with the decision: which was worse? My children living amidst the abuse, or growing up without a dad?

> *NOTES from Domestic Violence Group, Lifeline Broadbeach, 1993*
> Week 5, Denny: I'm depressed. Not a good week. I moved back to my unit and I feel much better. I haven't thought much about Rob at all. Before I left, we had a terrible argument; he made horrible accusations which went on and on and on. He apologised the next day but he's done that before, too. 'Eggs in basket' idea helped. I haven't been putting equal time into the children. My son (aged 8) isn't concentrating at school and he told the teacher that he worries about us fighting. That upset me.

Sometimes, after the group, I could see Rob trying to implement changes. It'd bring hope for a while, then confusion when another violent incident erupted.

Between episodes, as life went on, sometimes we'd have fun, go to the beach, go for a drive, play music together, he on the electric guitar, me on the piano. I'd bath the kids. Cook dinner. We'd eat sitting on the couch in front of the telly, or at the table. My children did their homework. Many days, we lived normal lives – all days, the dynamics of the violence cycle holding the relationship in place. Always, the undercurrent of me accepting responsibility for not triggering his anger. If I 'failed' – which happened increasingly with Rob, as he took me more and more for granted, my resentment of his disrespect grew, and I found it harder and harder to play the placating role – I dealt with the consequences.

'This is hell,' I'd say to Rob.

'This isn't hell!'

'Well you might be able to live like this, but I can't. And even if I could, I don't want to.'

How many people in the world 'live like this'? Battered inside, defensive, I trusted the world and others a little less now. *Are they trying to put me down?* I'd wonder of others. I didn't feel as safe, as loving a person. At family gatherings, I'd notice my sisters, unable to identify with how relaxed they were with their husbands, not on-guard, not living with abuse, but soft, safe, peaceful in their worlds, in themselves, unsuspicious of whether or not they were loved. Having energy bound up in defending myself, I didn't feel as lovingly attentive to my children either. *How can I give them what I want to, what they need, when I'm living in survival?*

One woman a week is killed in Australia by Domestic Violence.[3]

letter, 6 September 1993

Dear Rob,

Last Monday, after that violent episode here, as I told you, I rang the police. I want you to know what they said. The constable asked for my name. 'What will happen if I give it to you?' I asked.

He said they'd come around and arrest you straight away. They'd take you to the police station, photograph you, fingerprint you, and charge you with a breach of the Domestic Violence Order. While you waited for the court hearing, which at that stage was September 24, you'd have to stay at a friend's house, and wouldn't be allowed any contact with me meanwhile. At the court hearing, you'd receive a conviction, plus whatever sentence the magistrate decided. The fine would be at least $1,000. There could be a good behaviour bond, or a prison sentence of several months, depending on the severity of the breach, and the presence of cuts or bruises (in this instance, there were several). The officer I was speaking to had seen a range of sentencing, but with breaches, he said they were pretty tough. He'd seen a man get a three-month prison sentence just for parking in his car outside the woman's house. I'd already told him what'd happened that morning; he asked was I sure I wouldn't like to leave my name with him. I said I'd get back to him, adding I thought it was very unfair – *wrong* – that I should be the one to do the weighing up, that *you* had the DVO on you, and *you* had breached it *(many times)* – why wasn't it *you* who was doing the weighing up? Or why the hell hadn't *you* weighed it up *before* you were violent? Why should *I* wear all the flak when those actions are *yours*? He agreed with me and affirmed that every woman has the right to feel safe in her own home. He said that he could push his wife around because he's stronger, but it wasn't right to, etc. You've heard it all before.

So I thought and thought, and decided that because of everything that'd come from a breach, how some of your relatives would react if this got you convicted after all, and that *I* would wear it, not *you*, it'd be better if I just left.

NB: verbal abuse *is* breaching the order.

I learned from my marriage that love wasn't enough to fix it.

I learned with Rob that it was never finished. You could give them as much time and airspace as you had to give, but it'd never be finished. *That energy of trying to control you is never satisfied; resolution with it is not possible.* Abandoning the relationship and disentangling myself from it was the only option.

The abuse always gets worse.
Aggression leads to more aggression, not less.[4]
It's very hard for a violent person to stop.
DV is not about them losing control of their anger,
but about trying to gain control of you.

Our DV group facilitator said women are socialised to stuff their anger, be soft and forgiving, forever the diplomat, always the relationship maintainer, which means she feels obliged to accept his apology and overlook his flaws.

Couples counselling is no longer considered appropriate for DV, as it's recognised as a problem of the perpetrator, not of the couple.

letter, 20 November 1993

Dear Rob,

I've just been re-reading some old letters we'd written each other, some loving, some horrible. Still, they made me sad. As far back as the letters go (our first year), I've been saying the same things to you. Right through, I've tried to communicate them – that I'm not prepared to stay in a relationship where I'm treated with such disrespect. I've said it, and said it. And I've stayed in it for nearly three years. And nothing has changed. You've come to accept your abuse more. To begin with, you used to apologise, on your own motivation:

'*I know I have to stop speaking badly to you, Denny*' (1½ years ago – when we moved to our unit).

'*I know that if this isn't my last chance, I'm getting ever so close to it now. It's almost as if I have a "death wish" to lose my son and the woman I love... How can I get myself under control? Before it's too late... Sorry for the trouble'* (written the night I lent your work mate the van).

'Just as a flower is the start of a new life in plants, let these flowers be a symbol of the start of our new "life".' (26 Nov '92 flowers left for me on what you named Rob's 'turn-around day').

'About last night – I had no right to let my temper get away from me and give you the serve you got.' (Oct '92).

'I know I was a shit last night. All I can say is that I'm aware of my temperament problems and shortness and I'd love to be able to get it out of me. I wish I could show more self-constraint and just learn when to shut up... I've got to stop screwing up...'

And there are more letters with more of the same. I didn't write those quotes to hold you to them, or to shove them in your face, as you would me. I just feel sad, and this might be my last opportunity to share what I feel with you.

late 1993

Clairvoyants were beginning to emerge. I'd never approached one before. I wrote a letter to one.

I need to know what my future holds. Do I stay? Will he grow up? Are things going to improve? Or should I leave now? I can't take any more abuse, and it seems my health can't either. What's ahead for the children and me?

I'd got positive results in a pap smear and had to have a loop excision. Rob told me I'd got the pre-cancerous cells because I was 'a slut'.

There's a higher incidence of abnormal pap smears amongst abused women.[5]

At the end of my marriage, I arrived at similar stress levels, and was put on cortisone to help pick me up.

There's a higher incidence of DV perpetrated towards pregnant women.[6]

The first time I was newly pregnant, I had a loaded rifle pointed at my face. During that first pregnancy, I was pushed into a fibro wall that broke. When I was newly pregnant with my third baby, I took out a DVO about the incident where I was being strangled over the bonnet. I don't remember with my fourth, although there was much emotional abuse – even my father remembers being horrified hearing the verbal assault I was copping during that pregnancy.

17 November 1993

Two days after I've had the pre-cancerous cells excised, a phone conversation:

R: I don't accept that you have more rights over Ashley than I do. What makes you think you can take him away from me like you do? I'd love to do that to you and see how you feel. I'm going to have him this weekend.

D: You won't have him overnight.

R: What makes you think you can say that, and have total control; I have just as much right to say he comes with me…

D: I won't let him go overnight though.

R: Why not?

D: He's too young, he's only just been weaned.

R: What are you going to do about it, if I just come and take him, and you don't know where we are?

D: Over my dead body.

R: *If I have to kill you, I would do it.*

D: Goodnight, Rob.

I hang up.

It was not the only time he threatened to kill me.

Bit by bit, I worked my way through my barriers, grieving my ideals as I lived this reality. I'd given myself till the end of the year in the relationship. I did NOT want my sons modelling DV for themselves, nor my daughter growing up to expect it.

I was worn down, on borrowed time, but knew I'd be leaving. Sometimes I could feel my freedom within reach…

19 March 1994

Another episode: He's trying to push my head into a wall. I'm resisting, he suddenly stops, my head jerks forward, hits the wall hard – face first. He knew it would. I hear my nose crack. It starts bleeding. He leaves, satisfied.

…That smell – that headachy uncomfortable smell of your nasal cavity – like the shock of getting winded, of not being able to breathe… instantly that 'something's wrong' smell…

And afterwards, the slight raised bump on the bridge of your nose that shouldn't be there, that you catch sight of in your inner eyesight. And on the side of your nose, that slight dark bruising as the black eye begins…

Yes it hurt. But how does this end? There's nowhere left for it to go.

journal 29 April 1994

It needs to be recorded. A bit of grog. A bit too much perceived give on his part. Enter abuse.

My children are growing up so quickly. When do I leave?

A doctor on telly today said you leave at the first episode of physical or verbal abuse – *that's* when the decision happens. This year, I'll leave. *THIS* YEAR.

Don't forget your blood nose on the 19th March. Don't forget his injury was a hurt heel – from kicking *you*. (Yes, *assume* damage on my end – injury and bruising everywhere.)

Don't forget all the words tonight, parked on the side of the road again. 'Stupid' being the one he was drunkenly pursuing. 'Dickhead', 'goose', 'cockhead', 'cock', 'you're a joke', 'the most stupid girlfriend I've ever had'.

Don't forget Simon's nervous head shake and nod, that'd been gone for ages, that instantly returned by the time we'd got home.

You forget your rights – to respect, to be heard, to a peaceful home, to express your anger, to safety, to your self-esteem. You forget amidst survival. And don't realise you've forgotten.

***Children do not have to directly witness or be involved in violent episodes in order to be affected.*[7]**

We know this *now*. The research wasn't out when my children were little. DV wasn't even illegal till then. DVOs had just been introduced.

We know this now. And one in four Australian women still experiences it.

And more than one woman a *week* is killed in Australia from it. STILL.

Reflection from 28 Sept 2008

Women on the receiving end of domestic violence are shamed, of course from their partner, but also from society, and from the inside. 'How could they let it happen to themselves?' Your self-esteem suffers if you feel like you can't look after yourself properly. In discussion with my co-worker (not a parent): 'But didn't your husband *hit* you??' her assumption that it's so black-and-white, bellowing loudly across the room. Another (not a parent) sneers, 'Didn't it ever cross your mind to just *leave*?' Victim-shaming doesn't help. DV is underreported because people are afraid – of many things – and shamed. I felt ashamed of being abused when I was supposed to be equal to men. And the more equal women are expected to be, the more ashamed I expect the one in four still feels.

Out of interest, I was happy enough to look at life from Rob's perspective through those years as though there was no 'God'. But nearing the end, I'd begun to spiritually starve.

I was worn down, depleted, needed a stretch alone.

My girlfriend next door was going rafting down the rapids near Coffs Harbour. She'd recently freed herself from her unacceptable marriage too, and we'd done some outings to a local club.

Simon and Allie stayed with my parents while I spent the weekend away with girlfriends, white-water rafting.

Somehow, sometime, the raw truth HITS you in the face. Finally, you've had enough. You've become ready.

My own hindsight tells me it was because I was more relaxed, less vigilant, that he sensed he was losing power over me — and felt my indifference to his knowing. The fact that I was finding my freedom from caring, disentangling from that violently 'enmeshed' relationship, was so liberating. Separating from Rob on the inside of myself, I felt closer to him, almost compassionate for his traits and issues that were constricting him, churning out the DV perpetrator. His abuse continued. I'd done my grieving. I prepared myself to rear my children as a single mother. I knew I'd leave soon. I wondered how, and when.

28 June 1994

Dusk, a Tuesday night. I'd been grocery shopping and was putting food away in the kitchen. For many months, Rob had been sensing my growing independence: he was losing control of me.

A short argument escalates, immediately as usual. He's two-thirds of the way across the kitchen as I come from the fridge to reply to his abuse. A scuffle begins. He grabs me, restraining me by the side of the arms. I lift my knee to within an inch of his groin to make him flinch and back off, which it does. But he takes it a step further than he ever has before.

Instantly his hand swings at my jaw — and hits me. *Very* hard.

Two-thirds of the way back across the room, I 'come to' in a bent-down position. I've slammed against the glass doors. My eyes begin to open from darkness to a ringing in my ears. The realisation slowly dawns: *I've been hit.*

I try to straighten up. Too dizzy to be shocked, I gather my bearings. Turn to stagger out the door. Rob is yelling abuse. 'Go run away to your little friend, you fucking coward!' Reeling across the yard to the neighbour's house, my body starts to shake. The adrenalin's kicking in. My jaw begins to unfreeze. Something in the left side of my mouth starts to disintegrate. It breaks away from the back of my mouth, and crumbles down my tongue.

Into the palm of my hand, I spit: shattered fragments, splinters, a chunk of tooth.

The hit had broken my wisdom tooth in half.

Within three days, I've arranged a house to rent, and booked a carrier. I leave Rob for good.

There was a slow shift inside me as that decision was made: that I would not be staying in this relationship. Leaving wasn't a single action; it was a journey, based on all sorts of working through, a chain of inner actions that ended with me finally pulling my body out the door behind me. When I moved house, there was nothing more to process. I was free...

Domestic violence had been an issue for me until that day. When I left Rob, I felt that weight lift from my life. For the first few months, I was like a bird out of a cage. If it meant I was never in relationship again, DV was never going to be an issue for me again. Never.

CHAPTER 4

Mama Bear Solo

Your children are not your children...
They come through you but not from you
And though they are with you yet they belong not to you...
Kahlil Gibran, 'The Prophet'

April 1987

Simon, aged two-and-a-half, gazes intently under my arm as I'm reading to him.

'Mummy?' his huge brown eyes up close now, staring cross-eyed at my armpit, his toddler's index finger stroking bristles. 'Is that grass??'

Another story-reading afternoon, I feel a considered kick from my unborn baby – right where Simon's resting against my tummy. He doesn't notice. 'The baby kicked you, Sime!' He moves away; he thinks the baby's making room for itself. Baby stays still. Simon moves back against my tummy; baby boots him squarely again. 'The baby's saying hello to you!'

You and I are gonna be a team, the baby's saying. *Beware: I'm bringing a wicked sense of humour with me!*

Single parenting was not a role I would've chosen, one for which I'd had no modelling, but it was where I had my most precious moments as a mother. The calmer wellspring from which my treasured memories flow, single parenting equated to our freedom from DV. It still brings relief to remember how light the air felt when we moved out on our own. As a single mum, I didn't have to seek anyone's agreement about my child rearing – but neither was there any back-up, emotional or otherwise. I was the backstop and the front-stop; I was It. *'It'* took some coming to terms with.

After my third baby, the children and I stayed with my parents. Pete and I wanted our marriage to succeed, and we needed our own space. I decided on a fresh start, relocating with the children four hours' north.

1988–1990

The baby with the sense of humour is nine months old, Simon three, when we move to Gympie. It's 1988, and Queenslanders are cheap to rent where my children's godparents live. Other than Mary and Peter, we know no-one in town.

My husband Pete lives and works in Brisbane, and visits us on weekends. Within limits, I can rear my children with the support of a parenting payment while working on my marriage. I pull in our purse strings as we become part of a social sector that feels exceptional for the era.

I *love* our Queenslander on the outskirts of town, the first house I've ever rented on my own. We have no car, so we walk everywhere – to church 1km, playgroup, tumble fun, bible study 1km, the toy library 1.3km. I walk us to Woollies almost a kilometre away, pushing the baby in the stroller, taking advantage of their free home delivery for our groceries. To pay our fortnightly rent, we walk the 2km into town.

The baby's starting to talk. *Mum-mum, Dad-dad, Bub-bub, Nan-nan.* Then out comes Allie's first independent word: *shiiiiit*. It's more like *'h-h-h-hit'*, but there's no mistaking it. That sound had left an impression on our little voice-recorder. *Gonna have to watch my language now!*

I watched my language but the baby retained her fondness for words that reverberated on impact.

Under the macadamia nut tree in our yard, I'd spread a rug where we'd lounge for hours next to Allie's playpen. Simon helps his dad erect the swing set in the back yard. The gentle motion of the baby swing rocks Allie to sleep. Simon sits on the double seesaw swing, looking into the distance, alone. *His little brother should be on that other seat, God.*

Still a Christian, I'd work my way through my questions at women's bible studies, where no other women are single mothers, or admit to DV in their marriages. It's not two years yet since Joseph was here; I become the mother I'd met in hospital when he was born – the one who'd lost her baby son the year before and talked about it plainly. By now I'm full of questions – mainly *why* had it happened? Eventually most of the women have had enough, and one mother spills it. 'Look, babies in third world countries die all the time!'

'And those mothers hurt deeply too,' I reply.

'Yes but even if *I* was in a third world country with my children, God wouldn't let any of *my* children die.'

'Why not?'

'Because I'm a Christian.'

Oh the luxury, the privilege, the certainty of her unquestioned assumptive world.

My spiritual path separates from some of my fellow Christians at this time. I dig deep, attending two different churches and two weekly bible studies – one mainstream, one Pentecostal – searching, seeking.

I feel guilty not giving time to Joseph, as though his life and death could come and go, and I could get moving again quickly, like it hadn't mattered. I have no choice. My future drags me away from him. Life is busy with two small children on my own.

It's in the Queensland climate that Simon has an asthma attack, and the first of many hospitalisations with asthma through his childhood. Nebulisers, puffers and spacers become part of our lives.

After eight months, during a visit to my parents, Simon puts the hard word on his grandfather on one of their early morning jogs. 'John, would you give us your other car?' Suddenly this makes perfect sense to my dad, and we're able to drive back to Gympie in a little gold Sigma. What a difference a car makes!

Since Simon was a toddler, I've written notes to myself on how to be a better mother to my children. I continue to this day.

June 1988

Simon (*nearly 4*) needs your loving patience.

You need to get through your grief about what you've missed out with him, so you can let him go to enjoy the life he deserves, the full free life for which God intended.

This year, and there's only half of it left, is his last full year at home. He'll learn so much this year. Talk with him like another person. Enjoy him while he's here with you. Learn from him. Become like him; trusting, uncomplicated, real.

Get your sleep so you can be what they both deserve. Give Simon time – the moment is only here once, the opportunity gone forever.

Please God, help me do this now,
Simon's Mummy

God, be with the mother...
As she carried her child, may she carry her soul.
As her child was born, may she give birth and life and form
to her own higher truth.
As she nourished and protected her child, may she nourish and
protect her inner life and her independence.
For her soul shall be her most painful birth, her most difficult child,
and the dearest sister to her other children. Amen.
Michael Leunig

September 1988
The housing market is changing; our Queenslander sells suddenly. *No panic. Shouldn't take long to find another.*

It doesn't, although our rent in the next house increases slightly.

I'm having marriage counselling sessions with the minister. I love my husband dearly, and don't want to stay a single mother; I really want to be married and have a happy family. With the single parenting stress, weight is dropping off me.

Within three months, our next house sells too. The owner tells us we have to be out in ten days – on Christmas Eve. On advice from a solicitor, I inform the owner that we're covered by a 'periodic tenancy agreement'; we *have* to be given a month's notice. The letter arrives with three days to go: the new owners' furniture is being delivered, ready or not, on January 3rd.

On that very day, the removalists begin carting furniture in the front door as we're moving ours out the back door.

The godparents, Mary and Peter, had added our name to the housing commission list, and started looking.

A former Catholic Brothers' house, run by the Knights of the Southern Cross, a branch of St Vincent de Paul, has rooms available. A big old two-story timber building opposite the Catholic church, it has ten bedrooms in a row along the top story, with a shared built-in verandah; a chapel upstairs, a former bar downstairs; a massive wide staircase with carved railings right down the middle; communal kitchen downstairs, lots of fridges, a walk-in pantry and a big dining room with many tables.

And so, my children and I move into Emergency Housing. When we arrive, only one lady occupies a room up the end. Frances works full-time and spends weekends away. I choose the two bedrooms down the other end, and the children and I almost have the place to ourselves. Emergency Housing is not so bad.

For the first three weeks anyway.

Then Malcolm and Julie arrive.

Malcolm and Julie move as close to us with their three children as they can. They're loud, watch telly loud, yell at their kids loud, and fill the place with cigarette smoke.

We live in this arrangement for three months.

Then Tex arrives. He's loosely given the job of 'caretaker' of the premises. I don't know why. He's 'not the full quid', and takes the title seriously, deciding to do the rounds at 10pm each night with a torch, jangling a set of keys, knocking on our doors, insisting we turn off our lights and go to bed; then walking along the bedroom doors at 6:30 in the mornings, ringing a big bell to wake us all up.

It was crazy. I thought *that* had stretched me.

Tex's arrival is followed shortly after by two full-blown alcoholics, also homeless, who take the other two rooms closest to us around the corner. They keep to themselves, sleeping till midday, leaving to go out to drink, returning after midnight, loud, very drunk, sleeping till midday, going out to drink. We'd lost control of our environment. These were not bad people, they needed their emergency housing as we did, but living with full-blown alcoholism next door was where I drew the line. It was not the atmosphere I wanted for Simon and Allie. The five months of living with our diverse fellow humans in emergency housing we tried not to judge was coming to an end. We *had* to take whatever housing opportunity came up next.

So often timing is everything. 'Would you take a place out of town?' Housing commission asks. *I'd love to!*

Twenty minutes out, we have three acres to ourselves in Amamoor. The four-bedroom block house is our fourth place in two years. The preschool I have Simon enrolled at is a twelve-minute drive up the road.

One afternoon when I pick Simon up, a mum with whom I'm chatting looks down at my eldest child, now aged five. 'What a gorgeous looking little boy! He has such beautiful eyes.' She looks back at me, 'He has your eyes.'

'Actually,' – my standard reply – 'he has his dad's eyes.'

Simon's own explanation surfaces this time: 'Yes, I'm just having a little turn of them for a while.'

After two years, Pete and I decide to give living together full-time one last try.

Twenty-eight days later, the final episode of violence.

We will now proceed with a divorce.

Pete had shifted up from Brisbane and got work locally, so I leave the house for him. The children and I will move.

1990–1991

I'd left Pete before but maintaining the separation from him was very difficult. We loved each other deeply, and I knew my resolve would be tested. If I didn't move geographically, I wouldn't be able to stick it out.

On the southern Gold Coast, I secured a cute little A-framed chalet in a peaceful bush resort, koalas grunting in nearby gum trees, nocturnal animals climbing to our porch for the children to feed. We were now living near extended family in a familiar region.

I enrolled Simon in kindergarten at his grandmother's school; his Granny would be his first formal schoolteacher. The continuity of my parents in my children's lives from wherever we were, was a stability for them. Allie stuck close by me, only letting me out of sight when she got distracted chasing butterflies. I'd never seen butterflies land on people before. They landed regularly on Allie and stayed, I guessed because they felt some softness in her spirit.

I knew leaving Pete would be challenging, and a deep grief began to emerge that I felt would be impossible to survive.

28 February 1990

That emptiness is back. I feel nothing. I watch people happily living their lives that seem so shallow. Why do my children have such enthusiasm for life? What is there to be excited about? It's all superficial.

Reflection from 9 January 2011
Mine was a desperate grief: that poor 29-year-old woman who'd lost her baby son three-and-a-half years earlier, *forcing* herself to leave the husband she loved, to face an uncertain future as a single mother of two beautiful children.

25 March 1990
Again, the pain is expanding my vision – opens my eye to the inside of life. I'm seeing what Pete tried to describe to me, that God isn't contained just in Christianity, but is the life-force in everything. I'm seeing the 'God' energy everywhere I look – in every cell of life. It's liberating, broadening my beliefs.

Simon has another asthma attack, a hospitalisation, and I begin seeing James-the-counsellor who specialises in DV.

April 1990
Homework for James: I don't want to be overly controlling of my children. Are there any emergency protections for them while I'm unravelling learned behaviours and the judgements of Christianity in myself?
James's homework for me: practice not 'shoulding' on yourself.

After spending Easter in Sydney, I accept a Sunday afternoon drive with a friend in the country. Tony rocks up in his silver Honda Prelude. As we cruise between green meadows, sunshine beaming through an open sunroof, a little voice pipes up from the back seat.

'Tony?' Allie's almost three now.

'Yes, Sweetheart?'

'Do you have any kids?'

'No Sweetheart, I don't,' the unsuspecting driver smiles, endeared.

Allie comes straight to the point. 'Well don't think *we're* gonna be *your* kids.'

My snickers are hard to muffle.

25 January 1991
It's not what you say to Simon and Allie as much as the time you give them. Let them be satisfied before you take off to your next chore, let them decide when they've had enough of your time – prove that to them when you can; it's the FEELING you have about them that's conveyed. If your buttons are pressed, if you don't like them, they'll feel

it, and won't be able to like themselves. Make it your top priority, their self-esteem and confidence.

1991–1994

Another year, and we've met Rob, our time with him interspersed with single parenting episodes.

Allie's so bright that when most children are asking where babies come from, she asks, 'Mum, how do homosexuals have sex?' She's five, asks with naivety, trusting I'll tell her the truth. *If she's old enough to form the question, she's old enough for the answer* I decide, and convey to her what I know. She doesn't bat an eyelid, just fits the jigsaw piece into her mind, and continues onto her next wondering about the world.

It's not long before my fourth child, Ashley, is incredibly active, learning to climb before he can walk. His curiosity demolishes a room in five minutes, cupboard doors ajar, contents spewed across floors. Due to his speed, I eventually surrender to the house's chaotic state, leaving the tidy-up till Ash is asleep.

If drawers have external handles, Ash climbs. If handles are indented, in slip his little toes, and up he climbs – along kitchen benchtops, towards the fridge-top, where medications are usually kept. The dog's cortisone tablets quickly scoffed, register no effects in his system. His dad worries when Ash swallows a packet of my contraceptive pills.

'What did Poisons Information say?' He'd hurried in the door from work.

'They said he won't get pregnant.'

'Okay,' I smirk, 'they said he'll be okay...' He is.

Different story when Ash, in a nanosecond, breaks through the outer ties and inner childproof locks of the pantry. Two bottles of cooking essence later, Poisons Information informs me that some essences are 50% alcohol, and our baby might behave 'a bit hungover'. He does – he vomits eight times, sleeps for three hours solid, and wakes up hungry.

As it had been my third call to them in a week, Poisons Information wants more of my details...

From inside the DV, I continue steering my parenting.

16 March 1994

Whatever hardship in your children's lives or yours, THE most important thing for them is to feel acceptance, approval, friendship, and love – *unconditionally*. That will give them the framework to work life out for themselves. They're all intelligent. They'll come to you when they want to know things, and will ask you, if they feel they can trust you because you unconditionally accept them, and don't just project your stuff onto them.

You know what you like in a friend. Be that to them.

Enjoy life with them. Whenever you can, enjoy *them*.

1995–1998

In the midst of arguments with my husband, and my subsequent partner, a choice was assumed by both fathers. When angry with me, they'd vacate their parenting role, leaving the children with me. If I left, I'd take the children with me. My single parenting status was assumed – by all parties.

I didn't know how I'd cope with three to myself, but six months after my relationship with Rob had ended, living in the same suburb was not working, the abuse ongoing. The children and I needed to move away.

Four hours' south, Coffs Harbour was our destination. The new start was refreshing for all of us, Sime soon discovering the PCYC (Police and Community Youth Club), socialising there often. A fortnight after our move, Sime had his photo in the paper playing PCYC basketball. As many networks weren't up and running for children in single-parent families at the time, the PCYC was a help to Simon. I felt very much for him missing out on fathering.

By the time Ash started school, the consciousness was shifting. 'Kristal's mum and dad live in the same house!' Ash shared the oddity. *How about that, sweetie!*

Time and again, I applied for work, but nothing eventuated. I tightened my belt financially, decided to become a full-time mum that first year, sit on the hillside with my children, and observe life. It was a very painful year for me, facing why I was on my own again – *two* violent relationships. *How can that be coincidence?* I read books that'd begun to draw me, asked questions I hadn't asked before, journalling furiously, filling an A4 100-page notepad every month with new perceptions, and started attending Spiritual Awareness classes. My appetite was piqued, my consciousness expanding.

I did what I could to create a peaceful home, playing calming Enya and Iona CDs, to combat the effects of the abuse we'd lived with. I wanted us to stretch out, to enjoy the space to feel and be ourselves.

'Some adults think children aren't worth the time,' Allie says one afternoon. 'Do you think that?'

'No, Allie,' I shake my head directly at her. 'I don't think that.'

'I'm glad I don't have a mum who thinks that.'

'What's the meaning of life?' Simon asks me another day.

I ponder with him. 'To find the meaning of life...'

I sometimes feel their trust in me as a heavy responsibility, other times as an immense honour.

April 1995

After Easter in Sydney, I'm invited to race in a Women's Go-Kart competition at *Raleigh International Raceway*. My children, lined up along the fence with other spectators, cheer me on. They watch me tear around the tracks against sixteen competitors, secure a place in my heat, and come second in the final. It's satisfying for my kids to see me standing on the podium accepting a trophy, a boost for all of us to see me triumph. (Plus, it's massive fun!)

I'd chosen our property for the six-foot fence around the house and Ashley's escapism, but Ash slips his little toes between the fencing slats and escapes anyway. From wherever I am, I turn around at too much silence and he's gone – nowhere to be found. Heart-thumping stuff! I'd glance around the house and yard, sometimes having to grab the car keys, and drive neighbouring streets to find him. One day he's on the nearby main road, heading straight towards the busy six-lane highway, oblivious to the massive trucks and vehicles zooming past at 60kph. Aged three, he makes it there in less than five minutes. With long urgent honks on the horn, I try to arrest his attention. He'd apparently decided to take himself to *Macca's* for an ice-cream... Ashley earns the nickname, 'Houdini'.

At age two, I'd taken Ash to a paediatrician, who'd diagnosed him with ADHD. I provide as much stimulation in the home as I can, and attend a group for mothers with ADHD children, for extra tips.

Aged three, at day care, Ash draws a map of the streets leading to our home, then in a far corner of the playground, stacks foam blocks on top of each other next to the high wire fence. He's the only child to successfully escape the centre.

Aged four, I enrol him at a Steiner preschool; he lasts only a term. I keep getting calls from the teacher. 'He's scaled the fence again and run away. I can't leave the other children to go and find him.'

When enough time has passed without the domestic unrest in our home, when his neural pathways have settled a little, and when Ash eventually has 'enough' stimulation, namely school, the Houdini phase passes. I'm also helped by a guardian angel, a nesting magpie. Whenever *Houdini* tries to escape, it swoops on him. The bird soon trains the little escapist to stay behind the fence.

Ash's speed and climbing skills stay with him. In high school, he wins an indoor rock climbing challenge – fastest in his year to scale the high vertical wall (9.40 seconds). As he accepts the award, shaking the sports master's hand, I shake my head, laughing hard. Applauding audience members are clueless to those early *Houdini* memories inciting his mother's amused chuckles.

1995

My children love being read to. I read to them a lot, next to the glass-front fireplace, the four of us bundled together on the couch at night before bed: *Myths & Legends, Tales of Magic & Mystery, Gods & Heroes from Viking Mythology.* In *Mutant Message Down Under,* we go walkabout with an Aboriginal tribe, a little further across the Australian outback each night. Then relax in a book of *Children's Meditations.*

'Mum reads us medatashions on the couch,' Allie's school diary records. Allie begins reading a lot herself in Coffs Harbour.

Louise Hay has hit the scene. Around the dining room table, I play affirmations with my children, having each of us call out in turn, *I love myself, I respect myself, I approve of myself.* I know it'll take more than affirmations to counter the abuse, but despite my worry, a calm fills the air from the absence of all that tension. Our new life is liberating for us.

Exploring beyond prior spiritual boundaries, I have only one step further to take, to discover extended family already in these places. Initiated by the Reiki master of my father's siblings, I become a Reiki channel, and start sensing intuitively; it's opening my third eyesight. Frank open-minded discussions on broader spiritual topics with my aunt and uncles are a great support to my path. I'm devouring spiritual books, new information, and love what I'm learning.

The year I'm not working leaves me free to help with reading in the children's classrooms. My kids don't need the help, but they love having me there. Allie's hazel eyes sparkle with pride as we walk out of the classroom together for 'little lunch', her excitement tempered by the natural maturity she's always had. Chatting away happily, she retrieves her little lunch from her bag outside the room. While every other child pulls out a small packet of chips, popper or muesli bar, I watch as Allie takes from her lunchbox her sliced carrot and celery sticks. She's not self-conscious; she's done this a hundred times before. In the playground, Simon runs to meet us, carrot and celery sticks in hand too. 'Doesn't your mother pack you exciting food for recess?' I joke with them. Their eyes instantly divert to their shoes, shaking their heads – no – a response that seems automatic. Guilt crushes me.

That afternoon when they get home from school, Allie checks with Simon. 'Is Mum having a party?'

'Why?'

'Look in the pantry.'

A bag of 20 small chip packets fills a shelf, boxes of muesli bars, blackberry and orange roll-ups.

'I didn't want you missing out!' I try to shake the guilt from my mind. 'They're just for school.'

How long had they been embarrassed by their healthy lunches while all the other children ate fun, interesting food? I hadn't known; they didn't mention it.

17 August 1995

I'm seeing that our children teach us more than we teach them, if we're open to it. Awareness I had to struggle to develop in myself, they seem to bring with them.

Irrespective of their age, if my children are independent spiritual entities, making their own choices of lessons, then they chose me as I am now, not as I'll be twenty years down the track. That means that what I have to give them now IS what they're with me for. My lessons of honesty and respect will be important for them too.

This parenting bit is a lot tougher than I thought it'd be!

Be patient, kind and gentle with yourself, Denny – as the parent you'd like for yourself. We don't reach perfection; we only get 'there' by learning to love and accept ourselves right where we are 'here'.

A new definition of perfection: *unconditional self-love.*

Allie and I plan a fairy party. Next time the grass is mowed, under a tree on the front lawn, we build a round bird's nest from the cuttings, make a ring of saved clover flowers, spread a light blanket inside, bring her fairy toys, and eat lollies... a proper fairy party.

My daughter loves Pocahontas. Santa gives her the book for Christmas with Pocahontas paraphernalia.

I can still hear her eight-year-old voice singing 'Colours of the Wind'...

Coming up to Easter 1996, details arrange themselves before my eyes to enable Simon, aged 11, and me to take a road trip to the opal-mining town of Lightning Ridge. Ash spends the holiday with his dad. Allie, who's not an outdoors roughing-it girl (prefers staying clean) accompanies her grandparents to Sydney, to holiday with her cousins. Simon and I enjoy adventures of different kinds, and love that we can do this together.

All the way out, and back, we chat, listening to Simon's choice – *Nirvana Unplugged* – and my choice – Jethro Tull – in our little white Subaru. We take an esky of fresh fruit and lots of Easter eggs, stay at The Diggings with friends, and with my uncle who's a miner at 'The Ridge'. President of the Lightning Ridge branch of the 'Australasian Order of Old Bastards', he stars locally as the Easter Bunny, raising funds for the Children's Hospital. The Easter Ridge activities keep us entertained with billy goat races down the dusty main street, explorations down the mines, regular soaks in the bore baths, a trip out into the dry Grawin scrub, and a barbeque with locals on The Rise. Slightly elevated from the surrounding Ridge terrain, the view is perfect, light pollution absent in the Australian outback. The night sky on The Rise looks bigger out there, fills with a huge full moon and billions of bright stars across a perfectly flat horizon in a 360-degree view.

Simon and I love sharing this trip with each other.

A wound that never heals

Through the years, counting off every birthday, I picture how big Joseph would be, his personality, his head of black curly hair amongst his siblings', his eyes dark and round like Simon's and their dad's, his voice, filling that gap – that gaping hole, that aching absence – between his siblings, imagining his relationships with them, his coming home from school with them, milling around for afternoon tea, washing his clothes with theirs, sleeping in bunk beds with Simon, what his favourite food would be, would he be quiet, passionate, sociable? Would he be sporty?

No, he'd be quieter physically. He'd started life with a surgically corrected heart and would live a life of other leanings. Would he belt out Jimmy Barnes, or write rap songs like his big brother in his future? Or poetry like his little sister? He'd have loved music. We've all loved music.

The pain of Joseph's absence is with me every day, as I live the hurt of not watching my baby grow up. All those years, I don't speak openly about it, but keep him deep inside where he's safe.

From time to time through the years, I've had a recurring dream — a kindness from beyond — that I'm visiting a heavenly maternity ward, having a nurse of Joseph, his little body light as air, his soft head of dark hair resting in the crook of my elbow, his familiar face often smiling into mine. I only dream about him as a baby; he doesn't grow old. It comforts me that *I don't miss out on seeing him grow up.*

Allie arrives home from school. 'Kaitlin doesn't believe we're one eighth Indian. We *are*, aren't we Mum?'

'Yes, darling, you *are*.' Their paternal grandad was born in Calcutta and grew up with his grandmother at the foothills of the Himalayas. I love encouraging Simon and Allie's pride in their Indian heritage, the looks Allie inherited especially exotic.

The children have to sit state-wide and Australia-wide tests at school in English and maths. Simon, Allie and Ash all do well. All three of them sit at the bullet tips in their results.

On Sunday afternoons, we develop a routine of going to the Jetty foreshore where Simon, Allie and Ash burn off energy in the playground.

One Friday afternoon we venture to Trial Bay Gaol at South West Rocks, and camp at the bottom of the old gaol for the weekend. Lined up next to each other in Simon's four-man tent, our sleep is deep. The first morning we wake to the screeching of rainbow lorikeets whizzing over our tent from tree to tree through the campground. Like small children, the birds' excitement exudes out their shrieking, '*We live in the most beautiful place in the world!*'

Working life out, and why I'd been in pain for so much of it, occupied most of my private inner space. I'd observed before that being in pain sharpened my spiritual sight. Again, I tuned in to my intuition more, and took a quantum leap in spiritual learning, embracing more encompassing ideas about life, and about others, that suited my fair mind. I gathered a large circle of open-minded friends, some of whom were Readers with whom I clicked, and began to 'read' myself. In October 1997, I shared a stall site with friends at the Bellingen Global Festival, launching myself into the world as a professional Tarot Reader.

Many psychic Readers at the time were burning out after three years. Witchcraft laws all over the world were gradually being repealed, and there was a lot of underlying fear and clarifying of beliefs to address in the energy exchanges during Readings, of which we were at the coalface.

I also did Readings from home, and in 1998, worked on a psychic phone line – a challenge I enjoyed.

It was a great learning experience, deeply satisfying work, and a huge privilege. I still find it uplifting to speak spiritual truths openly.

My children were changing. I was changing.

In 1996, aged 12, Sime joins the Coffs Harbour Air Cadets, and takes two flights in a glider.

In January 1997, we head to outback Queensland. Simon has always felt a father-shaped hole in his life and wants to go and live with his dad; he and his dad have both wanted a period living together. Before we leave our Coffs Harbour house, Allie and Ash already in the car, I call Simon back inside.

I light incense, pull my Tarot deck, grab my feather, and fly by the seat of my harem pants, doing a little in-the-moment ritual, to acknowledge my precious eldest son officially leaving my care. Afterwards I realise it was just like an initiation, a youth's *rite of passage*, marking boyhood to manhood. The next time I see Sime, six months later, he'll have changed beyond recognition: his hair will be long, he'll be taller than me, and his voice will have broken. I'll glance at the youth on the bus I'm to pick him up from, then look past him searching for my son.

I wish my love could protect him as he leaves my care and goes out into the world.

We pack up the Pajero with his clothes, bike, new Christmas presents and head out towards the small outback town, to his dad's property. Simon has a curious adventurous independent spirit, so this will suit him. He's excited to get to his dad's place.

Right at the town's turnoff, we see a raptor that's been recently killed on the road. I pull up and look at Sime. 'We'll get a feather!' Sime's not sure; he's in awe of eagles. 'There are no coincidences, Sime. It'll be gone soon. We're part of nature too.' He follows me from car to road. 'Where's your army knife?' He pulls it from his pocket. I cut the three longest feathers from the bird's wing, hand the longest to Sime, the second longest I keep, and the third feather I give to Ash.

'If you ever miss me Sime, hold onto your feather, and you'll be able to feel me with you.'

Simon sometimes tells me on the phone during his stay with his dad that he's holding onto his feather. 'Can you tell I love you?' I ask.

'Yep!'

What a cutie.

Later that year, after nine months with his dad, Simon's ready to come home. The father-restlessness he'd had till then has dissipated. He jokes with his breaking voice, making it crack on purpose while the kids are singing together in the car. I love how unselfconscious he is about it.

Adolescence is now on my doorstep.

All year long, I'm on the lookout for great presents to lay-by for my children for Christmas. Each week from February onwards, I have a small percentage of my income deducted to a Christmas Savings account, so that Christmas is a spoil for my children.

27 December 1997

My dear little boy found out at 4am two mornings ago that Santa Claus wasn't real. Ash had asked Santa at a shopping centre in Coffs Harbour for one of his real reindeer for Christmas. Santa said he'd see what he could do. (Gee, thanks Santa!) The letter from the school Santa was no more help either.

So, my smart little Ashley put Santa to the test: if he delivered the goods – a live reindeer – then he'd know Santa was real. No reindeer = no Santa.

On Christmas morning, Ash woke at 4am, saw the presents at the end of his bed, and bounded out towards the door. 'I'm going to see if Santa left my reindeer!'

My heart broke for him. *I didn't want to stop believing in magic either, sweetie.*

Ash came back, hopped right into bed – 'Huh! Thought so!' – and went straight back to sleep.

October 1998

Of the lovely men with whom I was enjoying friendships, I entered into relationship with one. It turned out he really did consider himself more spiritually advanced than others. The night my children weren't home, out of the blue, he joined the DV perpetrators' list. In the worst episode of violence against me by any man, the catalogue of injuries he caused was prolific. When he tried to silence me, I stood my ground and spoke my truth. 'I will not have a relationship with a man who considers himself to be my superior!' With those words, he hit an edge, but he wouldn't cross it, so with no-one around, he hit me instead. My head bounced off the brick wall. He too broke my wisdom tooth – called it a gift from God. Amongst other injuries, wrists, shoulder, skull, jaw, I had a searing concussion for three days.

To have been hit by a third partner was absolutely heartbreaking.

It was not supposed to happen – again.

Or *ever*.

I have remained out of relationship ever since.

CHAPTER 5

Pursuit of Perfection

I don't suffer mental illness, I enjoy every moment of it
Allie Meek (26.8.01)

December 2000

I nose the Toyota into the park.
My stomach tightens. My breath quickens as I close the car door. At the solid glass entrance to the motley brick building, I hit the intercom.
Minutes pass.
'Child and Adolescent Ward.'
'It's Denny Meek.'
I tilt my ear towards the speaker, straining to gauge the atmosphere inside today.
'Yes?' The background voices are too faint to recognise.
'I'm here to see Allie.' I roll my eyes, desperate to shriek at the security camera, at someone, anyone. Don't you know this by now?! My sunnies hopefully mask the anxiety and sadness that seek refuge in my hostility.
A deafening buzz unlocks the door. I thrust it open, before the opportunity's gone, and trek along carpeted corridors to another set of doors – larger, darker beige, reinforced by thick silver plates – heavily locked as well. Another button to press, another permission to plead before they'll let me see my daughter.

Inside the next door, my tightness eases. Two teenage girls in track pants and T-shirts perch on the cream lounge. One is Tanya, a friend Allie's made in here. Smile.

Soon my daughter appears in the corridor. In flared jeans, her white halter-neck top highlights her olive skin, her brown hair falling past her shoulders, her smile gentle, hazel eyes peaceful today. She saunters into the hug we both need. I squeeze her, not too tight, and my chest drops with relief. She smells so lovely.

Allie and I head outside, seating ourselves at table and chairs by ourselves. Staff keeps an eagle eye on us through glass doors while we talk. Our backs to the main building, we gaze over the yard to the surrounding high brick walls, topped the entire length with generous rolls of silver razor wire.

If we choose our paths, then my daughter chose a massive challenge for hers. She was still a child when the crows began circling conspiratorially overhead, their vaguely identified issues mocking my powerlessness to stop them. The disquiet of watching Allie eating more the year Simon was gone, wondering about the father absence in her life, about the effects of living with domestic violence, her former stepfather's issue with fat women, my own anxiety in single parenting, little negative things she'd say, little worries she'd express, her high-achieving drive, her perfectionism, her artistic nature, her keen interest in her idols, her over-interest in food, diets and exercise – all homing in on her with too much intensity. Like magnets with her name on them.

No-one knew how much the crows rattled me. *Aaark, aaark, aaark.*

We try hard in our parenting to leave out the parts that hurt us when we were little, and add the helpful parts we missed. Allie was a good girl, as I'd been, and I didn't want her to feel it went unnoticed.

When she's nine I go to her room, sit on her bed, and give her a present.

From Allie's 'Autobiography:
Memories', Opportunity Class 1999

It was in a small necklace box that was wrapped in smartie paper and it was the most beautiful thing I'd ever seen. It was sooooooo shiny. Mum opened the heart latch revealing two pictures, one of me, one of her, that'd been taken when we went to Movie World.

'Thanks for being so good, Allie,' I smile in her eyes. 'I know I'm always busy, and you don't complain, you just entertain yourself. I want you to know I *really* appreciate that. I want you to know I *see* the very special, beautiful person you are.' A soul connection unfolds as we sit on her bed, two beings, chatting 'real'.

At age 10, Allie's offered a position in a Coffs Harbour OC (Opportunity Class) for particularly bright children, where she flourishes as a highly intelligent, creative student. Her perfectionism, common amongst the gifted-and-talented, is satiated enough until she's 11, when its appetite to conquer uncharted territory is piqued. This it finds in honing her padded body.

One day, Allie comes right out with it. 'Mum, am I fat?'

'No, sweetie. You're healthy.'

Healthy is a word she'll come to hate.

The crows will not be deterred.

Allie's Journal 6 February 1999
We hardly did anything today. I feel like I'm putting on heaps of weight and I feel so horrible. I bladed a bit today but I didn't have the energy to do anything else. I look in the mirror and I seem to be getting fatter and fatter and I hate it. I wanna go to some tropical island with a wise tutor who can teach me all this tricky stuff and I'd lose weight and be beautiful. I'm gonna ask mum if I can go on a diet.

Simon's been suspended twice this year and has become a school refuser. We need to move north for family support.

During our quieter year back on the Gold Coast, my children settle quickly into their new routines. Ash is happy, and within three months, Simon comes fifth in his maths test. Allie is ahead in most subjects and gets bored with her schoolwork.

Allie's Journal
Jeez, I miss the O.C. Everyone was so sensitive to each other's feelings, smart, deep.

from Allie's Story
I ended up attending one of my old schools. Everyone had established that community that grows during the first term, and I felt like an intruder. They were very nice, but I thought

they'd like me better if I was better looking. So the exercise continued and I became aware of how much I was eating. I'd ask mum to prepare my lunch a certain way, and went hungry if she did it wrong (which was *very* occasionally). Mum started picking up on things and confronting me about my eating and exercise patterns. I thought I was healthy though, so I brushed it off with excuses. They'll like me better, I'll like me better, and eventually, he'll like me better. I'd follow every bit of 'health' advice and exercise I could find.

(aged 12) Allie's Journal 21 October 1999
I cut ties with a girl at school. She called me a bitch, so I called her a slut. Oh, well. I've got more important things on my mind... I can't stop thinking about him. It's definitely a crush...

Allie spends the rest of the year stepping up her exercise, skipping in the mornings, running laps around the yard in the afternoons, and curbing every meal. She talks of diets, has long ago learned about cardiovascular workouts and becomes curious about calories. I'm agitated by the inevitable unfolding of an illness only I could see, could feel in our home, and couldn't get anyone to heed my concern.

By the time she's finished primary school, Allie's lost her 'puppy fat' and tells her diary, *'I'm quite close to my idea of the perfect body (for me)'.*

It would've been okay if she'd stopped there.

But she didn't.

She couldn't.

Allie's Journal 5 November 1999
I wish I was skinnier.
I wish the guy I like liked me back.
I wish I was prettier.
I wish these exercises would hurry up my metabolism.
I wish I was older.
I wish I was nicer. I wish I was popular.
I wish I was more open-minded.
I wish I'd lose my excess weight sooner.
I wish these wishes would come true.

It puts a strain on our household; one rebelling 15-year-old, a thankfully happy 7-year-old, and a 12-year-old whose fixation with food, workouts and exercise is thriving.

Arguments readily erupt.

Mum's Journal 27 November 1999

Four nights ago, I watched Simon succumb to anaesthetic. A surgeon sliced down his forearm to retrieve a severed tendon. At 9:35pm from the recovery ward, his first gesture was to lift his bandaged arm to show his splint. His other arm held a cannula. Best outcome as far as Sime was concerned. *'Now I'll have a scar!'*

Pushing each other's buttons the night before, Simon and I became embroiled in an argument. He'd turned his back, walked a few paces and punched a window.

I'm defeated. Anger – the stuffing down of it – is supposed to be an anorexia issue. *I don't know how to deal with it – mine, or anyone else's.*

Allie's Journal 15 January 2000

Did you know six minutes skipping is the equivalent to half an hour's jogging? Cool, huh? Looks like it paid off, too.

Allie's Journal 17 January 2000

...Ya know that horoscope book is just not working for me. Milton Black is full of it. Palmistry has me interested. I have crosses (*which represent stress*) all down my lifeline.

'Foods' – Allie's favourite topic. She'd spend hours in the kitchen cooking for us but never eat any of it herself. Her use of the word 'foods' irritated me. 'Food' is a mass noun. It doesn't get pluralised with an 's'. But that wasn't it. Adding the 's' broadcast her fear, amplified her obsession with food, overtly relaying her need to control even the grammatical rules by which she'd use it. With genuine authority and great interest, her thinning face would announce the word 'foods', yet so little would pass her fragile lips.

I lived around her illness; no shortcuts. I'd be particular about preparing her food, handling her plates and cutlery. I washed my own hands more than usual, used clean serving utensils from the drawer for her, and never washed up in dirty water. I wanted her trust so that Ano would not consider me an enemy. *I wonder if it knows I want it gone?*

Allie's Journal 24 January 2000

I need a regular schedule. I'm getting unfit. Regularity. Exercise half an hour every morning, and two intense all-over body workouts a week. I read this article which told me a fair bit body-wise. I need to eat and exercise regularly. Make it three intense cardiovascular workouts per week. I wonder if you can join a squash club? Each intense workout needs to be 45 minutes. So:

6.30 Get up
6.30–7.00 Exercise
7.00–7.30 Get ready

Always have lunch around 1.00pm and brekkie around 7.00am. Right!

It's never enough – an extra minute of exercise is better; 10 less calories is good, but 20 calories less is better. *'I'll keep it at 10 to prove to them and myself that I'm not controlled by the illness they say is bad. I have the control.'* Anorexia helps them have the control.

You'd think Ano would give her some peace when she gave it what it asked, but the more she obeyed, the more it wanted.

Allie's Journal 17 February 2000

I heard someone swear a lot and didn't like it, so I'm giving up swearing. Unless I get really, really angry...

Allie's Journal 29 March 2000

Yesterday Mum said I was anorexic. She probably doesn't care how damaging that is.

I worry about how vulnerable Allie looks and might feel. Today some boys in the bus line hassle her, standing close behind her, making lewd comments. 'You use carrots and bananas,' they hint. One describes what he does in the shower at night.

'If you don't have a girlfriend,' Allie shoots back, 'it figures!'

'No, you don't use carrots, you buy the real thing,' another continues.

'F** off!' Allie exclaims. They don't. She moves closer to the front of the line.

'You just want anal sex,' another says. Two of them jeer and repeat it. One picks up a stick and pokes her from behind. The duty teacher passes several times. Notices nothing. One boy says he'll think of Allie when he's masturbating in the shower that night. Allie's close to crying.

That afternoon at home, I conclude, 'You've gotta go to your year advisor first thing in the morning.'

The year advisor phones me. 'The matter's been "reported and addressed".'

Allie's staying closer to Simon on the bus, but days pass and the boys remain in school routine.

I phone a solicitor, then request an appointment with the deputy principal.

Across the desk, I hand the kind-eyed man a letter.

'If the four boys involved in Monday's incident with my daughter are not dealt with to my satisfaction, I will be contacting the Sexual Harassment Board in Sydney.'

The deputy fumbles in his bottom drawer, where the incident's been shelved under other reports. One by one the following weeks, the boys are suspended.

It's the significance of the battle I want Allie to feel, especially with the DV of her childhood. I want her to know such battles are winnable, that control of her circumstances is possible.

Already gaunt, Allie starts walking the 10 kilometres home from school.

Allie's Journal 20 April 2000

Today was beautiful, but I feel too full. I had two treats, an egg and an Anzac bickie, which is a bickie more than I should've had. Now I feel pretty terrible.

We discover at youth camp just how much Allie's losing.

from Allie's Story

To prove my fitness, and to get more exercise, I climbed Mount Warning (*an 8.8 km return trek*) with the group, in the rain. I was so *unbelievably* cold. I thought I'd die and was crying up the last stretch. I gave up trying to wipe my nose. But I got to the top, fifth out of 20, so I could go back and brag. Exhausted though I was, I sat for only a short while when I reached the top. And I made sure I was one of the first back down. I stood at the bottom of the mountain, trembling. It was FREEZING, but I was angry with myself because I didn't seem as cold as my friends.

That same overcast rainy day, we decided to go down the river rapids in tractor tubes. I jumped at the opportunity to prove my energy to everyone and myself (also to burn off fat). As soon as I impacted with the water, I lost all feeling of circulation. The group organiser, Tony, dragged me screaming, totally numb, onto a tractor tube. The other girls jumped on the tube and we went down the first rapids. I got cramps in both legs. They were temporarily immobilised. It felt like the muscles in both thighs had stretched. (I often got this feeling in various leg muscles. It was in fact caused by salt depletion.) Paralysed, I nearly fell off the tube. Tony had to grab me round the waist and drag me back up the side, otherwise I'd have gone straight to the water. He and the girls let me off onto the steep bank.

I trekked across this field, up a hill, all the way back to the campsite. I didn't think I'd make it, I was so indescribably COLD. I was past numb. At the camp grounds, there was no hot water for showers. So I got changed, rugged up as best I could, with more clothes, even with a beanie and doona. Yet I was still numb with cold, pure white, except for my nose and lips which were blue. I was so, so tired, but Alex, a nurse in training, wouldn't let me go to sleep. She made me a cup of tea. I nearly choked. It had sugar in it! I threw it out. I took ages to warm up. I was proud of how cold I'd been. Despite what seemed like hypothermia, I was really happy. It was proof that I had no fat at all to insulate me. And I'd still gone up Mount Warning.

Allie's cutting even more 'foods' from her diet, exercising excessively, obsessively, and continues to drop weight.

In mid-May, during an argument about food, the opportunity I'd waited years for arrives.

'You need help, Allie!' I yell. 'Why won't you accept help?'

'I *would* – if I could GET any!'

'Do you want me to try to find you some?' I quieten down.

'Yes.'

Thank God...

Late May 2000, we're referred through Community Health to a psychologist. But my relief is short-lived. Diane chatters recklessly about 'fats', and appears less intimate with this illness, whose covert activities have finally manifested for the medical profession to see. *I hope you know your stuff!* After this initial appointment together, Allie will continue seeing Diane weekly, alone.

At the second appointment, Diane tells Allie she doesn't have anorexia.

'What! Are you *sure*?'

'Yes Mum. Diane said, "You have an eating disorder, but it's not anorexia".'

I phone Diane. 'I have the utmost respect for you as the professional here – but I disagree. I think Allie does have anorexia, and I think she has a severe case.'

'Allie hears what Allie hears,' Diane implies she hadn't said this. She's to repeat the misdiagnosis to Allie several more times. It gives the illness a safe place to hide.

I have to sit back and play mum. I have to let the story unfold.

In June, I encourage Allie to a local GP to watch her body functions – weight, pulse, blood pressure, check her organs, listen to her heart – recording them in her file as he goes.

'How's her heart?' The GP doesn't answer.

'How's her *heart*?' I repeat, a little louder.

'Fine, yeah fine,' not looking at me.

'Is it – normal?' No reply.

Apart from her physical appearance, the delicate ribs and shoulder blades I feel when I hug her, I haven't a clue each week what's happening to Allie's body. I don't keep scales in the house. But the GP won't look at me, speak to me, or answer my questions. He'd done his three-month psychiatry internship: Anorexia Nervosa is the mother's fault.

In August, I'm able to have Allie seen by a dietician, who tells me not to let her prepare her own food. Allie likes the dietician, but by now, she won't eat food unless she's prepared it.

Month after month, three afternoons a week, I drive my frail daughter to these appointments.

How much do these professionals really know this illness??

from Allie's Story

Eventually Diane convinced me to reduce my exercise. So I did. To a workout in the morning and twenty dances every afternoon, of course with exceptions. I began to enjoy sessions with her though felt we never really got anywhere with the illness. I refused to call it anorexia nervosa, as neither she, nor my doctor, called it that and Mum was just panicking (in my opinion).

Mum's Journal 23 June 2000

When things go wrong with your children, your perfectionism questions you, undermines you, bringing guilt and anxiety.

I wake up daily to these harsh facts that have to be dealt with, and I'm the only one on the planet taking any responsibility. Like a reverse version of *The Little Red Hen*, everyone contributes their pathological ingredient then jumps ship when the going gets tough.

I'm so angry. Diane's misdiagnosed her, the GP won't speak to me, no-one would listen when I saw it coming, and now won't acknowledge that I knew for years what I was seeing.

Inwardly I'm always railing.

I had no idea at the time that my anger, along with the isolation, horror and fear Simon shared with me, was normal for the family of an anorexia sufferer.

(aged 13) Allie's Journal 28 July 2000

I've lost weight in the past six months. Two months ago, I was around 47–45½ when I started with Diane. I'm now 43kg.

I'm sick of being cold. Everything else is okay, but I hate the cold. And the confusion. Mum says I have anorexia. Diane says I have a problem. The doctor says my iron and cholesterol levels are low and everything else is perfect. I don't know if anything is really wrong. I like exercise and hate fat. I like the shape of my face lately. It looks narrower and more mature. If my body was toned differently, it'd be perfect, but it's nice. I feel like I'm slowly going further downhill. In the last week I've woken, wondering 'Will this be the day I can no longer walk?'

If I lose my cool with Allie, it's a further excuse for her to not eat. It becomes my fault, my motherguilt concurs, and Allie doesn't take responsibility for it.

One afternoon, my inane comment escapes and it's over in a second. 'Fine then!' she exclaims throwing her dinner on the floor. Unplated food

traverses a further metre across polished boards. Surveying it with a frown, she peers up at me. I wanna scream. But Allie'd known the rules since she was two. Her Ano knew the rules too...

'Don't talk to me while I'm eating' was already a household rule. Add: *'before or after meals either'.*

The murder of crows has arrived. Perched on my daughter's gaunt frame, they face me, eyes gleaming. *Ark, ark, ark,* they mock. *What're'ya gonna do?*

Allie's Journal 20 August 2000

I've just seen how dangerous my attitude can be. I thought I'd put weight on around my cheeks, so I went into a I-hate-my-body thinking frenzy. 'I'll only eat calorie-controlled food!' I was thinking. 'Great, now I can cut back!' 'I need more exercise!' That's so dangerous. But there were thoughts like: 'It's good for your body.' 'You need it.' 'Now, you have fat to burn' which is good. Mum suggested it was fluid retention and I remembered what the dietician said. Then I relaxed a lot. But I'm starting to see what a threat I can be to myself. I'm glad I'm not following through. It's just so dangerous.

Mum's Journal September 2000

I stood at the bathroom mirror this afternoon. Out the corner of my eye, I watched her prepare her dinner. For her 'half cup of greens', she tore around a lettuce leaf to fit the circumference of the cup, then pushed it down into the bottom 'half' of the cup. She's not doing baked chicken breast in foil anymore. Spinach and carrots – still okay – egg white too. Egg yolk – bad – potato and pumpkin long gone. Forget avocado, butter, oil – THE worst. *Does it think she can absorb it by osmosis?* A teaspoon of skim milk powder now instead of a tablespoon. *How does her exercise not exhaust her? Leave her depressed from no energy?* Her Yoplait fruit-of-the-forest no-fat yoghurt (everything has to be fat-free – not 99% but 100% whenever it's available, definitely no more than 1% fat), her tins of Sustagen and Ovaltine – all get prioritised in our shopping. The boys and I continue to leave food in the house if there's a chance she might eat it.

Allie's Journal 5 November 2000

You know, it's strange. I've done what needs to be done, and more. I should be pleased with myself. But I feel rundown and depressed. My heart aches.

I'd stopped going into Allie's appointments with the GP, but I'm desperate. The time comes to talk with him privately.

Before I can speak, he cuts in. 'I'm not letting her drop below 40kg.'

Allie reaches 40kg easily in the following days. Eating little now, she's lost the fat pads under her eyes, now shadowed red, her cheek bones protruding. She's skin over bones. The young GP has never admitted a patient to hospital with anorexia before.

I phone him again.

'Yeah, she's reached admission weight, but I'm just gonna let her do her yearly exams. They're very important to her...'

God Almighty!

'She'll be in for about six to eight weeks.'

To do her exams, he lets Allie go another fortnight falling under admission weight. These professionals seemed to want her to like them. *Why would they need to be liked by a sick teenager? With her outgoing personality, she liked them all anyway!*

When Allie goes to sleep at night, I tiptoe to her door and listen. *Is she still breathing?* Now I'm worried she'll die in her sleep. I'd be as objective as I could, trying to tune in to her psychically, scanning her body for any danger areas. *What's going on inside there? Surely something's suffering?* I'm hardly game to check. Although she never mentions it to me, I keep picking up on her 'chest'.

Allie's Journal 17 November 2000

Two weeks ago, the doctor decided to admit me to hospital. Mum knew, but didn't say anything, to not stress me for the yearly exams. I went to the doctor yesterday and he just came out with it. Apparently the other girl they were treating was suffering heart problems and her BMI's higher than mine. [*Body Mass Index = height/weight ratio*]

The GP just let me off because I was trying so hard. I could've done so much better.

I went to school today and spent possibly my last day there for this year. Oh, boy.

Mum thinks it'll be easier once I get some fats back into my brain. I won't be so depressed. I have been terribly lately. But I look in the mirror and see veins, bones, etc and still don't care.

I suppose in a lot of ways, I was expecting this. It feels like something's over. Or that it's the beginning of the end.

ADMISSION

20 November 2000

Towards the end of Allie's first year in high school, she's finally hospitalised at the Gold Coast Hospital in Southport. Allie is 13, so she's in the children's ward.

They describe her body as cachectic – in an emaciated/wasted state.

By this time, her organs have surrendered the last of their fat to her vital organs – brain and heart. Even those two have begun to slow, evidenced by her slowed slightly slurred speech, called 'prosody'.

She has 'bradycardia', a slowed heart rate of 38 beats per minute at rest.

Her respiratory rate, at 16 breaths a minute, is slow.

She has low blood pressure and 'a significant postural drop' – her blood pressure falls further when she stands up.

Her core body temperature is low. Cold has become her body's default state.

Her fingers and hands, feet and toes show lividity – a red colouring she's been gathering at the extremes due to poor circulation.

Her skin is crepey. She's moderately dehydrated.

Her hair is thin and limp. Loss of nutrients.

She's never had a period and doesn't mind. Any indication that she's winning her war against fat is a victory for anorexia.

Over the last few months, 'lanugo' has appeared – fine downy hair – on her face, arms and back, a warming mechanism when there's no insulative fat, usually found in advanced cases.

At 167cm, she's taller than me, and on admission she weighs 38.2kg – a BMI of 12.

Her team have never before seen an admission for Anorexia Nervosa this sick.

Tests over the following days show Allie is 'neutropenic' with anaemia (low white blood cell count), low haemoglobin (an iron-containing protein in red blood cells), and a low platelet count (colourless blood cells that help blood to clot).

Her echocardiogram shows that because of the types of essential micronutrients in the 'foods' Allie had eliminated from her diet, together with some cardiomyopathy – weakening of the heart muscle – she'd accumulated 2cm of fluid inside her heart lining.

Consequently, Allie has a large 'pericardial effusion' on the right side of her heart.

Day One: sitting next to Allie's bed, waiting to meet her team, I look at where we've landed. I feel so guilty – about *everything*. I've tried so hard, since I saw this illness first hovering when she was nine. I've taken her to all the appointments, tried to redirect my mothering, the things I've said, the ways I've felt, thought, behaved, especially with her. I managed to curb myself, though not to perfection, I achieved considerable restraint. I'd been fighting it on my own at home all this time, yet I could not stop this unfolding. And here we are: hospital. I've held back the tears in front of Allie all year, but it's all in my face now, and the tears are forcing their own way out. It makes her cry to see me crying. At that too, I feel *so guilty*!

That night, I don't want to leave her.

For the first eight days, Allie's on strict bed rest. No getting up to go to the toilet or shower; it's bed pans and sponge baths at her bed. A nasogastric tube is inserted through her nose to her stomach through which she's fed special nutrient fluid. She's on a heart monitor that's set to alarm at 36 beats per minute. It goes off constantly because Allie's heart rate keeps falling.

from Allie's Story
My heart rate dropped so low in my sleep I could've died. I always thought Mum had handled it, or barely thought much of my problem. She'd been told to stay off my back. But that day in the hospital, she cried. I didn't know what to do. I hated myself.

It's left to me to inform the GP about her pericardial effusion.
'How did she get *THAT*?!' he asks the mere mother.
'Ah – *Anorexia*.'

He and Diane both seemed to think that gaining my daughter's trust would get them across the line. Neither said they were sorry at having missed such vital diagnoses.

Allie's Journal 24 November 2000
I've been getting 'round in a wheelchair to the toilet for the past two days and I even had a shower today! I stood, though I wasn't supposed to. Linda figured out a reward plan with me. It includes things like going to the toy room, to staying home

overnight. The kitchen stuffed both lunch and dinner up, but instead of feeling like crying, I asked the nurse to reorder. God gave me such strength.

Eight days later, when she's physically stable, Allie's transferred to the psychiatric unit in St Vincent's Hospital, Robina. During our first talk, the psychiatric registrar asks us questions about contributing factors. Joseph's short life and death a year before Allie's birth. Allie's dad's breakdown in 1997, her paternal grandmother's depression, potentially predisposing Allie with a genetic vulnerability to mental illness. Allie's high-achieving artistic nature. Family perfectionism. Several lots of DV. Subsequent father absence. Religious tension towards our family unit from extended members around Mum's Tarot work. No shortage of stressors contributing to this illness.

Days later, Allie asks me to bring a little blue pot from her bedroom.
'What for, sweetie?'
'To plant a seedling... I'll keep it on my windowsill.'
'Good idea!' An encouraging symbol for her recovery to health.
The following night, staff catch Allie draining her tube-feed into the little blue pot.
Shock.
Hurt. She hasn't pulled anything like this on me before. She wouldn't normally buck the system, disobey authority. *Is she responding to being treated like a naughty child? Is this how anorexia behaves when it's cornered? Does she see it?* I'm frightened how far its tentacles have grown around her mind, how strong its hold. *It's the illness doing this, not Allie.*

Without the little pot, she quickly learns to reduce the rates/speeds, clear the 'volume fed' and pour leftovers down the loo.
We're in this thing deep.

Allie's Journal 6 December 2000
I don't like lying. I feel terrible. These people are lovely to me and I betrayed their trust. I threw away over half an apple. I would've done more. I plan to turn the tube down. I'm not proud of myself. Not at all.

I saw the dietician yesterday. She decreased the tube by one hour and increased my feed by one slice of bread. And said they can't make me eat my crust!

13 December 2000

Allie's allowed out for a few short hours to attend the high school's end-of-year presentation awards in the civic centre. I take her school uniform to the hospital. Her nasogastric tube's removed beforehand. No evidence.

Many times Allie appears on stage to collect award after award, ever so pale, red around the eyes, in a coat that's way too big, out-of-season for summer.

Anorexia's proudest accomplishment tonight is nothing academic — not Allie's top achievement in English, or in design-and-technology, or in Japanese, or in visual arts, nor her outstanding achievement in maths, science, or history — it's getting a perfect score in physical education. Allie hadn't got an 'A' in Phys Ed for her half yearlies — a blemish on her otherwise perfect report. She hadn't been naturally athletic; this is something she'd had to work for. She got there alright.

from Allie's Story

> My meals were supervised from the beginning. I'd tried to show initiative that I could do it, resist temptation to throw food away, but they didn't believe me.
>
> They put me on 'specialling' in my new room: a nurse sits and watches me all night while I sleep, and comes to the bathroom with me. I felt I'd lost the last of my privacy all because of what I'd done weeks before. But I reasoned myself out of depression...

24 December 2000

Allie has 24 hours release for Christmas. She's allowed home for the night of Christmas Eve, so she can wake up at home on Christmas morning. After Christmas lunch, I discover she's slipped away from the family. I search the house, upstairs and downstairs. Eventually, as I approach the downstairs entertainment room, I hear the whirring of my dad's gym bike. Allie's perched on top — peddling — the slave doing the bidding of the illness. I try to hide my panic.

On Christmas night, Ash with his dad, Simon and I drive Allie back to Robina Hospital by the agreed time.

Inside the locked doors, I sign my name, we kiss and hug Allie goodbye, and Simon and I return to the car. We drive away, leaving Allie — enclosed in that razor-wire psych ward on Christmas night.

As I drive, the cabin starts to fill with the sobs neither Simon nor I can contain.

from Allie's Story

Each time I got leave was like being resuscitated. I felt a new push to get better each time. I loved getting out. It was the only time I was truly happy.

Allie's Journal 28 December 2000

They took me off 'specialling' last night. They'd had a nurse sit with me overnight to make sure I didn't screw 'round with the tube.

I was dreading being weighed today. I was nervous going in the weighing room, kidding myself, hope against hope, that I hadn't lost weight. Inevitably, I had. Then they did my 'obs'. And my blood pressure was 65/40. The head psychiatrist came and listened, and decided on the spot to send me to GCH.

So I'm back on the tube 24/7 on strict bed rest with the pan. I don't go back to Robina until I'm 47kg and then they'll get straight into therapy.

Mum came and met me at the GCH. She looked like she'd been crying. She looks like that a lot lately. I feel guilty for what my problems have done to her. She looks destroyed.

Mum's Journal 28 December 2000

Backwards and forwards, gaining and losing.

I told Allie I was going to the toilet, locked the door of the first cubicle, vaguely aware of a workman next-door. There was nothing I could do. I sat on the closed toilet for half an hour and cried audibly, sobbing and sobbing.

When I came out, Allie was worried about where I'd been. She noticed my swollen face, then felt guilty that she might've caused my sadness. It's a terrible hypersensitive cycle.

Allie's Journal 3 February 2001

I asked Mum to bring my *BN* shorts, which she did. I put them on the following day and they were tight around the butt and waist, and the padding sat on the edge of the shorts. I skitzed. I took them off, dressed into my PJs, sat on the floor behind the curtain and cried.

I hid in the end room for ages.

I wanted to die.

Mum's Journal 4 March 2001

Allie was transferred back to St Vincent's a month ago. She came home for three hours today, a right she has to earn by putting on a specific amount of weight. I have to sign the Patient Leave Register whenever I take her out, with all the details – the date, where we're going, what time we're leaving, my signature, and then the same when we return – as though it's not my right as a mother to do this, as though I've become answerable to someone holding my daughter. She feels like a prisoner. It hurts.

26 March 2001

8.00pm. Phone call from St Vincent's. Allie's missing. Tanya too. St Vincent's has to file a 'Missing Persons' report with the police. *Missing. How did that happen? Why? Surely they couldn't have scaled those high brick walls? Climbed over that razor wire?* I drop on my bed, picturing a fragile Allie and Tanya darting through Robina streets in the dark, throwing backward glances. *Why would Allie do this?* 'Stay by the phone,' I'm told, in case she rings. My stomach feels punched. I'm soon in a foetal position. *How could she think escaping would help her?* I thought we'd been through the worst. *Allie – where are you??*

Allie's Journal 26 March 2001

Jessica, another sufferer was admitted today. Shocked by her appearance, Tanya and I ran around unnoticed for half an hour, before locking ourselves in the seclusion room, dragging a mattress into the middle of the floor and running a marathon around it. We're forbidden to exercise, so we were in hysterics. I cannot remember so much fun through my entire admission.

Later, we took books and jumpers, climbed into a cupboard where we hid, planning to stay until morning. But our consciences pricked us. We climbed out, the nurses pounced, and separated us into two 'time-out' rooms.

My favourite nurse informed me that the police, and our parents, had been searching for us.

Three hours later, I snatch the phone.
Found! Hiding in a cupboard...
I curl up on the bed, sobbing. Utterly spent.

from Allie's Story

Though we can have a negative influence on each other, we sufferers can also be the best thing for one another. Jess chose a full-fat diet instead of the tube. With our plain-boiled chicken and veggies, no flavourings, Jess sat opposite with sausages and gravy with roasted vegetables. She wouldn't procrastinate, she'd just eat it. It had an impact. Tanya and I soon started trying the menu, instead of always ordering special diet foods.

It was hard on Jess, though. It's hard on anyone. She later confided how sick she sometimes felt and how fat. There's no hiding from it.

As I gained weight, I gained rewards. Shopping, gym, visiting cafes, became an everyday thing. Nearing 'my' goal weight (the hospital's number) became a lot harder. I begged to be discharged 2kg from goal weight, or to maintain briefly before moving on. Not permitted.

But I tried – increasing my food intake, wary of my exercise, and trying to remain stress free. I was bitterly disappointed when I stepped on the scales and was less than 1kg from my goal weight. I'd tried my best and it wasn't good enough.

Again, the head psychiatrist became insistent that I trial 'Zoloft', an antidepressant. Again, I stubbornly refused. It's funny, when you don't obey, you're stubborn, but when you're obedient, you're determined – determined I'd get through it without being pumped with chemical crap.

I kept my mind to myself, deciding not to confide anything in the staff, put on a fake smile and unhappily ate my way to that disgusting number that would privilege me with the title of 'normal'.

I looked forward to family therapy, to feel the tug of the lifeline in our hands, to finally receive the support we desperately needed. I wanted to discover where I was going wrong in my mothering so I'd have something concrete to work on, to throw my effort into fighting the illness with Allie. I wanted someone professional to take Allie's side so I could express what it was like for us to live with. I wanted Allie to have her say – all of it – in the safety of a therapeutic environment, to feel formally heard. I wanted the boys to have their say about what it was like for them, to alleviate the helplessness we felt in living with anorexia, to voice the changes they hoped for.

Where did the 'family therapy' idea come from? That we'd be getting it at Robina? Or *anywhere*?

Weeks passed. Months passed.
'Family therapy' never came.

> *Mum's Journal 28 March 2001*
>
> Allie is almost at goal weight. We're now into month five of her hospitalisation.
>
> Her psychiatrist sees me regularly for support, and Allie not at all. Allie's owned her illness, acknowledged it's not physical, has begged for therapy since admission – until a month ago. Now she feels like a fat blob, and couldn't be bothered helping herself. Stripped of all control. Nowhere to go but rebellion. Doesn't care.
>
> You'd expect that being hospitalised for four-and-a-half months for a mental illness, she'd have received intensive psychiatric therapy. Therapy was delayed until she reached 45kg, because she wouldn't have had enough fat around her brain to concentrate. 'Cognitively impaired' is the term, yet second in Year 7 a fortnight before admission. She's had little therapy – except for *Group*. I'm grateful – they've saved her life – yet gutted they haven't addressed the mental illness. I watch her eat, not much more than when she was admitted, in the same obsessive way. Her talk is still of body, foods, weight. She's as 'anorexic' as ever.
>
> I feel let down by the hospital for not *healing* her, for treating only symptoms, not causes. Still sick, she'll battle this for years. I'm told the longer it continues, the worse the prognosis for recovery, slipping into a chronic diagnosis, with the 20% death risk.

I hear of a support group for anorexia sufferers. A thread of hope tugs. Peta Hartmann, a young psychologist, has led the group for eight years. A former sufferer, Peta's now doing her PhD in Anorexia Nervosa.

Each Thursday night, I start signing Allie out of the psych ward, taking her to the group nearby.

Slim, petite, and energetic, Peta appeals to Allie. She seems honoured when I ask if she'd take Allie on as a patient. Peta's never had a patient as young as Allie.

I engage the services of the Child & Adolescent Psychiatrist we'd met early in Allie's hospitalisation, Dr David Furrows. He agrees to see Allie once a month and oversee her team.

'Mum? When I reach my goal weight – 52kg – would you consider discharging me?'

Allie's only 13, but her team have set her goal weight at 54kg. Being pushed to an adult BMI would've generated horrendous panic.

'I don't want the illness to manipulate you...'

'I know, sweetie... I'll think about it.'

But Allie's goal weight comes and goes, and with it, her trust in the team – and in me. I don't take her out at 52kg. Her anorexia frightens me – it's bigger than me, wants her life – but apparently, I wouldn't have been allowed to take her home before she'd been officially discharged. (David's kindness later relieves my guilt, saying that had I tried, Child Services would've been waiting outside the door.) By the time she comes home, she has weight under her chin.

Allie doesn't forgive me.

Reflection from Mum's Journal 2004

Now that Allie's psychiatrist is head of the adolescent unit at Robina, he's changed procedures so that anorexia patients are handled differently than Allie was (three years ago) – not pushed up to an adult BMI, given therapy when they ask for it, and not have all control taken away. The changes were introduced because of how Allie's case was handled. He says Allie's and my relationship was pathologised at Robina, e.g. Allie was told the heart necklace I'd given her, that'd meant so much to both of us, was seen as my reinforcing the 'Good Girl' role in her; and that we were being squeezed into a model that didn't fit us, when we were two strong-minded, strong-willed, independent intelligent females who were predictably going to lock horns at this time in Allie's life. He says *he's* learnt a lot from seeing Allie and me over the years, and has benefitted both personally and professionally from our therapeutic relationship with him. As an assistant professor in Child and Adolescent Psychiatry in Brisbane, he includes examples of Allie's anorexia in his lectures.

Allie's Journal 23 April 2001

To be discharged from hospital, I must display the ability to maintain my weight for a fortnight. This was hard, as I was allowed to exercise freely, eat when I 'wanted' and basically do what I wanted. Weeks before, Tanya had been given the same privileges, hadn't eaten, exercised like mad, and lost 3kg. We'd been given a 1kg fluctuation space. The next weigh-in, I'd lost 1.1kg. I was devastated. I silently prayed they would miscalculate and be deceived that I'd lost only 1kg. They didn't. Regardless, I continued to maintain my weight, started kickboxing and tried not to worry. Two weeks later, I was blessed with the surprise that the 0.1kg didn't matter and that I'd be discharged that day. They weren't as pedantic as I believed.

DISCHARGE

I'm scared about bringing Allie home, scared our family dynamics won't be 'unpathological' enough to keep her safe. *We might make her sick again.*

Mum's Journal 9 May 2001

A fortnight since Allie came home, a new grief emerges. She's sicker than before admission. Her rituals are a little more extreme. She used bowls instead of plates before, and teaspoons – now she uses the smallest bowls and the tiniest teaspoons. She walks round the house, now openly taking the longest way, from bedroom to kitchen, to bathroom, and back, eyes downcast. I don't know if she's aware it's more obvious to us. Anorexia's rituals are supposed to be a secret. They've increased. Before she eats, she prays over her food, hands clasped, for longer periods – up to 20 minutes. She just obeys anorexia on auto now, like a robot. Although technically her organs are all fine (except her heart, but her pericardial effusion doesn't compromise the function of her heart), and four-and-a-half months of nasogastric tube-feeding has rebuilt her body and she looks physically good, she has a *pallor* which hasn't been adequately explained to me. A worrying look. I saw these behaviours as manipulation when she first came home, but it seems half the time she's just not there.

This is such a shock, after the five months we've been through. A shock that reverberates through me, bringing grief close. I've cried every day this week.

I feel I've lost my daughter, perhaps for a very long time.

In the following three months, Allie loses half the weight they'd put on her during her five-month hospitalisation. It falls off. She reaches readmission weight readily.

Allie's Journal 1 June 2001

I've been discharged from hospital for two months. And already the threat of readmission hangs. It has for the past fortnight.

This illness has become dangerously close to an OCD (Obsessive Compulsive Disorder) episode. I pick up a teaspoon and if it's the wrong one, I have to select another, lest I get fat. Everywhere

I turn I have to get it right, lest I get fat (I apologise if my mentioning the word 'fat' stresses anyone). It's everywhere. I get so frustrated. But if I don't do it, I get a horrible feeling that affects everything, my mood especially. I'm writing all of this to let anyone who suffers the same know: you're not alone.

Mum's Journal 30 July 2001

What a day! Allie was to be readmitted to hospital.

Yesterday, I'd collected the GP's referral with reports from cardiologist and psychiatrist. I'd drive her, after the boys had gone to TAFE and school.

When I went to her room, she wasn't there. I looked everywhere – house, yard, neighbourhood... She'd disappeared. Phoned friend, GP, hospital, finally psychiatric registrar – who tells me to call the police.

'My daughter is missing,' I say, 'physically and mentally unwell – she's supposed to be admitted to hospital today'.

Simon comes upstairs. 'She's not missing. She's at school. But you're right about the "mentally unwell" part – the whole household's fuckin' crazy!'

I get off the phone, divert the argument Simon needs to have with me today, and head to the school. Allie's pulled out of class, and we have a showdown in the same room I've had two previously with her brother – only she doesn't know they're supposed to end peacefully. Surprisingly, she stands up, and on it goes.

'I'm not going hospital!'

'There's no choice, Allie. The State won't let you die – neither will I.'

When the deputy principal knocks for the third time, we leave the school grounds, inspiration hitting me at the car. 'Would you speak to your psychiatrist?'

Yes.

Breakthrough!

By phone, David negotiates a compromise: Allie will be admitted tomorrow to GCH (Gold Coast Hospital) – not Robina.

OMG! When I can finally draw breath, I laugh that Allie has 'rebelled' by going to school.

I've already called anorexia 'The Good Girls' Rebellion'– ©Denny Meek.

READMISSION

31 July 2001

Dr Furrows set a readmission weight of 47kg. On readmission, Allie was 46.5kg.

(Aged 14) Allie's Journal GCH, 9 Aug 2001

Okay, I was warned. I pushed the limits. But this time it's not so bad.

I was to be readmitted on a Monday, but, for the first time in my life, I put my foot down. My psychiatrist promised he wouldn't push me above a weight I'm comfortable with, and that I could go to GCH, not Robina.

Now I'm happy here in GCH — relieved to be here. I needed a break. I'm not fighting the weight either. I needed help, to put a bit back on; I couldn't do it. There's no forcing — I still don't have to eat if I don't want to — they're working with me.

Of course I get stressed, seeing the figures go up quickly, the bloating; the intrusive thoughts still affect me. But I'm coping. And I'll be out soon.

In hospital, Allie does her schoolwork by correspondence. Several days a week, I drop her work off at school, and pick up the next folder her teachers have prepared.

No, the school authorities don't know where she is. With letters from her psychiatrist, we've gone to great lengths to keep the sticky, misunderstood AN term from being stamped on her school file.

Allie's Journal 15 August 2001

I'm 0.6kg away from discharge. I've been gaining 0.2kg for the past few days, which is what I've needed to handle it mentally.

Yesterday, a Red Cross volunteer came around while I was having afternoon tea. Having nothing to talk about, she bent down, read aloud 'ENSURE PLUS, MILKSHAKE' (STYLE) and asked, 'Is that like a fattening thing?' Yeah, thanks. Makes it a whole lot easier. She's lucky I didn't chuck it out, there and then. I was pissed off and almost <u>defiantly</u> took another mouthful. Which scared me shitless. Eating in spite. I've never done that. I was scared of getting fat, but I know God would never let that happen. I'm so grateful for his love, for faith.

12 September 2001

'I think we got it,' Peta tells me after the appointment runs well overtime. Allie rarely cried in these sessions, but this day she came out looking fragile, her eyes swollen. Peta looked unusually drained, pale.

'*It?*' I repeat. *We're nailing anorexia down to one cause?*

'*One* of the big things.'

The sadness in the air grabs me. Had something bad happened somewhere in Allie's life I didn't know about?

'When you were with Ashley's dad,' Peta started – *Oh shit, oh no* – 'you were having an argument in the kitchen one night?'

'Yes.'

'He hit you.'

My heart's pounding. 'He did.'

'Allie saw it happen...'

'*Oh NO!*'

My forehead falls in my hands, eyes squeezed against the sight.

'I wondered if Allie had seen it, but... We left straight away – packed up, gone – within days.'

'She knows you did the right thing. It's just that she couldn't stop all those things from happening...'

from Allie's Story

I didn't believe this illness had anything to do with control. Not for me. I believed it to be something else. I almost always did what others asked, always put others ahead of me. How's that for control? But then the idea was put forward that it wasn't a feeling of 'want of control', but a subconscious feeling of 'lack of control'. I couldn't stop my mum and dad from fighting. I couldn't stop the break-up. I couldn't stop us from moving in with my stepfather. I couldn't stop his abuse toward Mum. I couldn't stop him from hitting her, and instead felt like a guilty bystander.

My psychologist would say they were things that weren't up to me to handle. I don't know why I felt I had to.

SECOND DISCHARGE

Mum's Journal 3 September 2001

After five weeks, Allie's discharged again. She's cranky, blaming me for things, doing the rebelling she hadn't done more overtly. While Psychiatrist

Dr Furrows understands how tough this is, it relieves him to see Allie go through normal adolescent rebellion. He has a calming effect on both of us. Talk is not cheap to him. He said that the illness will change the form in which it manifests. Previously it was praying, and walking a certain path through the house – that's eased, and now the trichotillomania has increased. [*Trichotillomania, a type of compulsive behaviour, is an overwhelming urge to pull out hair at the root from places like the scalp, eyebrows, eyelashes. Since Allie's first hospital discharge, she'd begun nonchalantly pulling out her eyelashes. She'll keep up this behaviour on and off for years.*] David said that just as I'd explained that the dietician didn't understand Allie was incapable of making herself do certain things because of the illness, so the manipulative behaviours she's now displaying are also part of the illness. (That was a help.) He also said that from what he could gather, I was handling the situation at home quite well. And that was the best thing I'd heard all day.

Mid-October 2001

At Lifeline in Broadbeach, I join a Therapy Group for Women Exploring Anger. Three hours on Thursday afternoons, for two months.

The subject of anger needs addressing in our little family. How it was handled in my household as a child (judged a sin) worked for my parents, but doesn't work for us. How it was handled by my children's dads (violence) was destructive. We have to keep finding ways that work for me and my kids.

Allie's anger towards me continued. It was awful. She pressed my buttons; I pressed hers. Rearing teenagers is hard enough, but it felt like I'd lost my daughter at St Vincent's – that we'd lost our relationship. I wanted Allie back, but I had to try to help her recover from a deadly illness *and* rebel against me/individuate. I didn't appreciate at the time that Allie's anger expressions were normal to her recovery, the rare breaks in intensity like rainbows through storm clouds.

Allie's Journal 11 April 2002

After my hospital episodes, I was able to regulate my eating patterns enough to stay out of hospital. My aunt and uncle (who's a doctor) ordered calorie fortified fat-free supplements to help me and I started buying supplements from the supermarket. They formed the basis of my diet.

Aged 15, her first high school year without hospitalisation, she's dux of Year 9.

We continue to share our home with anorexia – her obsessive eating, exercising, little notes on the fridge: 'Do NOT hold the handle if you've been touching fatty foods!' I still drive her to fortnightly psychiatrist's appointments – but she's learnt to maintain her weight on her own. She holds it just below the lowest acceptable BMI.

Late in the year, Simon comes home from work and joins me in the kitchen. At Currumbin Wildlife Sanctuary, where he's now doing carpentry, he's building a boardwalk. His energetic strides in the door announce the days he's been working on it.

'How are you today, Mum?'

'Oh, you know...' I hug my torso and shrug.

'What?'

'...feeling like the worst mother in the world...'

'Why's that?' he persists.

Another reluctant shrug.

'Allie?'

Single nod.

'How come?'

I love seeing him confident. He's growing up, and we love our on-the-level chats. Besides, I don't have the energy to cover it up today. Out it spills: 'It's hard not to feel like her anorexia's my fault.'

'That's silly,' clarity beams from dark shining eyes. 'I used to blame myself too, because when we were little, I used to call her fat. But I realised I can't make her better, she's the only one who can. It's Allie's to deal with.'

'Yes but I *feel* like she wouldn't have got anorexia if I'd been a better mother to her.' The words tumble out my mouth before I can catch them.

'How can you *say* that?!' Simon glances around our hippie mansion. 'Look at where we live! Look at the places we've always lived. You've *always* provided beautiful homes for us to live in. You've never not paid our rent. You've never not paid our bills. We have *never* gone hungry.' I didn't know he'd noticed all this. 'I can't imagine anyone in the world being a better mother to me than you have been. No-one else could've taught me the things I needed to learn, in the ways *I* needed to learn them. Don't – *don't* doubt you're a good mother.'

Speechless, I walk to Simon and hug him.

What a beautiful young man.

It does pick me up. I feel able to continue.

Missing Persons

You have that glazed, far distant look again
It's not all the time, it's just now and then
That you go somewhere else, and leave us behind
For that curious world, inside your mind

I can understand it, I go there too
When difficult emotions are well overdue
To be dealt with in private, eased and abated
And by thinking, accept, that they're all somehow 'fated'

But sometimes your desire to go there is strong
It's not that I judge you or think that it's wrong
It's just that for you it's a powerful yearning:
My fear is that one day you won't be returning.

Those gone before you now spend most their days
In a pleasant but chillingly distorted haze
It's their way of dealing with so-called 'reality'
Their hearts just too tender for this world's mentality.

I know the temptation when you're feeling so bad
To contemplate concepts that send others mad
In order to gain at least some understanding
As you work hard to fathom emotions demanding

Sometimes I feel like I'm teetering too
And sense that connection between me and you
I don't know what brings me back from the brink
But that it comes down to the way that we think

Is this a choice? At times it seems not
How do EXternal origins govern the plot?
But please try with your will, despite your misgiving
We want you to stay in the land of the living

Your destiny lines the palm of your hand
Free will? Perhaps. But I think it is planned
That these choices our mind and our character bend
Will work out, as they are meant, in the end.

Denny Meek 12/08/01

CHAPTER 6

A Withdrawal

*I have seen death too often to believe in death.
It is not an ending – but a withdrawal.
As one who finishes a long journey, stills the motor,
turns off the lights, steps from his car,
and walks up the path to the home that awaits him.*
Don Blanding, 'A Journey Ends'

January 2003

Simon tiptoes upstairs to chat with me at the round table, before work. 'Guess what I did last night, Mum?'

'*Umm...*' I beam a naughty smile at him. He'd left with cash in his pocket.

'I wouldn't waste my money on *that*!'

'You'd never *have* to, sweetheart!'

'Guess again.' I observe a little more seriously my handsome eldest son, looking like his dad. Simon writes in the air with a buzzing sound.

'A *tattoo*! Show me!'

Shirt comes off, the massive yin-and-yang he'd wanted, freshly inked across his back. My insides grab. The two halves have been separated, one half on each shoulder, his heart behind the gap in between. 'Oh wow!' I slip excitement over unease. 'You've got your angel's wings!'

It's been a worrying few weeks.

A fortnight earlier, Simon had driven up the road from work for smoko. On returning, he'd stopped for an elderly lady coming out of a carpark in a Camry, who owed him right-of-way. She saw him, stopped – Simon assumed to give him right-of-way – and he proceeded. The old lady suddenly surged headlong into Simon's car, slamming him into a telegraph pole.

The police officer's never seen a suburban crash cause such damage. Simon's 100% in the clear, but his pride-and-joy – his 1976 VK Valiant Charger – has been totalled. The old lady, shaken, is taken to hospital by ambulance; Simon limps back to work with a sore knee.

For days, Simon didn't complain, didn't protest, didn't pull inside himself, just kept limping to work, normally. His knee gradually improved, but he didn't rail at the injustice of losing his beloved Charger. He'd owned it for two short months.

The morning after the crash, I woke at dawn, unsettled. I'd had many worries as a mother. The last few months, I'd been sensing something about Simon I didn't want to feel. All his life, we'd talked about meaningful subjects, more recently about how hard it can be to make yourself stay in this life when you feel like leaving. An extended family member had recently survived a suicide attempt. We felt very deeply for them, and Simon saw the reality of what nearly happened.

This morning, troubled there was nothing I could do for my son, I wrote him a poem.

<u>Simon's Charger</u>

For half my life, it'd been my desire
To own an old car, still propelled by fire
Not just any car, but the real 'Queen Mother'
A Valiant Charger – it could be no other

I was eighteen years old when it came to me
Through a friend of a friend… it was meant to be
Black, and with two doors, extractors, a V8
I knew by its sound, I need never be late!

She just wanted to go, this black Charger of mine
Twin exhaust, a sunroof, and a shape so divine
No need to push it, just knowing her power
My respect for her rare make, it grew by the hour

I fixed up its hiccups, there was more to be done
Irrespective, my Charger was second to none
Tried not to be proud, but I just couldn't help it
And to boast at our rallies, she fully deserved it

But one day as fate had it, I couldn't believe it
An old lady – my Charger – she just didn't see it
And although the crash was through no fault of mine
The door of my Charger closed for the last time.

For all of my life, I had wanted to be
Owned by a young man, whose heart wanted me
With zest and with passion, an eye for detail
He'd know when he saw me, his hopes I'd not fail

I'd had sev'ral owners, who were good to me
Keeping me maintained, with new things to see
But the heart of the young man was what I still yearned
And with years of good service, this want I had earned

The young man came in and soon took me away
A new power I felt from my engine that day
His fresh expectations I'd gladly fulfil
With might from his life and pure strength from his will

On the power from his heart, I ran better than ever
Such respect from a young man and love, I'd had never
Appreciation in common, each day it would seem
An honour to serve him and fulfil his dream

We hung for a short while, young man and his Charger
Contentment complete, till the old lady's merger
But t'was with satisfaction, I departed in glory
This last stretch of life, the best part of my story.

Denny Meek 4/01/03

'Thanks, Mum.'
'Sweetheart...' My head dropped, my hand helpless at his shoulder, I stood weeping for him. Crying in front of my children wasn't something I did, but it felt like someone had died. A sensitive deep soul, Simon took

life personally, searched for its meaning, and the loss of his Charger was a significant one for him. It was unusual for him not to get angry, smash a chair against a tree, vent his hurt in some way. He was not in a depression; he was being too good. My worry stirred deep.

We'd driven around looking at other cars; naturally the Charger proved hard to replace. For some reason, prospective buys kept falling through. The car-less fortnight frustrated Simon.

And now, what I've been feeling for months surfaces before my eyes in the fresh symbol, divided, on his shoulder-blades: a separation from deep inside...*'doesn't wanna be here,'* suggests *that* 'lens'.

It wasn't always like that for Sime. As a child, he woke early every morning, his eyes wide, shining their readiness for adventure, his busy enthusiasm for life contagious. As an adult, I'd feel better when he just walked into a room, his practical presence shrinking my petty worries into perspective. He spoke his truths readily and expected the same of others. Yes he'd missed a dad through his years, yet there was rarely a shortage of mates in his room up the back of the house.

The day after his tattoo, an LH 75/76 Torana ultra-blue is parked roadside for sale. Within an hour, after a test drive, Simon owns it.

It had needed a bigger carbie, which sits on the front passenger floor. Sime doesn't mind the mechanical project next day of replacing it with a mate. By day's end, he looks good, although my anxiety doesn't abate.

That night, for some reason, the four of us gather in the big bathroom in front of the mirror. When Simon has me Bepanthen his tattoo, I can feel Allie and Ash noticing my sadness. *They're your feelings,* I tell myself, *let's not project them.* There was no way I could know that within 24 hours, our little family would be irrevocably changed. To this day, I learn to distinguish my worry from intuition.

Next morning, a Monday, there are two cars in the carport again. Simon can drive himself to work today. Our routine is back to normal.

'I thought I'd take Allie and Ash camping for a few days before school starts,' I tell Sime that afternoon.

'Would it be okay if I have a mate or two stay while you're away?' Simon's impromptu party in Coffs Harbour at 14 springs to mind, then his out-of-hand 16th birthday party. '*Mmm...,*' I shake my head. 'Sorry, darling...'

How many decisions do we wish we could go back and change?

If I hadn't been in a motherly hurry that afternoon, if I'd stopped to think, to feel, to appreciate his space more... if he could've spoken a deeper concern directly to me that day...

As he had when I first mentioned an unborn Ashley to him... in our little bush chalet, when it was just Sime, Allie, and me, and I'd sat my six-year-old eldest down on the couch.

Glancing at my tummy, he paraphrased my words. 'So... you're pregnant?'

'Yes, darling.'

'Wow.' His dark eyes sought mine. 'That's great, Mum.'

'You think so?'

'Yeah. It is,' he nodded slowly. 'It's great.'

I didn't know where his wisdom and clarity came from. Even at that age he seemed to view the situation like a sage. I was relieved to see Simon growing a clear self inside the sensitive young boy who'd been processing his parents' divorce, his little brother's death, and learning to live without his dad.

Or when Ashley was born, and he and Allie came with my parents to visit us in hospital... Simon loved having a baby brother. Gathered around the bed admiring a newborn Ashley, Simon piped up. 'Would it be alright if Allie and I start calling Rob "Dad"?' Simon knew his need. Rob, a little taken aback, smiled shyly. *What an honour.* 'I guess so!'

Or that night at the dinner table with my parents, Simon looking into middle distance... 'I feel sorry for Mum. She's got a new baby boy and she's probably up in the hospital wondering if he's going to die, like Joseph.' Such empathy voiced itself from Simon's quiet depths.

But not always. Sometimes it was anger his integrity fuelled. When a gentle mate in high school was being bullied, Simon stepped in. A fight broke out between the bully and Simon in the playground, a crowd of kids gathered around. The deputy asked him afterwards what the fight had been about, but Simon kept his mate's confidence, choosing a suspension instead.

Not all his suspensions were so innocent. In Year 7 with three other curious boys, Simon was caught making a little homemade bomb behind the science block. Not such a crime at first sight – until it's discovered they're inadvertently standing, at the time, over the gas mains. The principal at his first school observed, 'I'm not saying Simon *causes* mischief in the playground, but when it happens, he's never far away...'

One detention in Year 9 *was* a pure power battle. Suspected of wagging class, he and a couple of mates in the playground were approached by a teacher. 'Pick up those papers.'

'I didn't leave them there,' Simon stood straight. 'They're not mine to pick up.'

'You *will* pick them up.'

'I *won't* pick them up.'

'I'll *make* you pick them up.'

'Good luck!'

'*Good luck*', in Simon's inflection, becomes a family saying.

The detention – 'failure to follow a teacher's directions' – didn't deter Sime. He didn't attend detention, so he got another suspension, which he didn't mind either. He didn't like blindly obeying authority for the sake of it.

A year later, he thought this'd work on a bigger scale. At schoolies in Surfers Paradise, a police officer directs Simon and his mates off the footpath. The mates follow the directive; my son doesn't. To his surprise, Sime has to join the big world: a court appearance, 'contravene a direction given by police', and a six-month good behaviour bond. No more blatant brushes with authority follow.

Right through school, Simon's teachers, while frustrated at his 'not reaching his potential', often commented in his school reports in almost veiled admiration of his social life in class.

Maths Yr 7: *Usually works well, but occasionally spends work time socialising with his friends.*

Music Yr 8: *His good work is quite often overshadowed by his ability to distract others in class and then treat lessons as social events. He has a lot of talent in this subject but is certainly not working to achieve his full potential.*

In Year 9, his history class is given three questions to answer.

'Question Two: *How were the pyramids in Egypt built?* Simon, would you read your answer out to the class?'

'From top to bottom, by aliens.'

'That's not right,' the teacher corrects.

'Yes it is,' Simon counter-corrects.
'Where did you come up with that?'
'From one of Mum's books.'
'Just because you read it in a book, doesn't mean it's right.'
'Well that's where you get *your* answers from – from a *book*.'
'*Well*... I'd like to read your mum's book...'
'I'll bring it in for you.'

Simon's very bright, had received the maths award at the end of primary school, can achieve great results in any subject, but doesn't always interest himself in academic study. His first teacher remarks: *Amongst other things, he likes to work things out for himself and do things his way.*

His kindness gives without counting cost. My last birthday: six boxes of chocolates instead of one. Hands clasped behind his back, he stands watching while I open a miniature bottle of Estee Lauder perfume. 'Thank you, Sime! This is my favourite – *lovely* to have a bottle of it!' Sime pulls his hands out from behind his back and passes me another wrapped present: a large bottle of the same perfume. *How did he know?* Generous with his siblings for birthdays and Christmas, he gives presents that really mean something. On birthdays and Mother's Day, he makes me a cup of tea – just how I like it – and brings it to me, *still hot*, in bed.

We love our meaningful discussions. A deep thinker, he ponders every experience on his path, with the courage to feel his difficult emotional states, and quietly takes my mind places it hasn't been before. We talk a lot about life itself. He'd like to go to China to study with the Shaolin monks. Sensitive to people's spaces, he looks inside, not just *at*, speaks less rather than more, his few words representing whole pages of thought. 'Life's too big to put into words,' he says. He seems to connect more deeply with people from his soft interior this way. 'You've been such a beautiful eldest son to me,' I note my incidental use of past tense. 'Such an angel!' One time, Simon flaps his hands, trotting lightly on tiptoe, as though flying out of the room. His dry humour makes me laugh.

The music that flows in his veins finds expression in teaching himself guitar. When a drum kit's being assembled in his room, I brace myself. I assume hearing him learn to play will be painful; I'm wrong. Amongst the songs he accompanies, and the tribal-sounding rhythms he composes, he never misses a beat. He becomes a reality rapper, and writes his own rap songs, including one to Joseph.

The morning in mid-2000 I'm eating breakfast and get a call from Telstra, the music goes quiet.

'I'm just ringing to let you know – as we're obliged to – that we're taking you off 1900 numbers.'

Oh no, think I sarcastically, *I'll really miss my 1900 numbers*. 'Why's that?'

'Let's see,' telephonist browses our file. 'This time yesterday, your bill was $79.60. This morning it's... $864.50.'

'There's been a mistake,' I assure her confidently. 'We don't ring 1900 numbers.'

'Do you have a computer?'

'Yes.'

'Do you have the internet?'

'*... yes...*'

No!!!!! Simon and his mates had been in the computer room the night before, for a couple of hours. Several times, they'd shrieked and guffawed loudly, extremely entertained by *something*... Surely that wasn't it...

'Are porn sites on 1900 numbers?' I squeak.

'Yes they are.' Her concealed sniggers trickle through my explanation.

Apparently the night's venture isn't just for entertainment; it has an enterprising purpose. Simon, aged 16, has scrolled through several disclaimers that he's over 18, downloading clips onto floppy discs, intending to profit by *selling* them at school.

Angry, disbelieving, beside myself not knowing how to handle it, I'm admiring of his entrepreneurial streak – all at once! My dad offers to help, talking to the boys at the round table. He finds what they've done 'understandable', but organises them to come and work for a half-day on our property to 'pay it off'.

As direct as he is kind, the night before my 40th birthday, Simon's perceptions surprise me. He, Allie and I sit up chatting in front of the fire, and at midnight, I jokingly ply them for a speech. 'You've done a better job as a single parent than lots of two-parent families,' Simon starts. 'You love your children and you speak real to us, not down to us just because we're your kids. You treat us like we have a brain. You give us room to be ourselves. You get what you can for us – which is what we need anyway – and you make *sure* we don't miss out at Christmas and birthdays.' He's not joking. 'You're smart, you're deep, and you like having fun. You're a real individual. You think for yourself and encourage us to do the same. You just keep going. Heaps of people would've given up by now, but you never have.' How had he noticed all this?! Mouth agape, I look at Allie to say, *Don't you think what he just said is incredible?!* As though asking for her speech, she says, 'Yeah, what he said.'

Many parents don't get such moments. I *knew* I was lucky to have that one.

Simon's depth enjoyed alone time, but he also loved socialising. Very few days of the year in high school did he not have mates in his room up the back of our house. It was a convenient house structure that allowed him to have friends over without much disturbing the rest of us.

Except when he was angry and wanted to let me know. Then Slipknot's Corey Taylor would scream loudly, directly and very personally down the hallway – right at me: *'MOTHERFUCKAAAAARR'*.

I was grateful to have reared my children in an era that considered we might choose our own parents, and that our children might be *our* teachers. I know I learnt more this way. It allowed me to respect my children at a level that felt right to me.

Few find anger an easy subject to address, but because we loved and trusted each other, Simon and I continued learning about its purpose, and healthier expression with each other. At the Women's Anger group, anger had challenged members' lives – either too much personal expression of it, or too little - most of us the latter, having had to learn a placating relationship with anger. Domestic violence inhibited a natural expression of anger for me and my children. I'd wanted us to consciously embrace our own anger more as part of our humanness, not avoid interacting with it, be manipulated by it, leave one of us to carry the mantle for it, or cast it into shadow.

Mothers from violent relationships often worried about their sons modelling violence.

For his 15th birthday, I gave Simon a punching bag. It strengthened his body, and gradually his character, as he learned responsible direction of anger. In an angry moment alone, I decided to try it, and saw just how much self-discipline Simon had developed. To walk away – in the opposite direction – to punch the bag instead of the person, to learn satisfaction from the process – all took *so* much self-responsibility, I could only admire him.

But when '*MOTHERFUCKAAAAARR*' roared for me, I'd roll my eyes and storm to Simon's room, clueless how I was going to approach it. Although triggered myself, it was terrifying to march myself towards anger, readying to front it, instead of away from it. Each time an argument ensued, from the midst of the anger, I'd steer us in a healthier direction. 'Simon, you don't have to *swear* at me!' I'd yell. 'Be angry! Express yourself! But don't *abuse!*' 'SAY what you're angry about!' Bit by bit, I was able to help Simon learn to express his anger respectfully, help myself bear its presence, help us both stick to the point, and discover what it had to say to us, until we were having still loud but healthy arguments that ended in resolution and a heartfelt hug.

After an earlier argument, my tender 16-year-old leaves a note blu-tacked to the top of the stairs, next to my bedroom. As always, his maturity, insight into himself, into relationship dynamics and life, astounds me, warms me.

> *Sometimes it's easier to put thoughts and feelings in writing and leave it to the other person to read, because sometimes our tone of voice, facial expressions or body language turns a conversation into a fight.*
>
> *I love you Mum, I love the cool person you are, I love the fact that you understand what most mums don't, I love the freedom you give me, although there's a part of me that wants you to be more strict, or have more control over me. I understand that you want to help me, not criticise me, but living in this world I've learned to think the worst of people, and as soon as I hear what I think is someone criticising me or telling me that what I believe is wrong, I go into instant attack mode. That's when I don't hear a word anyone says and all I can do is abuse or yell or swear. I find it very hard to take advice on life because it sounds like the person giving the advice knows what life is all about and I don't have a clue. I know I don't take enough responsibility – a lot of that comes from being a teenager. Although it might not look like it, I'm working on that. I don't know why I'm on this earth and sometimes I wish I wasn't, but when I come to the realisation that I have the ability to end it, something tells me to stick around because I don't think the*

answer is on the other side. I believe we are ready to die when we have the answer. I'm so grateful that you are a part of my life Mum, although I might not show it. You are one of the coolest people I know and you're one of my best friends. That will never change no matter what happens. I just want you to know that I do understand your reasons for saying and doing what you do, and I believe that most of our disagreements come from misunderstandings and miscommunications. Anyway I better go to bed so I can wake up in time.

Love Always,

Simon.

I was honoured that Simon credited me with teaching him to communicate.

An honour... except he didn't communicate a vital worry to me when he most needed to. I believe he wouldn't have wanted to worry me with it.

I'd seen the Father Wound (from *father absence*) early in Simon's life. When our marriage finished, night after night, Simon would sob, 'I miss Dad, I want Dad'.

In the years to follow, I'd sometimes observe that my youngest son lacked this wound. Other single mothers said they'd observed the same in their sons, even in twins – raised in the same environment, one son would have a 'Father Wound', the other would not.

My dad tried to help fill the gap, sometimes having Simon stay over on weekends. When Joseph was in Prince Charles Hospital, Dad had looked after Simon, bonding with him as a toddler, and had maintained the closeness through the years. On holidays, Simon would go jogging with Dad in the early mornings. Dad would take his grandchildren to the pool, mountain climbing or camping. He helped Simon study for his school certificate, and bought a Mitsubishi Triton duel-cab ute at the end of Simon's TAFE year, to help him secure a carpentry apprenticeship. After a few months, it needed to be replaced with a runabout Nissan Skyline. Which was replaced by the Charger. And eventually the Torana.

Dad helped many of his grandchildren learn to drive. One sunny afternoon's lesson with Simon, heading down the highway with its 100kph speed zone, Simon was sticking to his 80kph learner's limit. From a distance, a driver zoomed up behind Simon, blew his horn, and started tailgating him. Sime knew his L-plates were showing, stayed on 80kph, and kept looking ahead without moving a muscle. His calm self-control impressed his grandfather. Then Dad noticed Simon's right hand had left the wheel, elbow resting on open window ledge, hand positioned upwards, his middle finger extended. Dad says he thanked God he wasn't wearing his clerical collar.

As a Charger owner, Simon joined the Gold Coast Valiant car club, and drove in their rallies.

Schoolies week 2002: At the lights in Surfers Paradise, Simon and three mates are in the Charger, beside a late V6 Commodore, drivers daring each other, revving their engines loudly. Schoolies drape from balcony windows on all sides, cheering them on. The lights turn green, the cars take off, the roar from the crowd only just audible above the engines, mainly the Charger's V8. The gun-metal grey classic fangs off the new techno-beast – and WINS! The crowd goes wild, thunderous cheering blasting from every balcony.

Simon liked being in a man's world. He enjoyed his pre-apprenticeship in carpentry at TAFE.

The dads and I had encouraged the children's love of nature all their lives, especially in rescuing animals. As with his own dad, Simon's gentleness found sanctuary in nature. At 18, there was only one place he wanted to work: *Currumbin Wildlife Sanctuary.*

Simon began as a groundsman, working with gentle souls like himself, soon referring to colleagues as his 'work family'. Amidst welding, shelving, maintenance on work utes, bobcat operating, and a few laps' train driving, Simon asked every day if there were any carpentry jobs for him. So perfect was his attention to detail, he'd topped tech drawing in Year 10, and sailed through his carpentry pre-apprenticeship. At the Sanctuary, he was given the boardwalk to replace. 'With no-one watching,' his boss said, 'he completed it with such precision, skills so exact, that he did a better job than the original carpenter, 15 years earlier. He didn't need to finish his apprenticeship to prove himself a carpenter.'

And so Simon now has his fourth vehicle, a Torana. At work that first Monday, he asks his boss if he can speak with him privately. Monday morning busy-ness steals the opportunity.

That afternoon, after I tell him I'd like to take Allie and Ash camping, Simon leaves to have dinner with work friends. He opens the door of his

Torana, finishes our chat with a few parting words, a slight smile, shines out his dark eyes at me, and leaves.

And then he slips through some kind of portal.

How does it all come screeching to a halt? A sudden end to all this beauty, intelligence, talent, sharp wit, humour, love, vitality, unspeakable depth, awareness, realness, unrealised cleverness, 'potential'.

A sudden end to such an immeasurably loved soul?

∼

> *A suicide is a puzzle, that cannot be untangled,*
> *for there is rarely something simple in its causing –*
> *rather, a multiplicity of threads*
> **Kathleen Stuart, 'The After Life'**

And here, the lifeless body, the beautiful face so familiar, communicating with me only hours before, animated, loving… now cold, unmoving on a mortuary trolley.

My gasps tear at the police officer's shoulder. I sign his papers. *Yes, this is my son.*

Simon! Where are you? What pushed you??
I know the Charger crash was a blow. I saw how anxious it made you. We'd talked about life, speculated about this, but I didn't think you'd do this.

The thought of his pain is unbearable.

The telling. The shock. The re-telling, over and over. Gasps, whimpers, stunned silences, as vulnerable humans interface with Death. In that first week, through exhaustion and the impossible new reality – *'Simon has **died**'* – we're laid bare in ways we never are any other time; humbled, mortal after all, the profound closeness it brings with others, a rare deep comfort.

Perhaps this is manageable? whispers the Shock.
Perhaps it's Strength? Hope plies.
Maybe Death isn't as big a deal as everyone makes it out to be? Denial's soft tones echo.

In moments, I feel him nearby. I'm not used to him this way. *Does he have a home? Does he sleep at night? Is someone close to him whenever he needs, to let him know he's incredibly loved?* …the same wonderings after Joseph died. *I can't suddenly stop being his mother.*

My world has fractured, and in between the cracks slowly oozes the world of grief.

My trusted friend Joan, minister of a Christian Spiritualist Church, takes Simon's funeral service. A psychic medium, Joan tells me Simon is speaking to her nonstop. First words – *'He's saying he's with the one who had the short life'* – are immeasurably consoling to me.

Graveside after the funeral, I read aloud a children's book about the journey of a water bug from a quiet pond; he climbs a lily stalk and to his surprise, discovers he's transformed into a dragonfly.

[Water bugs and Dragonflies, by Doris Stickney, The Pilgrim Press, 1997]

Pete, Allie, Ash and I step from under the gazebo to release blue helium balloons.

As mine drifts upwards, it happens: between me and my balloon, the precious little insect buzzes.

'DRAGONFLY!' I yell, pointing.

Simon could not have imagined the comfort this would bring to everyone gathered. But he was always considerate: why would he not try to reassure us? For many of us, this did.

Three days post-funeral with many more assembled, Currumbin Wildlife Sanctuary places a plaque beside Simon's boardwalk and dedicates it to his memory.

Three nights after Simon's death, news rippling through the suburbs, his best mates chat around our table. Paul mentions other teens 'sucking up to' him, feigning closeness with Simon they hadn't had. 'Oh, the *Competition!*' sparks Mykaela. *Who's the closest? Who's hurting the most? Can we grab some of the limelight?* An observant little circle... It is not yet possible my son is no longer amongst them.

Simon's mates visit us regularly in the following months. We share our grief around the balcony, chatting, philosophising, listening to music, reminiscing, laughing, relating deeply, forging invaluable friendships. After a while, they don't have to mention Simon's name; I can see him in their eyes. They love him.

5 April 2003

Paul said he believed Simon had given a lot of thought to suicide over his previous few years – that each time he thought it through, perhaps hundreds of times (not planning it, just where he stood about it), he processed it a bit more, until finally he'd covered the subject – from a deeply philosophical level, to a point of acceptance about it. So by the time those final triggers converged on him, his thinking about suicide itself was already complete.

I think this is insightful of Paul. It's a 'big picture' perspective. Paul wondered if those closest inherit a part of a person when they die.

If so, he felt he'd inherited Simon's mind. Not long after, I heard Paul say Simon was always looking at 'the bigger picture'. I'm grateful he articulated this.

It was three months before I could do a grocery shop without crying, even with Allie and Ash. Simon had beautiful manners, always expressing appreciation. *'That was a lovely meal, thanks Mum.'* I hadn't had to miss his dad as much – or Joseph – when Simon bore their defining feature: Indian heritage shining through their big dark eyes. Now the dark eyes were gone, taking with them too much history. I cried washing our clothes without Simon's amongst them, I missed his smell *(except his socks!)* the occasional waft of cigarette smoke, the sounds of him about the house – his absence an aching presence with which there was no negotiation. It challenged me wherever I tried to position myself in it.

13 February 2003

The moments of grief and what Simon's passing means to us change continually. Every day a slightly different angle, a little more intensity; through the comings and goings, a greater dawning perhaps. I welcome the tears: they're a direct connection to my love and grief for Simon, and the quickest way through. I realise 18½ years was a long time for me to have had my son in my life, and yet it seems so short.

30 March 2003

It's felt over the last week like I've been holding onto my sanity by a thin thread. It's *very* scary. At times I've felt physically shaky, like my body is on the verge of collapse.

Trying to wrap my mind around having lost two children is stretching my head a lot more now.

I'm amazed at how I kept up my gratitude. I didn't do it as a practice, it just made me feel better. I was being honest about *everything* I felt, not just the dark stuff – and I felt closer to Simon in it.

12 April 2003

How lucky am I that I wasn't left wondering what sort of man my first baby would grow into? How satisfying to have officially completed rearing him, and be blessed with an extra year of being official 'equals' with him, living in the same house while loving and respecting each other on that level; how fortunate to have spent 18½ years sharing our lives. To think of all the experiences we shared, the places we lived, the 'clothes' we grew out of, the emotions we felt, thoughts with which we grappled, choices we made, the lack of choice life hoisted on us, the pain, laughter, sadness, happiness, discoveries, frustrations, achievements, the peace – and the final peace… the thousands of days life gave us to experience together.

It's better to have loved and lost at 18 years than at two months.

An unknown factor

I appreciated that many factors contribute to a suicide, but there was one I hadn't known about. Simon was bullied during his final weeks. It was a picture I had to piece together afterwards.

In late March, Simon visits Mykaela in a dream, asking her to come and visit us. During conversation the following week, she mentions an unfamiliar name. Within 24 hours, two others randomly mention this name to me – a young man living in our suburb. By the third time, my ears prick. *Okay Simon, what do you want me to know about this lad?*

I start enquiring…

On the morning of his death, Simon had approached his boss at work requesting a private talk. Some people were after him. But Monday mornings were extra-busy, the boss had details to organise, and later, when he had available time, Simon was out working. After knock-off, Simon drove home, then to a work colleague's place for dinner. He confided in Maddy that he was being hassled by a young man in our suburb, and didn't know why. En route to Maddy's house, he'd sighted him with his girlfriend (with whom Simon had a brief flirtation two years earlier). He'd slowed down to show them his new car, hoping the lad might express interest. Instead, he started screaming at Simon, 'I'm gonna f**kin' kill you, you f**kin' ***!' Several times he screamed, 'I'm gonna f**kin' kill you!' kicking the passenger's door with the bottom of his shoe – twice. 'Maddy, I'm too scared to go home.' Maddy wanted to ask Simon to stay, but was a guest in the flat of a co-worker with whom Simon had been friendly, who was now pointedly ignoring him.

Simon left after dinner, dropped by work to pick up some items from a cupboard, and headed to a shop, passing those on the footpath with whom he'd had dinner. He pulled up, the engine idling, Maddy's boyfriend, an auto-dismantler, listening. 'You need smaller jets for the carbie.'

'Next weekend...' Simon replied. He'd already spent the previous day replacing the carbie with a mate. Although he didn't tell them, they were standing in the spot the Charger had crashed a fortnight before.

Later that night, the sentence found its way amongst others onto a small page, *'I cannot make anything work out'*.

I'd watched my children all their lives for indications of their dad's vulnerability to mental illness. I'd eyeballed Anorexia Nervosa years before it manifested in Allie. When Simon's boss, then work colleague, told me he'd said someone was 'after him', I worried it was a paranoid delusion. Simon's mate told me Simon had bought a mobile from the lad and wondered if Simon still owed money on it. The bully had shown Simon a gun he kept in his car. He was known to police.

Three months after Simon's death, a possible inquest hadn't yet been ruled out, so Simon's cars had remained under tarps on our property. I asked Maddy to come for a chat. Putting the picture together, we checked the Torana for evidence of the bully's 'kicks'. No dents in the passenger's door, no scuffed paint. But close inspection revealed the underside of two shoe prints: thick patterned rubber from a chunky-soled sneaker — right where he'd described. We knew whose they were.

I'd been quicker to believe my fear — that this had been a delusion. Simon had tried to communicate his legitimate fear the day he died. No-one heeded. And here was proof. Now from the other side, he'd wanted me to know. Yes, it'd hurt him that the girl he'd liked had ignored him. The Charger crash *had* wounded him deeply. My dad saw the crash site: 'That's where Simon died.' I felt the death blow had been dealt there that day. And I felt *dreadful* assuming the bullying wasn't real. He didn't want to tell me about it.

A fortnight after Simon died, I'd had to make a statement to the police about why I thought he'd taken his life. Several months later, when this new information came to light, before his case came before the coroner, I went to the police and made an addendum statement.

Time and again, I've revisited this 'trigger'. *'This is my escape,'* Simon had written that night on the small loving note he'd left the three of us. It was unlike him to accept intimidation, but in my Reading down the track, he said he 'preferred the gas to a bullet' — adding that his death 'wasn't just one thing, it was 2 + 2 + 2 + 2', and how he *felt* about it all. The bullying wasn't *The* cause; it was a trigger — perhaps the final straw.

This is how it's been for me living with suicide. *Perhaps it was the hopelessness of living with anorexia? Perhaps his sensitive personality could've managed life's blows if he'd had a secure father figure? Did the domestic violence factor more directly than I've thought?* I'd spend months believing one cause was 'The Reason', before moving onto another, just as convinced the next motive was 'The *Real* Reason'. Underneath I felt a gutted helplessness about the contributing factors all converging at once. 'IT' never resolved itself. Even now 'The Reason/s' revisit, tightening my breath, fuzzing my vision, before I can ease Simon and me from their insoluble rumination.

In May, I acquire the phone number of a 'Survivors of Suicide' support group, and try hard to get there, but it's not happening. I'm not gutted. It's the death of a *child* part that's harder for me than the *suicide* part.

The following month, I wander into a local chapter of a bereaved parents support group, *The Compassionate Friends*.

Nine mostly older women natter around a comfortable lounge room in the facilitator's small home. The meeting starts with reading TCF credo aloud together. Three sentences in, *'Our children have died at all ages and from many different causes, but our love for our children unites us'*, I cannot continue. My head drops; I cry through the rest of this brave, sad, pointed declaration. Gentle, unafraid, facilitator Lorraine suggests each member introduces themselves and briefly tells their story.

'I'm Carol,' a younger mother begins. 'My son, Samuel …was seven… He drowned at a Christmas pool party.'

A profound level of shock swamps me. I stare, unable to respond. Suddenly I realise the door's shut, and I'm part of this group with staggering stories to tell.

'I'm Joan,' begins the next woman. 'My son Jamie died in the Prince Charles Hospital when he was twenty-five.'

…*'from all walks of life, from many different circumstances'*… the tales continue.

Joseph's story's not hard for me; I'm used to it, but I tiptoe, wary of the disenfranchisement of grief for babies. 'Simon's death has sensitised me about Joseph's death. Losing Joseph was harder for me' – I say on that day – 'because I didn't get to rear him. Simon I had a close relationship with, a small satisfaction in my grief. I feel Simon around me, get little signs, know his voice, his caring personality. His life was just finished; he was a highly sensitive young man who didn't have to stay.'

I'm only four-and-a-half months down the track; my grief processing will keep changing. In moments I think I'm doing well. In others, I'm definitely not...

For four years after Simon's death, TCF monthly meetings eased the isolation. It was a relief to talk past the lump in my throat, to admit how bad it really was. Around the table afterwards, sipping strained leaf-tea from china teacups, poured from teapots warmed by knitted tea-cosies, the uncensored discussion continued. Sharing mock chicken sandwiches, profiteroles, lamingtons – good comfort food – the bond with other parents forged deep, the chapter leader heaven sent.

Many times, at the end of my rope, Lorraine would happen to phone, and then talk for hours. *What have I done to deserve this angel in my life?* I'd wonder. Her passion to care astounded me – that she wanted to learn more, to tend sensitively, individually to us all. In 2011, she was awarded Citizen of the Year locally for her work with bereaved parents.

How different to my journey after Joseph's death. I was not so alone now.

The shock would've ensured I didn't feel suicide's stigma initially, although people's questions, assumptions and speculations irritated me. *Did he have girl trouble? Was it drugs? An undiagnosed mental illness? Was he in trouble with the law?*

I learned that some TCF members believed mothers of children who'd suicided should attend a separate group. They resented us: their child *wanted* to live; ours 'threw their life away'.

Suicide's stigma was inconspicuous, but alive and well.

As soon as Simon died, sleep eluded me. It was exhausting. From then on, noises woke me with a jolt. I slept with my ears and eyes covered, a habit I couldn't undo for years to come.

20 September 2003

The chasm between my inner and outer worlds widens. I wish there was a separate language for these experiences.

Pulled inside to process my grief, others no longer see where I'm at. How could they know what they're looking at when they interact with me? They shut off to my incomprehensible losses, keeping them safely compartmentalised in their 'Death' section, relating normally to the rest of me as though my children's deaths haven't seeped into all the other parts of me too. They don't know how far into my inner worlds I've slipped. They're not relating to me at all, but to a hologram of who I used to be.

5 October 2003

I'm frightened – about being in the deepest loneliest valley of grief for my precious son; of the constancy and intensity of emotion here – especially the sadness and desolation. I'm frightened of *not* grieving properly; that I may have totally missed what this life's about, that my fear and stubbornness and strong-willed insistence on my own way may have led me in the wrong direction, and taken my children with it, that I might reach the light at the end of the tunnel when I die and discover I'd wasted my life and all this pain, and didn't make any progress in my soul. I'm frightened I'll discover at my life's end that I'd been shown the key – of unconditional self-love – and much knowledge, but was too 'naughty' to do what I was supposed to do in this life; that I've professed love as the answer and not lived it; that life isn't at all what I've thought; that it's not alright for me to be as individual as I am, and that I merely justify what I want because of my fears. I'm frightened I mightn't be nearly as 'light' as I think; that I spend way too much time and energy in my head and almost none of it in my heart; that my fears prevent me from living the life I'm supposed to be living.

It's *frightening* here.

Christmas had always been the happiest time of year for us. That first year I shopped for Allie and Ash, I saw presents everywhere I would've bought for Simon. The sight of the Christmas tree pierced the three of us with unspeakable loss.

21 December 2003

These days are much harder than I anticipated. Waking up, I'm okay for the first few moments. Then I remember it's Christmas, and it stabs me, as though it's happened afresh.

I take myself back to the beginning of the year and wonder if it all really happened…

Did you really not come home that night, Simon? Did the police really knock on my door at 3 am? Did they follow me through my darkened house, sit down with me, and tell me you'd *died*?

Was that really you lying on that hospital trolley? Were you really 'DEAD'? Did I really bend down and rest my cheek against your cold face??

Did the fumes from your carbon monoxide saturated body permeate my head and stay with me for months? That smell that came from everything from then on – flowers, cooking, thin air?

Were they your beautiful olive-skinned hands, that'd grasped my finger tightly as a little baby, that held my hand trustingly as a little boy, that learned to draw, to write, to build, to create, to play a guitar, to drive a car, to forge their own rhythm on their drums, that crafted a boardwalk so skilfully, that you lovingly left as a legacy to the world; that made and brought me cups of tea, and held me in loving hugs? Were they your beautiful hands that took vacuum cleaner hoses to the beachfront, cut them meticulously and positioned them perfectly into place? Was that your beautiful right hand that wrote its final letter to us, then turned on the ignition – its very last task – before coming to rest forever in your lap?

I haven't seen you since then Simon, we have framed photos of you around the house, and I feel immensely sad when I look at the Christmas tree.

I guess it must be true...

That first Christmas, I told God, 'death shouldn't be so final.' We should be allowed a few hours' visit once a year, maybe Christmas Day – to hug our children, share drinks, nibblies, cry again when they leave – but be comforted and at peace, knowing they were alright.

27 March 2007

I dreamt this morning that our whole extended family was sharing a long table.

Bright lights are on. It's dusk, Christmas Day. Simon's with us, visiting from the other side.

I'm walking behind seated relatives, seeing the back of Simon's (No. 2) shaved head. 'Would you like to hear what it's like on the other side?' he asks Dad. 'I would!' I exclaim.

Heading to the corner of a lovely room, I see a small cute boy with dark eyes. (Joseph?) I pick him up and cuddle him. 'He's *very* cute!' someone comments. I sit him on my lap, and pick up a children's book to read to him.

A scene instantly inserts itself, a grey merkaba – a 3D star shape – which Simon's showing us are on the other side. There are spaceships, UFOs that look like that. Looking away, I catch sight of a grey object the same shape and size as he's shown us, and the interconnectedness of that coincidence confirms it for me. *Great!! I wanted so badly to believe all that stuff was real.*

Sime would soon have to return. I want to spend some time with him first.

Outside, mythical Japanese figures approach to take back the departed children at the end of Christmas Day. The children hold hands in a big chain. As Sime joins them, I rush to say goodbye. He's little again, three or four years old, wearing his yellow jumper with black stripes, his hair neat, his eyes dark, round, shining. He's not happy about leaving, but he knows he has to go.

As the chain of children passes, I call out, 'Bye darling! I love you!' He's heard, but it doesn't make him happy. I try to lift his mood: 'See you next year!'

The dream ends.

For me to wake up was just like NDEers (Near Death Experiencers) finding themselves back in their body. One NDEer cried for three weeks having been on the other side, then returning to this life. It was heavenly being with Sime. Realising this reality again as I began waking up – lifeless without him, having just called out to him, having parted *again* – was beyond words.

I cried buckets.

Christmas Eve 24 December 2003

Mum's work colleague phones, thinking of us.

'You said at Simon's funeral you felt privileged to be his mum, but I think he was lucky to have you as his mum. You let him be who he was, and that's the sort of mother he needed. You didn't squash his free spirit.'

This means everything to me; it was always my intention. *Still is.*

First Anniversary

A quivering well fills my torso. I'd had a goal, an unconscious bargain – 'Just get through the first year', I'd told myself – and now that we'd made it, I could lift my head to see what was left. The *finality* of never seeing Simon again hits hard from an infinite number of angles. *He's nowhere on this planet. You must live the rest of your life without him.*

At Currumbin Sanctuary, we'd turned around to see half-a-dozen of Simon's friends.

23 January 2004

I take Lee to the edge of the boardwalk; we sit on the path. I ask him what he makes of Simon's death. Looking timeless and tender, Lee says he thinks it'll hurt forever. Says he's a bit angry with Simon. I tell him about my friend Nick, who'd shot himself when we were young, how deeply it'd hurt me, how I was angry towards Nick for a decade. The poor young people. Eighteen years is young for something this huge. I tell them how grateful I am that they love Simon, and allow their hearts to be hurt by his death – how I appreciate that I'm not alone in my grief as I'd been with Joseph, that Simon had had a life where he could grow to independence, and is loved by people I'll never know, who'll carry the sadness of his death for the rest of their lives. Their poor young gentle hearts.

I'm grateful too for the boardwalk, that many thousands will walk along Simon's amazing craftsmanship, read the name of its builder, and think of him. In those moments, he will not be forgotten.

14 June 2004

On my good days, I'm amazed by the newness and clarity I feel, the strength and purity of my resolve to move forward and make a beautiful life for Allie, Ashley and me, and help others with the pain I've suffered through my life.

But the ups and downs continue, and the next day it's so hard to keep that resolve fresh – when you and it feel weakened by lack of sleep, your thinking processes blurred through worry because Ashley's more withdrawn or Allie hasn't come home the night before, a bill must be paid that'll empty the savings account today, the car will need servicing next week, and no long-term plans have been made to address the financial situation, because you're incapable of committing to such a thought at this stage, let alone the reality of it.

Why can't I *see* you, Sime? I wish you could walk up the stairs and say hello just now. As if that would fix this mess of having to sort through life, and what it means when your child dies early. I'm too far through now for it to be 'fixed' by anything (déjà-vu – two decades ago). At times I'm a little more used to the idea of your not being here, as bad as it can feel to say that. I pay for it, at the times I can't stand the thought of your being gone. Then it's so profoundly sad, I beat myself up for ever thinking I could do the rest of my life here without you. It's insanity, this notion – and reality – of Death.

27 June 2004

I've reached places I arrived at after Joseph died, that I thought I wouldn't be visiting again. I gave myself a hard time for years back then, thinking I was doing my grieving badly – an emotionally clingy, maladjusted human being. After a long while, I felt pressured into hiding the severity of my grief and the huge sense of loss I always carried about it.

Allie and Ash are individuating, and it's very hard not to take it personally. I'm losing all my children, and have been feeling like the biggest failure as a parent.

13 October 2004

I feel like Moses-and-the-children-of-Israel, roaming around lost in the desert for 40 years, looking for the Promised Land. My mind's on the job *all* the time, searching my soul on the inside and this world on the outside, for meaning and purpose to live again.

All day long I look for the key that will make sense of what's happened and what continues happening in mine and my children's lives, the key that will make the penny drop, simplify things down again for us, in *some* way justify our pain, and help us keep living.

My concept of 'God' had been evolving my entire adult life, especially since my marriage ended, but it was my innocent beliefs that were suffering now. Talk of spiritual things we couldn't know irritated me, the sacred ground under my feet, especially as a Reader, now tremoring. By this stage, my assumptive world, that still expected *some* fairness, was feeling greatly violated. Inside, a *Dark Night of the Soul* had descended.

All I could do was vent – with no resolution.

25 September 2006

CONVERSATION AT GOD

I've wanted to talk to you for a while, God. I'm angry with you. You know why. I can understand people not believing in you anymore. It feels like I'm in a Cargo Cult when I do. Words say nothing, but they're all I have – and I *will* speak out against this injustice. My son would've. So would yours.

I'm done suffering in silence just so I can be 'gracious'. What does grace matter? Where's your 'grace'? Expecting me not to venture into the taboos that keep me from questioning you? I'm supposed to take it all lying down?

No reason vital enough justifies this much hurt! What were you thinking when you invented the conditions of this planet? How did you come up with 'Death'? What convinced you it'd be such a great idea to take a person away from here and never let their loved ones see them again?

How do you decide who's worthy of your miracles? Why do you appear to lavish them on some and not on others? How is this LOVE???

I never thought I'd stop believing in you. When I was a child – and thought like a child, and reasoned like a child – my entire world was based on your being real. I don't even seem to be on the same planet I grew up on now.

I don't wanna hear the 'Footprints' fairytale again. No-one's here, carrying me. I'm in this alone. Dropped into the same quagmire that took me a forever to climb out of before. Why is it alright for me to be back here again? Don't you think this is cruel of you? Others look at my life and think so. But we're not meant to say it aloud. Why can we ask these questions when we can't have the answers?

I can't go forward with you, try to establish some sort of relationship with you, trust you, value you – when nothing makes any sense to me, and when it looks to me like you don't value me. Yes, my sons are in a better place, but how are these repercussions alright for me? I'm supposed to accept being an inferior half-breed with a dispensable psyche, who bows to its maker and then thanks you every day for your love?? Tell me how Love CAN stand so supposedly close by, watching – counting every single greying and multi-coloured hair on everyone's heads (because that hair count really matters) – and not take that pain away??

How did I end up on this planet? Is there some extremely critical lesson I'm stupid enough to have to learn only in this way? Tell me why you thought this insanity would be such a good idea?

Why have you abandoned me? Why are you so irrelevant now?

I no longer know about your love. I do know this: Death is real. It's the only thing I know, isn't it? No matter what I say, my boys are not coming back.

End of story – Yours and Mine,

Respectfully,

Job

I no longer hold that a change in beliefs under such duress means your faith has been 'weakened'.

24 May 2006

I feel like a very embittered person, especially next to some others at my support group who are further along the track. Sometimes conversing with them, I watch myself to see if I can respond in ways that don't reveal my bitterness at life. I can't really. *I was a beautiful person once*, I'd think, *but this has destroyed me. I have no faith anymore, no good will towards people, towards life, I'm extremely cynical. All I feel is raw anger, and it's so hard to hide. Yet another casualty: my beautiful self. I don't know how they do it – perhaps they don't question as much as me – but I'll never again be as uncomplicatedly beautiful as these women.*

6 May 2007

Dad reaches his hands out either side, as a hot Sunday lunch is served. 'We usually get the visitor to say grace,' he smiles playfully at me.

'You do NOT!' I give him the don't-do-that-to-me look.

After Dad's prayer, my aunt addresses me directly. 'Are you a believer, Den?' She clearly considers my 'rebellion' a disrespect to my parents' beliefs. I avert my eyes, silent. 'Do you believe in God and an afterlife?' Quiet, I look at her, my stomach tender. 'Yes or No?' she presses. 'You either are or you aren't.'

I'd protected my parents, letting them glimpse only a fragment of my struggle, hinting that the 'meaning-making' conflict after such devastation was not straightforward; but no-one grasped the extent of the Dark Night, could gauge its destruction, or recognise that next to my sons, my spirituality was the biggest secondary loss of my life.

'*I don't know.*'

While we eat in the now-sober air, I lose my battle. My aunt reaches across the table. She holds my hand, silent, as I weep.

~

24 September 2012

I said at your funeral that I'd continue to take comfort in those words you kindly spoke to me, Simon. You were such a strength in my life; your integrity was amazing. I hope you're benefitting from that now. You were a very beautiful eldest son. If we choose, thank you for choosing me. Thank you for all the lovely things you said to me through your 18½ years, for all the learning, for the precious lifetime we shared together. I love you, Simon. I hope you are happy.

CHAPTER 7

Beauty and The Beast

*I was in the barth and I wobbild my tooth and it came out.
It did not hurt not a siggol bit.*
**Allie, Kindergarten
aged 5**

January 2003

Within weeks of Simon's death, life began to change significantly for Allie. She was picked up and carried for a while by older friends who'd known Simon and wanted to comfort her, which she needed. Naturally it worried me when she began staying out late, then sometimes not coming home at all... A month before his death, Allie had come dux of her year at school. A popular student, she'd been elected to the student representative council – a position of responsibility and trust – one we'd soon see she wouldn't be able to fill. She began to rebel, including wagging from school, and letters began arriving from the deputy principal about her absences from class. Near the end of third term, out of 150 school days, she'd missed 50, and collected several suspensions.

In an unexpected irony, Simon's death speedily precipitated Allie's recovery from her anorexia, dwarfing all that'd been important to her till then. Within a month, she'd got her first boyfriend. Within four months, she'd put on enough weight to bring on her first period, which then triggered a torrent of hormones. Amidst normal teenager-ing, recovering from anorexia psychologically and physically, rebelling, and grieving for her brother, she was up and down and all over the place.

'Is she blaming you?' her psychiatrist asked me, Day One after Simon's death.

'Not yet!' although I sensed what lay ahead.

There was no blame about Simon's death, Allie didn't suddenly lose her insight, beauty or depth, but our relationship began an uphill climb, arguments erupting in air thick with worry. I often wouldn't know where she was, or if she was safe. She got her hair cut, dyed, got piercings, spoke to me in ways I never had to my parents, and swore more than ever. To onlookers who glimpsed two strong females in a most stressful chapter, it was no surprise. To me, amidst grieving for Simon, it felt impossible. Allie needed to push against me, and she needed me to stand firm.

She did keep up her dance class, which was a great outlet for her. An all-rounder, Allie really got dance.

'When you dance, you're no longer a human being,' she wrote, *'but an extension of the music, in physical form. You don't dance to, flow on the music, or let it move you. It flows through your veins, controls you, dissolving you from the inside, until you're just a part of it: you actually are the music.'*

She kept her appointments with Dr Furrows, and confided in him, which was a blessing; someone had their finger on the pulse.

'Behaving impulsively can be hormonal,' David explained. 'I know it's hard, but if you can let go her "needling" you rather than reacting, it might help long-term.'

Allie and I used to say to each other often, *Thank god for David*.

4 August 2003

I know the best help I could be to Allie is to not entertain so much self-doubt, and, when I can – be loving in my strength, instead of guilty about it, or always seeing her vulnerable side.

Best for both of us if I drink from the Holy Grail, the cup of unconditional self-love.

Allie's sleep suffered alongside mine. By mid-September, David suggested antidepressants for her, something neither she nor I would've previously considered.

15 September 2003

When Allie was first admitted to Robina, they wanted to pop her on antidepressants, almost – it seemed – as a matter of course. She chose to plough through that anorexia chapter under her own biochemical steam – and to feel her own choice was very important to her.

Now in another setting, she's interested in medication. It's the first time in my life it's suddenly made sense – in fact, it looks like the only merciful thing. She deserves, and wants, the help.

16 September 2003

Allie's just started antidepressants. Having not had a full night's sleep since Simon died, she slept for sixteen hours straight. I've been filled with a huge sobbing feeling all day, so sad for her – for all she's been through, for the huge challenges she's still in the midst of, this year alone. It's all been so out of hand for her, and she's been letting me wear the lot. I hope things will improve now if she can at least get enough sleep.

She needed, and wanted, to just stop.

Even Allie's felt like I have lately: we just wanna cut all our ties with the world and be left alone, in our own space.

Allie loved her work at Supré clothing store, not attending class as much. Her year advisor kindly offered to gather estimates from her teachers for her school certificate.

1 February 2004

When Allie's having a hard time in the world, she projects it onto me. In that adolescent fault-finding-with-your-parents way, we bounce tensely off each other. I guess she at least has some way of coping. I can't bear to think of how it is for her, having to fight (and there's a lot in that) her illness, and learn to live without her brother.

'Why do you have to always criticise me?' I throw out one day. 'How will I know what I don't wanna be if I don't?' she throws back. Her self-awareness floors me. I feel so inadequate.

She just has so much on her plate to keep going, not to mention the pressure of doing her best at school over the next two years, to win that scholarship she wants. My stomach knots for her.

I've said to Allie, I don't fully understand why things are like they are between us. I've always over-identified with her, projected more onto

her than the boys, felt excruciating guilt about that, and wanted more close moments than we've had. It's been a stormy adolescence with all these problems; last year was a shocker.

I miss Simon's unconditional love. He didn't used to judge me…

Occasionally Allie and I get to talk about our grief. 'I feel really bad for you and Ash that I'm still grieving so deeply for Simon,' I tell her one day out near the clothesline.

'Maybe you're doing it on behalf of all three of us,' she says, 'so that Ash and I can get on with our lives.'

I smile at her. *So insightful!*

29 March 2004

This year since school's gone back, our routine's been the same: no visitors, not much talking, very little activity; and at night, dinner in front of the telly, zoned out, the three of us huddled together in the corner, consuming copious quantities of chocolate (we're all addicted now) – a type of shocked togetherness.

With the death of a child/sibling, life becomes more unpredictable. It loses its order.

We need this space to ourselves.

5 April 2004

Glancing back over this journal, I see that Allie and I have established a closeness in this time.

Simon's death takes a lot of handling. A feeling persists that something's wrong, and we don't have rest from that, although the intensity's kicked back a notch.

Allie still needs to rebel, a slightly scaled-down version of last year.

None of this can be expressed in words. The feeling of how *impossible* it is to get to the end of some days – let alone of the experience (wherever the end of that is) – cannot be described. Just as miraculous is that we can get up next day and keep going.

Allie chose subjects for Year 11 that'd enable her to study medicine, because she was bright, and could, but her school attendance didn't return to 'normal'. By mid-year, pressure was mounting, while grieving and rebelling were prioritising themselves.

In May 2004, Allie sat her half-yearlies. She didn't bring me her half-yearly report in June, in which three of her six subject teachers had requested interviews with me, nor the weekly school newsletter reminding us of parent-teacher interviews that week.

17 June 2004

Allie's not doing well academically. She just needs my support. Ashley's growing, and is withdrawn. They're both okay when I'm okay. My poor deserving children. I'm scared of how hard it is for them because of how hard it is for me. I feel guilty about my inadequacies. It's like we tell ourselves spiritual stories just to make life bearable; it doesn't matter that there's no sense – there *isn't*. The lives of this little family can be crumpled and impossible, struggling to live on with SUCH meaninglessness, in a world of people who don't have to live with these unfathomables, and the fucking mess it makes of your life.

In late July, I received a letter from the principal and deputy, requesting a discussion ASAP. I wrote to Dr Furrows: Allie's disrespect was pressing my buttons hard, I wanted to change my 'holding' pattern of rescuing her from her bad decisions, and I could see another crisis looming.

David assures me the stretches we go through of not talking are normal. We're in our own spaces; it's not cold-shoulder stuff, but like we're dancing around each other, not connecting. It grieves me terribly, always has…

Bereaved siblings would feel as though their lives are not being celebrated. Bereaved parents are painfully aware of this, but that awareness doesn't automatically give us the energy to do anything about it. The rock-bottom self-esteem from being so deeply bereaved makes it all worse.

How can she grow up when I keep assuming full responsibility for everything she feels, thinks, and does?

2 July 2004

About seven or eight weeks ago, I began cooking again. Big in itself, as those at TCF acknowledge, but for the first time since before Allie's anorexia, she's been eating the meals I've cooked: a big deal.

Also big are the arguments we've been having. Allie (*now 17*) well and truly stands up to me, yelling swearing at me. When things are settled between us, our rapport is loving, close, and she's her normal beautiful funny self.

Allie's always been strong-willed and independent. She's said a few times of later years, 'I just want to experience life for myself!'

(Saturday) 7 August 2004

On Wednesday afternoon, Allie came to the lounge room and sat with Ash and me. She hasn't spoken to me much the last few weeks, but began talking while I hand-sewed. The things she said were a bit shocking, horrible. Without getting baited energetically, I just stated they weren't true. I was determined as much as possible to stop reinforcing the holding pattern; writing it out helped a little. I don't know what was precipitating it.

As I started preparing dinner, I asked Allie if she wanted to eat with us. When she's unhappy with me, she won't let me cook for her. 'No.'

Some time after 7pm she stood at the pantry door, looking in. I'd done a shop the day before, so I knew there was food.

Next morning, when I went to get her up for school, she was vomiting. *Was it because she hadn't had dinner the night before?* She didn't know, she said, *'maybe'*. She stayed in bed that day, vomiting intermittently.

Later that afternoon, I phoned the doctor's surgery, thinking I might take Allie for a shot of Maxalon, but they'd stopped taking calls at 4:30pm. I wrote down the After-Hours number in case we needed it. Apparently Sydney hospitals were inundated by people with a 24-hour bug.

Next day (Friday), Allie didn't look like heading to school. She spent the day on the couch in front of the telly, looking a little better. But after the 24 hours was up, she vomited again, and more, so I phoned the surgery and asked my GP brother-in-law to come on his way home.

He came about 4:30pm. After he'd done his obs and talked with her, he said he wasn't going to give Allie Maxalon because she needed to go straight to hospital. He could call an ambulance, but they'd take her to the nearest hospital, and he thought she should go to Southport where her file was. *Why does she have to go to hospital?* Because when he asked her had she taken anything, she said she'd taken Panadol – and quite a lot.

Panadol is not a good thing to overdose on. Six at once can do liver damage. Forty kept down for 36 hours can kill you. It causes intra-cellular bleeding (i.e. you bleed to death internally), if the 36-hour IV flush-out doesn't do the trick.

Allie took 98 Panadol.

Just in case, she left a note under her bed. I found it a couple of days later. Written on Winnie-the-Pooh paper, it said: 'I'm not trying to kill myself. I just want to escape for a while.'

(Saturday) 7 August 2004

One day at a time till we see the extent of damage to Allie's liver. Results from 'A & E' last night (*Friday*) show the presence of certain enzymes that track liver damage. When Allie was admitted (48 hours post-ingestion), the enzyme level which is supposed to be between 0–45, was 850.

Today we find out if it's improving or still getting worse. The mortality rate from paracetamol overdose increases two days after ingestion, reaches a maximum on day four, then gradually decreases. I'm told you only need 10% of your liver to function.

Today's (*Saturday*) blood test, another twelve hours later (60 hours post-ingestion), the count was 3800. She's on a drip to keep flushing out her system.

I have nothing in me with which to react. My head was on her bed, spent.

(Sunday) 8 August 2004

Today's count is 1300. They say it's peaked, and is on its way back down again.

(Monday) 9 August 2004

Allie is home. She was discharged this afternoon at 3:30pm.

Her psychiatrist would've liked Allie go to Robina adolescent psych unit from Southport hospital. We've had a hard run, and home was where she wanted to come to. It was too much after a close call like that to launch into analysing it all straight away. A stay in hospital sounds like a break – a respite – but the reality's different, especially at Robina. Southport was good; Robina would've been depressing. In any case, Allie just wanted to come home…

In the days Allie was in hospital, we talked. We went from not talking much the days before, to spending hours each day, side-by-side, communicating. Southport hospital was in a different state, a long way from our sad grieving home; it was easier for us to talk there.

(Wednesday) 11 August 2004

There's nothing 'wrong' with our relationship. We're two strong independent females, who like a lot of space. We love each other and always have.

This episode has shifted things. Allie said she doesn't really want to study medicine. She wants to follow her passion: fashion. She'll probably repeat Year 11 next year. At last, the pressure of her getting through school without stopping is off.

Post-Panadol overdose, Allie said she'd been depressed. She was mourning the life she'd had before Simon died, her academic orientation, her relative innocence. She felt like a terrible best friend not being able to resolve her girlfriend's relationship problems, and guilty abandoning her friends to spend time with her boyfriend and his crew. She was sick of the awful state our relationship was in. And she was really angry when she took the overdose which was 'just the catalyst'.

My motherguilt with Allie had always run in overdrive. Grieving Joseph from her conception, guilt about that, perfectionism, and partly because she was the female child, this episode was no different. *How could I have let this happen to my precious daughter?!*

Somehow, there was no permanent damage to Allie's liver.

The stress since Simon's suicide began to manifest physically for me. A week after Allie's overdose, the results from my blood count returned a problem: thyroid disease. David said thyroid troubles occur so often after a major stress, it's beyond coincidence. It means medication every day for the rest of my life. Complaining to Dr Betty only earns me a slap on the wrist. *Dr Betty's right. 'Taking daily medication is nothing.'*

11 December 2004

Last night, when Allie mentioned Joseph, I took his photo album and scrapbook to her. When I went back to her room after a while, she was slowly turning pages, crying. 'I don't ever want to go through anything like this. I couldn't do it...' She cried a lot.

This morning she said that going through the books last night, felt as if someone had just died, as though she'd just lost someone.

That *was* the atmosphere into which Allie was born.

How desperately do we crave a happily-ever-after ending? Despite the reality of all we've experienced? Is that what fuels our hope? Maybe just a break from the stress?

Allie's overdose cleared the air for a few weeks, but in the end, there'd be no shortcuts: Simon was gone from our lives. We couldn't suddenly change the fact, or 'get over' it. Grief is hard work. So is adolescent individuating.

Allie had lost several main anchors in her life, Dr Furrows explained: her dad, Ashley's dad, and Simon, who'd been like a rock for her – but her being able to blame me, dump on me, and fight with me, was her mainstay. She'd sometimes say to him, 'I know I'm wrong, but I'm not giving her the satisfaction of admitting it to her!'

Allie could no longer swallow tablets, so was off her antidepressants. She got another job, and kept her social life busy.

The following year brought a fresh start: new school subjects for Allie, and high school for Ash.

Despite medication, my thyroid levels took a long time to bring under control, my anxiety meanwhile intensifying.

5 April 2005

When Dr Betty suggested anti-anxiety medication a fortnight ago, I wondered how I could politely swap doctors. Understanding my thyroid condition better now, I've decided it's the decisive intervention my rapidly spiralling circumstances need. It'll hopefully address my sleep situation, heart palpitations, panic attacks, and the slow rate at which my anxiety and stress levels are continuing to kill my thyroid.

I didn't think I could live past last night. Thought I was going to die – even in the waiting room – a thought I've had often this year. Part of me did die last night – the part that believed I wasn't allowed to accept help of this nature. I love my children, and want peace and gentle loving harmony for us all.

I'm proud of our courage.

Thankfully, Allie and Ash did quite well in the half-yearlies. *Something's functioning right.*

Towards the end of the year, Ash comes dux of Year 7.

5 December 2005

Allie formally finished school today. She'll do Year 12 further down the track. She started a new phase of her job this afternoon. More adjustment for all, but I'm relieved for her. It's a good change.

18 March 2006

Allie came and sat down yesterday afternoon, and we had one of those rare real talks. The female thing makes everyday clashes harder for Allie and me, but during those chats, you know it's a timeless one. I'm relieved to see Allie's qualities strengthening, especially when I'm deeply struggling myself.

Towards the end of 2006, the house we were renting sold. It was a grief to leave the home we'd shared with Simon. Out to the neighbouring green valley, we moved to a 12-acre farm.

Under the paperbark tree in our new back yard, I'd see Allie talking to 'someone' on the other empty chair while having a cigarette. I always assumed it was Simon, glad to believe she knew his death didn't have to end their relationship.

She started Year 12 at a different high school so she didn't have to go through with students who'd travelled through several years below her. New teachers took a while to recognise her talents.

My dad takes his turn at a driving lesson with another grandchild, on a narrow windy road where it starts to hail. Instead of pulling over as the other drivers do, Allie picks up speed, unable for the storm's noise and hailstones hitting the windscreen, to hear Dad screeching, 'Slow down! Slow down!' Through the whites of his eyes, wipers barely coping with the water, Dad notices visibility at about three metres, Allie rocketing along instead of following instructions to stop. Finally, the hail eases.

Allie pulls up, and smiles at Dad. 'We got through *that*!'

(*And my parents thought* their *children were headstrong!*)

In late April, Allie and I watch *The Sea Inside*, about a quadriplegic man seeking euthanasia. Afterwards, we don't need to clarify our positions to each other. They haven't changed: *a person's right to end their life, for whatever reason, must be respected.* Allie doesn't think people really want to die, even those feeling suicidal; it's that they don't wanna keep living their life. Sometimes, ending their life seems the only way to end the pain.

I love her depth.

A week later, Allie stays overnight with a girlfriend who lives with her disabled dad. Less than 24 hours later, Ashlee's dad takes his own life. The following Friday, the day she's supposed to submit a textiles-and-design assignment, Allie attends the funeral. I ask a TCF friend who's going, to keep an eye on my daughter.

Allie talks to me about it afterwards. It was big for her, touched her, she's talking about Simon. She's okay, but I tread carefully.

The following Monday, in one of those deep chats, I tell Allie how her frequent swearing at me affects me: *doubles me over physically.*

'I didn't know my words even touched you. I thought they were like water off a duck's back!' She can show depth and such insight at such moments – which I told her I respected a lot. 'I always thought you were closer to the boys,' she said, 'and that it was easier for you with Simon.' I felt awkward – terribly sorry for her. 'I read an article about how mothers are often closer to their sons because they had an unconscious fascination with what they weren't, i.e. male.'

'I did feel close to Simon. It's often like that with fathers and daughters too,' I said, then felt sorry I'd mentioned something she'd missed out on. Allie had always been close to Simon. After he'd died, she said she didn't have hugs with anyone else like it. Thankfully she missed that I was saying it actually hurt me that she couldn't take much comfort in my hugs then. Instead she went on to summon a memory she often enjoyed. 'He used to hug me every day.'

'When I was pregnant with Joseph, I was expecting – and hoping for – a girl.' I was so glad to tell Allie this. 'I'd even lined the chest of drawers (of baby clothes) with pink tissue paper before I went to hospital.' She seemed quietly pleased. 'It hadn't always been easy for me with Sime. I had my challenges with him too; he and I had to learn rules of communication. The violence for which I left Dad started to menace with Simon at one stage, and I didn't know what to do. You can leave the partner – the other parent – but you can't leave the child; you *have* to work it out. Every relationship with each of your children is different, just like every love, every boy you're with. I thought you and I always respected each other a lot, and wanted to be closer, but maybe we were also a bit scared of hurting each other. I think our relationship hasn't been as spontaneously free to express affection.' Allie looked a little bit hurt, 'but that wasn't how it was for me as a child, nor for my mum as a child, nor for generations before her I suspect. But you and I enjoy other aspects to our relationship that are good. On balance, I think we do alright.' She agreed.

Allie brought up her time in hospital with anorexia – twice – I wasn't sure why. Her eyes glassed over in that dull way they used to when she got sick. I didn't know what was connecting her to it, but her need to speak of it was strong, so I went with it.

'When I was in St Vincent's, in the adolescent psych ward, and they were pushing me up to an adult BMI, I knew you could sign me out earlier if you'd wanted. I broached the subject with you several times in there and could see it was upsetting you, so I stopped bringing it up.'

Was she implying she'd lost her trust in me then? I felt sad she was looking vulnerable. I explained as best I could, what it was like for 'us' (mainly Simon and me), to watch her slowly dying in our midst, and not be able to stop it. I didn't want to remind Allie of the sad memory of her Christmas in hospital, when Simon and I dropped her back, and cried all the way home.

'I had to play Mum in that situation, not psychologist, and entrust you to the mental health profession to save you from it. It was a bit scary to see how powerful that illness was. I didn't know what was best. I *had* to trust their decision. I could see how sick you'd been, and that if I'd let it, that illness would've taken you. I was fighting the Grim Reaper for your life.'

I mentioned initiations in tribal times, how a boy especially, or girl, at the start of adolescence would be taken away from the main tribe, and put through rites that symbolised their launch into adulthood. 'When Simon went to live with Dad at age 12, it was like that – as was your anorexia. I knew that separating process towards independence and becoming an individual had to begin sometime.'

Allie's insights had shown such mature understanding, I told her.

'I don't have reason to live this life,' she said.

'Neither do I, sweetheart.' Living with Simon's death, we'd spoken openly at times like this to each other. 'I don't know what helps me keep grinding through whatever's in front of me for the day. Maybe it's inherent in the life-force? I think I hold hope beside me that life'll become better, that I'll have reason one day. For now I live for those who love me, to spare them grieving my death. I can't make sense of this life and the things that've happened to us. But when you get through your hard times and things are a bit easier again, you get distracted by life, and not having reason doesn't seem to bother you as much.'

Of course I've had opportunity to wonder if levelling with my children so honestly was a bad idea. I've had time to question my every move as a parent.

Allie was born mature. She was thinking these thoughts even if we didn't talk about them. It's others being real with me I've most appreciated in life, and this is what I gave my children.

We have a long hug – always longer than the boys.
She's so soft, feminine. Always smells so lovely.

Two days later, she takes the day off school to study for her half-yearly chemistry exam.

Allie was heading for a scholarship to the Whitehouse Institute of Design in Sydney. She intended to do the first half of her fashion degree there, and finish at its sister college in Florence, Italy. In her half-yearlies, her textiles-and-design teacher docked a mark for a question she'd answered accurately, but not as the teacher wanted. 'She's got no right to dock me that mark!' Allie fumed. She knew how to reach perfection; it was sitting in the crosshairs again.

Midday, I answer the phone to a woman asking for Allie. 'Who am I speaking to?' An unknown name... Instinctively protective, I let the silence amplify. It's her teacher...

I call Allie.

She picks up; she's being read the riot act, feigning cool... 'If you don't get last Friday's assessment task in to me within 24 hours, you'll get a zero' ...'*I was at a funeral*'... 'If you don't get a letter to me within 24 hours about your attendance at the funeral, signed by your mum that she drove you there, and your friend who accompanied you, you'll get a zero.' – i.e. *Forget the Whitehouse scholarship.*

1pm: Monique comes over, signs the letter, and takes Allie out for a break. I shake my head as they drive off. *You took the day off school to study for tomorrow's exam, Allie...*

Finally, when the sun's stopped shining on our side of the hill, I hear a car... She's back.

Inside, within minutes, she emerges from her room, crying. 'Can I have a hug?' I roll my computer chair out so she can sit on my lap.

I regret not hugging her tighter then, warmer, rescuing her from those consequences, again.

Back in her room, sitting bedside, she weeps; she'd intended to be home sooner. Allie looks at her desk, her chemistry notes unstudied. 'Why can't I finish anything I start?' I'd heard her say this before but regarded her as rather infallible... except I do know a perfectionist's critic can be merciless.

She'd been on her L's for a while, had her 50 hours up, and went for her driving test the month before. Theory, no worries; practical, I had a *feeling*... Dad and I sat in the RTA, waiting anxiously. In her reverse park, Allie's tyre nudged the curb (which of course ours *never* do). *Instant fail.* Sometimes I think today's test standards are ridiculous...

Allie had already repeated Year 11, pulling out before finishing her first attempt, taking subjects she was interested in second time around, instead of the harder ones of which she was academically capable. Now in Year 12, this was the second time she'd tried to sit her half-yearly chemistry paper. In another fortnight, she'd turn twenty... entering a decade her brother never had. Time was intensifying.

'A friend said to me recently' – I hoped to ease her tears – ' *"look at the situation and try to take the emotion out of it".'* I hoped she could put her mind to chemistry tonight. I'd been a good last-minute crammer.

'I'm feeling too emotional at the moment...'

'I've recently discovered that *eating* helps me feel better.' (A dry joke for all we'd endured: eating + emotion => anorexia), 'I made a nice dinner... you might feel better when you *eat*...'

A delicate smile through drying tears.

Allie texts girlfriend Kara, and starts applying make-up in the bathroom mirror. 'You're going out?' I try to stifle concern.

'<u>Yes</u>.' *No more questions, mother.*

Allie suddenly gets busy in her room, carrying a bag of stuff to her car. 'Would you please take some photos of me?'

'Sure. What's this for?'

'My HSC Art major work.' Since that's why I'd bought her the camera, I don't question. She looks so beautiful, several times her eyes sparking into mine as I snap away.

In the lounge room, starting a DVD – *The Beat My Heart Skipped* – eating dinner, Allie comes to hug me. *Out again, Allie... second attempt chem paper tomorrow... dunno how you're gonna get through this one.* Of course, I say nothing. I've been trained.

'Love you, Mum,' she heads to the door, ' – very much'.

A weird profound panic grabs me. *'Love you'* is normal, *'very much'* is not.

'Ditto,' ...our word from *Ghost*... 'Don't be home too late.'

'Yep,' says Allie.
I can hear she doesn't mean it.
She shuts the door.

And that's it.

~

*Let me not pray to be sheltered from dangers, but to be
fearless in facing them.
Let me not beg for the stilling of my pain, but for the heart
to conquer it.
Grant me that I may not be a coward, feeling your mercy
in my success alone;
But let me find the grasp of your hand in my failure.*
Rabindranath Tagore

mid-morning, mid-May 2007

At the table, I'm updating my new recipe book, feeling calm and centred, for no apparent reason. Naturally we'd like to assume we're finally getting on top of things, coming to terms with life as it is.

Then a car pulls up in my driveway... *Oh thank God – Allie. Maybe her chemistry paper's later than I thought. Hopefully she stayed overnight at Kara's. It's probably them.*

Sounds like a second car. The engine turns off. Glancing out, I notice there are not two heads, but three – conferring closely to each other, near the car. *Maybe it's not Allie...*

They start walking steadily, three heads close together, in step, towards the house; two men in formal shirts and ties. *Maybe it's to do with the school?*

I start to get up. Before they reach the door, I peep around to check the third person.

It's a police officer.

When Simon died, and I'd told the story of opening the door to three police officers, some replied, 'You must've *known* as soon as you saw them.'

'No – I didn't.'

'Well...' they'd reconsider, '...yeah... Why would you?'

I'd had four years to ponder that.

Why would *you assume three police officers had come to deliver such news?*

Because you'd seen it before.

I look at all three of them heading, with unrelenting deliberation to my door, my eyes settling on the policewoman.

'Oh no,' I blurt. 'Oh no. No. No! Oh god, No!! Oh God, NO!' My protests don't budge their beeline into my life. 'Oh No! NO! Where's Allie?' I gasp at them. I look out at their cars, vain hope she might be there. *'Where's Allie?'* The sombre air around them tells me she's not there. 'No! No! Go Away! GO AWAY!' They're undeterred. 'NO! **NO!** GO *AWAY!*'

That's how I know.

Allie's gone.

Backing back to my couch, I sit. I grasp my head, gasping 'No! NO!'

'Maybe we'd better come in,' the policewoman says through the flyscreen door.

'You'll have to let yourselves in... I can't move.'

The policewoman comes in first. I stare into nothing, patting the couch next to me. She sits; I grasp her around the neck in gut-wrenching shock, clinging to her like a leech, stunned tears around my eyes.

'Allie has passed away.'

'*No!*' I continue gasping. 'It's not true!'

Paula needs to breathe. 'How?' I release her neck, grasping her hands instead. She doesn't seem to want to tell me. Wants to ask me a few questions first. She doesn't know I know. I need to know *how*. There are ways that could've made it harder for her. 'Please tell me!' Allie's been to a funeral five days before. 'Tell me please!' I wanna make sure she didn't suffer. 'How did she die?'

'She gassed herself in her car.'

'*Oh thank God.*' I breathe out, head in hand. *This method's easier for her. It was about Simon, not something else I didn't know about.*

These police officers have not done their homework. They have no idea the bomb they're dropping on me. They don't know why a mother would utter *'Oh thank god'* when they've told her that her daughter 'gassed herself in her car'.

The story takes a bit of explaining.

The procedures. Had she been depressed? Was anything upsetting her? Is there someone they can call to come and be with me?

Again, my sister and brother-in-law...

I place an embargo on phone calls, visitors, contact with others. If I didn't have to talk about it, didn't have to relay it to my outside world, maybe I could stop it being real? I can't do that onslaught again.

Again, the hospital, mid-afternoon.

Sobbing over Allie's unmoving body, frozen beauty on mortuary trolley, saturated with that smell – that *'carbon monoxide' smell* – I had no choice. My mind had seen it. My hand had signed it.

Yes officer, this is my daughter.

Too late.

Next morning, I phone Monique. Crying with her in my room, I'm reminded – because *you forget* – just how much death humbles you, brings you close together. I realise it has to happen, the madness embraced: Allie's mourners must invade, make it real, start the process, let the pain in, comfort each other.

After Day One to myself, I lift the embargo.

As it was with Simon, hundreds of phone calls on top of each other all day long, visitor after visitor, my children's dear friends, flowers filling the house, impossible fatigue through amazing perfume, appointments, late nights preparing for *another* funeral. I cried in exasperation at Allie's and my perfectionism, the unexpected suicide, terrified of not getting Allie's funeral right for her. I was her voice. This was Allie's death now. *Allie's GONE!*

The word 'bizarre' reached my ears. It irritated me. Did people think this word was comforting?

The term 'copycat' was being bandied about. It aggravated Dr Furrows and me. 'Copycat suicides aren't about copying a *method*,' I'd sigh frustrated, 'they're about copying an *identity*.' *Lucky you for my patience.* 'Allie was her own person, with such self-possessed maturity! She wanted the same exit as Simon, but they were different people, with different lives.' David would later add, '– whose deaths happened for different reasons. Brother and sister – not *"copycats"*!'

Some phoning condolences were sure they were voicing my feelings: 'How DARE she do this to you?!' leaving me to defend Allie's actions before I'd begun to process how I felt.

'She didn't *"do this"* to me,' I'd retort, 'she *"did it"* to herself, and if we're going to respect Simon's right to leave, we'll respect Allie's too – as we respected her life. She's not accountable for all the deaths leave us with! People have a right to leave if life gets too painful for them.'

'If it gets too hard for you, Denny,' a few said, 'we'll understand if you need to go too. No-one would begrudge you...' It was never an option. Each time I'd lost a child, I had another to single-parent.

For many, the thought of the deaths was just too much.

I was grateful for the shock.

As we arrive in the mourning car outside the door of the church, in the habit of wrenching coping mechanisms from wherever I can, the thought comes through the fog: *I can do this. It's the same church. I've done this before.* Now reaching the door, the atmosphere inside calm, I'm glad I've had them play Allie's Dido album; it's brought the feel of Allie to them. *We can do this. I've done it before.* Ash puts his arm around me as I've told him the day before to do. *There we go.* I look up. *Ugh!* This is *not* the same! That's *Allie's* photo smiling at us from the coffin! *This is ALLIE'S funeral! Ohmygod!* The floor starts falling from under me as I start to buckle over. 'Say something!' I fix my eyes on the minister, panic descending. 'Quick! *Say* something!' 'God loves you,' she looks right in my eyes. 'Yes!' 'God loves you, and Allie loves you.' '*Yes!*' I've been a good mother, she tells me, my daughter's proud of me, she's with us, and God has his arms around me. It mightn't be true, but I need to believe it. She hugs me, tells me to take a deep breath in, then breathe it all out, another breath in, out. One more... and I'm okay. To the front of the church, I glimpse Pete. Twenty-three years earlier, we'd exchanged wedding vows, right where the coffin of our last child now stands. 'There's my husband.' I keep my eyes on him as we start the slow march up the long aisle to the front of the large tightly packed church... dear Ash beside me, only just fifteen... to Allie's chosen song, 'In the Arms of the Angels'.

Standing by the open grave that holds my two teenagers' bodies, one on top of the other, I hug Mykaela.

*'You're the only person I can say this to,' I whisper. 'Maybe when these last few have gone to the wake, no-one'll notice. There's a space down in that corner. See? ...It wouldn't be comfortable, but I could fit. It's **my** grave. I don't wanna leave my children here. I just want the others to go now so I can get down in there where I belong. It's the only place I wanna be.'*

'I know....' Mykaela looks away. '...I don't blame you.' ...the truth... a comfort.

I don't leave yet. Next to the grave, I drop to one knee, my head on the arm of a mourner's wheelchair, and sob and sob and sob.

Like the hailstones, pelting hard on Allie's windscreen, we somehow push ourselves.
'We got through that', Allie.
Now the hard part: to grieve you, to learn to live without you.

My journalling didn't register a hiccup. I just kept writing, scraping the top off my feelings and thoughts, allowing them room, helping express, clarify, explore, addressing my children directly. To keep my support systems in place kept the wheels rolling, which helped begin processing my grief for Allie.

17 May 2007

The guilt's going to be very hard darling, especially as time marches on without you, and the shock wears off. The shock makes it feel manageable.

I was conscious of being on anti-anxiety medication; it dulled me a little, for which I was grateful.
The shock was more about having lost two children to suicide now.

30 May 2007

It's sort-of not as completely shocking this time – the suicide thing, the gassing thing, the death thing. It's the *fact* that Allie's gone now, forever, and halfway through a year that could've brought to fruition, major rewards for all her struggle. As she said, if I get that scholarship, it'll all be worth it…

I don't think anyone has ever had as many hugs in one day as I had the day of Allie's funeral. It was beautiful. But from two nights after, I haven't been able to sleep on my right side, because I've had RSI in my shoulder from all the embracing, sore wrists from holding 400 people in tight hugs.

19 May 2007

A TCF mum phones. She thinks 'certain sensitivities are inherited genetically with mental illness'. I baulk at the mental illness connection – at that *assumption* people make with suicide. She said she hadn't meant they'd inherited mental illness from their dad, or even the susceptibility for it, but perhaps the *sensitivities* present alongside mental illness, that make it really hard to bear this world.

This deep sensitivity mightn't just accompany mental illness. My friend Nick (*who suicided when I was 22*) had it. But it explained my experience of rearing Allie and especially Simon – of that sensitivity I could never fully protect in them, nor feel like I could successfully teach them to protect in themselves.

26 May 2007

I'm glad you have Simon there to show you Allie, how to be in the ethers. I believe I feel you around. Thanks for blowing the bathroom light.

29 May 2007

I haven't dropped my cynicism about all things spiritual. It's been overridden for the moment by everyone's loving support, and by my great need to believe my three Meeky children are together, and happy.

I'm scared of going back into the Valley. I'm afraid of starting that journey that will have me question what sort of mother I was to you, Allie.

I've been there already with Simon.

I don't wanna go back there...

5 June 2007

I notice how supported I feel at this time by the Universe. Everything I need is where I reach for it. That happened with Sime too.

My psychic receptivity is heightened again at this time. As far as I know, most of what I see with my little eye is accurate. It's as though I currently live in that dimension.

7 June 2007

The SHOCK is eerie. You *know* the gates of hell have just shut behind you. It seems to wanna lull you into a false sense of security, let you look at the death, feel nothing, allow you any foolish thought you may have that you *can* manage this. Hard to trust the process will lead me where I need to go down the track. I feel like keeping on with the goals I had – like going back to work, travelling O/S... I don't feel stopped by this yet.

Gees I wish you'd got through that stretch, Allie. I wish you were still here to play in the world, to enjoy the feeling of conquering. I was so *sure* you would! That your path was different, that you weren't destined for suicide too. How did you slip through that portal? Was that okay? Do people die only when they're 'meant to'?? Is it as belief systems I know of, think? Psalm 139:16, World English Bible – 'In your book they were all written, the days that were ordained for me, when as yet there were none of them.' The Hare Krishnas: everyone is born with a certain amount of food, a certain amount of wealth, and a certain number of breaths. Is this for suicides too? Were you destined to die then, Allie? Parents who lose children seem so expendable, in so many ways. What are they to do with their mental constructs on life?? And their ability to make them accurately? Truth is important to me.

Allie had six months of appointments booked with Dr Furrows, so I kept them. I needed the support, and a clinical relationship slowly developed that welcomed both intellect and a respected friendship.

Before Facebook, Allie had a MySpace page. At the time of her death, she listed her Heroes as 'My Mumsy, my brothers &; my mates☺'. David tells me Allie admired my strength, which was partly a bad thing: she thought I could handle her leaving.

7 June 2007

Dr Furrows is certainly of the opinion that suicide is individual, and not necessarily precipitated by mental illness. He believes mental illness was not a factor in Allie's suicide. 'People want to tie off loose ends neatly. They want neat explanations, not have to become uncomfortable.' He said, 'To reduce this to a "low self-esteem" is to over-simplify it.' Before Allie's funeral, he described her as having 'the most beautifully complex mind'. I showed him the goodbye Allie left in her little journal for us. 'She asked for her decision to be respected,' he noted. I like that he drew my attention to that.

11 June 2007

I saw Allie get through so much stuff that was harder than this stretch. I saw her cry so many times, as she saw me. We just thought that's what the other was doing – getting through our rough stretches. I banked on it.

Allie had been Dr Furrows' favourite patient. He understands the contributing factors; he just wished the final trigger had been a bit more 'worth it'.

But it's the *straws* that break the camel's back. To this day that's how I experience suicidal spaces: *the straws*...

The 'triggers'... mid-May already, Year 12, slight panic, nearly twenty. Not enough study for second-attempt chemistry that day, that she'd stayed home just to study. Her girlfriend's father's funeral five days

before, his death the night after Allie had stayed with them the previous weekend – *a bit close to home.* Textiles teacher's phone call that day: get that signed letter to me within 24 hours, or you'll get a zero. *The Sea Inside* three weeks earlier: *yes, everyone has this right. What are we struggling so hard for anyway? Simon's just across that veil. A fine sheet of organza brushed aside and there he is. And Joseph, the brother I didn't meet, whose absence I've felt all my life anyway. Just the other side of that gaseous cloud, where I wouldn't have to study to tell you what the cloud's made up of: relief, reunion, acceptance, love...*

I get it. *For Mum, it'll be those elements plus reason, sense and meaning.* To my core, I get it, sweetie.

2 July 2007

The fact that Allie and I had stormy interactions pass between us, and did four years of grief together, alongside each other, means that I believe on the other side, she understands these difficult grief spaces. I also trust the female bond – enjoy it, but mourn it too.

5 July 2007

Allie, how are you? I'm starting to really miss you. I know it's only gonna get worse. You're never coming back.

I don't wanna feel my grief more and more, as you leave these ethers, to feel your absence more, to feel you gone. I wanna be able to feel your cheek on my cheek, from you sitting next to me. I don't want it to be like this, Allie.

6 July 2007

Simon, I'm losing Allie. I know you'd care. I'm just starting to descend into the hard part. The temptation beckons to distract myself by socialising and leaving the house. Bed is nice, although waking up is starting to get hard. I've been breathless at times every day for the last week (panic breathing). I'm still in the midst of thankyou cards and wish I wasn't. I'm sick of thanking people. It's a brain strain thinking of a thousand different ways to say, 'I'm so grateful'. I think the thankyou cards mean the end of Allie's dealings with the world, and *I* don't wanna deal with that. I don't want that end that means the beginning of my hard work – to go down to the levels where I can't feel her, to feel guilty about everything; I wanna remember nice stuff. I don't want my grief for her to deprive me of remembering our beautiful times.

I did go down there. I did suffer. It happens slowly, the grief, the suicide questions, the *What Ifs*, seeping below the surface, as though they have their own deal with 'the real you', the one who might've known more, who surely would've been able to stop this outcome you're living with, this escalating pain you're in. It was different for each child, but as inevitably as I loved them, the deep grief space for them claimed its time with me.

20 November 2010

As I scoured her motionless body that last day for a breath, a flinch, a twitch, anywhere, she looked asleep.

A baby again, in her brown timber cradle, apricot lining, Princess Allie, newly home from hospital, in her pretty white going-home dress. I'm watching her breathing; she won't die from cot death, or an undiagnosed heart abnormality.

At four years, asleep in the bottom timber bunk, her big brother in the top bunk, also sleeping.

At thirteen, asleep in the timber bed that had been Simon's. She sleeps on her back, deathly still, extremely thin, elegant hands folded neatly across her flat stomach.

At nineteen, asleep again, in the afternoon sun, tired from the months of effort of getting herself back to school for her HSC year.

And now, a fortnight till her 20th birthday, and these familiar sleeping limbs, impossibly still. I beg a muscle, some tissue somewhere, to dispel with just a tic, what this scene asks of my sanity – that this resting pose, this mahogany cradle – is her final home.

After Simon died, I found it hard to continue working, and at the end of that year, I eventually stopped. Now I enjoyed my part-time work. I needed and wanted to keep busy. I didn't want to grieve Allie the same way I had Simon or Joseph. I needed to process it differently.

Having said that, chocolate is still my primary coping mechanism. People ask, 'How do you *do* it?!' *'Faith'*, *'meditation'*, *'God'*, they expect.

'Chocolate,' I reply straight-faced, irritated at their overt fascination with my uncommon circumstances.

'Chocolate isn't my weakness – it's my strength.' – © **Denny Meek**

4 August 2007

I just realised I won't hear you play your little trinkety pieces on the piano anymore.

The theme from Titanic sounded sad before you died. It's way too sad now.

5 August 2007
I'm glad you learnt how to fight me, Allie. That'll rest so much more comfortably with me when I think about the pain of your earlier teens. Good girl for rebelling. We had a life, didn't we?

11 August 2007
Albert Facey, of *A Fortunate Life*, escaped death many times, including at Gallipoli.

What determines which body of the hundreds running, the small metal bullet will enter and kill? How is it that many people died and he escaped – many times?

What *determines* that?

17 August 2007
My confidence in my parenting is understandably shaken. Should I always have respected my children's freedom so much? I *want* Ashley to be happy. I feel for him having no siblings left. It's hard not to see the period of time since Simon's death as that I mustn't have handled it well with the kids, or Allie would still be here.

I acknowledge that even if my love had been perfect, it wasn't enough to keep my children here.

Then I survey their lives from a different perspective, not that of my grief critic, and note that I saved *all* my children from death many times over – Simon, Allie, Ashley, *and* Joseph.

Through days, weeks and months, such thoughts and feelings subside and re-emerge on an endless circuit.

For years after their deaths, I'd see Simon or Allie in public, usually driving a car, so that the image of their face was slightly opaque through the glass, and I'd have to stare for longer, couldn't take my eyes off them as my heart rate soared, until some angle or feature would prove to me it wasn't them. 'Acceptance' to the unconscious mind takes a lot of work.

Allie was my only daughter. I ached for the female energy in the house.

Our hugs were longer; we were not self-conscious about our bodies next to each other's.

I miss the bip of your straightening iron, Allie.

4 January 2008

I know Ashley's gone to sleep numerous nights since Allie's died, hearing me crying in my room. I don't know how he manages. He's lost his mother too. I can't think about it.

11 September 2007

I dreamt Allie came in and lay on the bed with me, as I've so wished I'd done with her on her last night, when she was sitting on her bed crying... I gave her a hug, we lay down facing each other and talked. She was saying something about our relationship, telling me we'd chosen it beforehand – together – and 'as individuals'.

It's always perplexed me that our relationship was allowed to go on, feeling challenged. The only notion that made sense was that it was maybe 'karmic'– i.e. by prior spiritual arrangement – and that's why, try as I may, I couldn't change it.

After Allie died, her girlfriend Talia had a 'dream' that she and Allie walked down a road for hours talking about life and what's to come. Allie told Talia she wouldn't be able to remember what was said, because it would affect the way she thinks about life.

In the year after Simon's death, Mykaela dreamt Simon told her that the visits he makes in people's dreams are real. He was looking good, more and more himself.

I dreamt I'd been with Simon. 'Right?' His face, dark shining eyes, energy up close, all conveying: *'This is where we're together'*. I got the impression that when*ever* I sleep, I'm in a realm where our being together, for the *duration* of my sleep is a given.

27 July 2008

Last night, I dreamt about my kids. All night long, they filled my dreams. They were young and happy; it was colourful and playful.

That was beautiful, thank you kids.

9 August 2008

I dreamt my kids and I were in my childhood home, going to live there.

As though she was referring to the time from Joseph's death onwards, Allie said to me, 'We've both been damaged in different ways.' She put her arm around me as I started to sob, and was very sad with me. Simon had sat down the other side. I realised my dreams are also a safe place for me to cry out tears I need to cry, as well as a happy meeting place with my children.

26 August 2008
The last two nights, I've had dreams about just Ashley and me – which means it's starting to sink in: it really is just the two of us now.

30 August 2008
When you're awake, you think that's real, but when you dream, you feel *that's* what's real, and it's often more real than the realness you experience when you're awake. It's as if Allie and I have worked on our relationship from behind the scenes in my dreams. I feel more confident about our love for each other these days.

I related to Allie in spirit a lot, talking to her in my journals, dreaming of her, thinking to her in the ethers, and I received hellos from her – which built that bridge between us quickly. I was familiar with relating to my boys those ways. Whatever my beliefs about God, I accepted those ways of relating as valid.

At the end of the year, I contacted the high school Allie had attended for six years. I was aware Simon was being formally remembered in the world, but Allie was not. The principal and I came up with a Year 11 memorial award in Allie's name: *Encouragement for Creativity*.

Seven months after Allie's death, at a private family-and-friends gathering, Currumbin Wildlife Sanctuary dedicated a plaque at Simon's boardwalk in memory of Allie too.

18 June 2008
People tell me I'm doing really well. What does 'You're doing well' mean? Denial's not a choice. My defence mechanisms don't ask my permission before electing themselves Head of the day's Coping Mechanisms. How do people know what to value in grief?? What does 'doing well' mean?

29 August 2010
I've observed how angry I've been at times: during Allie's anorexia (at the world), when Simon died (at the fathers), to three years after Simon's death when I wrote 'Conversation at God' (at Life) – and I've been proud of myself that another death could come after all that, and I could show grace to the world, and feel less anger rather than more… as if it's a reflection on some fineness of character with which *I* might be responding, rather than just how it all happens.

I grieve my children and always will, but I also recognise a grief for myself and my life – not for the house and possessions I didn't own, or the career I didn't have – but for the horrible states, the shadowy corners, in which I've had to dwell inside myself, for so many years of my life, for the awful person you feel you must be, to have all these dark thoughts and feelings going through you for several decades of your life. A sadness for lost time – spent surrendering, allowing my true responses – for a lighter self I can't retrieve.

In late 2007, I needed dental crowns, so I made a trip to Thailand, sharing a room in Bangkok with a girlfriend from TCF who'd since moved back to Melbourne. Sarah and Allie – our beautiful daughters – had both died in their teens, and it was a comfort to share this female loss, far away in a bereaved parent world, anonymous together in a foreign country. Allie found many little ways to let me know she was with us there.

At the end of 2008, Ash and I headed to Tasmania for a holiday, gearing for a bigger trip planned for 2009. My sister and her husband had contacted extended family, suggesting contributions to fund an O/S holiday for us. In May–June, Ash and I flew to London, then toured Western Europe for a month. It was the trip of a lifetime, impossible though it was to leave my grief behind. I took moments wherever I could, ducking into churches along our path, leaving candles lit all over Europe for my children, shedding tears in some of the most magnificent cathedrals in the world.

11 June 2009

May I never forget standing in Piccadilly Circus, watching Ash and cousin Mel chatting, as the 17-metre lettering lights up in red behind them with a message only I can see: '**HI MUM**'. Thanks Allie!

19 June 2009

I found it peculiar when we got back from Europe, that everyone was so keen to hear about where we'd been – to know what we'd experienced *externally*. I'd been traversing a very uncommon landscape *internally* for the last 10 years, both landscapes eliciting reactions, but they wanted only to hear about the physical landscape, the external geography.

During one of our deep phone conversations, my dear cousin, a psychotherapist in Sydney, asked about my grief journey. 'You've been where not many people go. I feel you've been to the edge of the world where the dragons are.'

20 June 2009

Logic has no appeal to Depression. Since Allie's death, when the suicidal space offers me its comfort, it's been a given that it's my fault. I can cite all the reasoning I've accepted before – that 'if Simon was still alive, Allie probably would be too'. That what David said – 'Allie's death was not about me' – was true, etc. But down in the sticky mud of depression, none of that affects me. I think, *I may have been able to save Allie that night if I'd been braver, stepped across the tripwire to her bedroom, not taken her individuating space personally, just loved her, just asked her, 'What can I do to help you?'*

It's only an acceptance of the world of logic again when I'm coming out the other side of the depression that gives me a reprieve from that blame.

Irritation. My primary grief response.

Within two years of Allie's death, I was getting deeply irritated at my support group. I resented their lack of understanding of my situation, didn't feel supported, and there always seemed a competition to talk. We needed a talking stick. Although I had nowhere else to go to just *be* a bereaved mum, I rang the facilitator, readying myself to pull the pin on the group.

10 September 2009

As it was after Simon died, it amazes me that sometimes it's just one individual in this world who helps me take the next step through my grief. Sometimes it's my parents, sometimes Dr Furrows, last night – Lorraine. By her stories and words, I'm reminded to feel; she gently shakes my heart awake again. When I think I get the rest of my world sorted, she helps me look outside my own pain, and helps me care, if even minutely, about other people again. She reminds me it's grief '*work*', and helps me recognise some of my experience, like irritation, as fear. My irritations are other things as well, such as injustices, but I see that one was my fear of isolation.

So I went to the group today.

As I'd 'seen' beforehand, it *was* easier than I expected, although still hard work – not letting all my energy bleed into irritation, and eventually forcing myself to speak.

I cried as I spoke – about how I used to talk a lot at the group after Simon died, but have spoken very little since Allie's death. I felt newcomers who'd joined since needed to be heard. Some people are talkers, some aren't,

I said, I'm a talker, and needed to *express* myself. The last few meetings my need to speak had welled up so greatly that I felt I'd burst, to the point where my body was physically hurting (in my chest above my heart, in my back at the top of my lungs): I knew I had to speak.

Another reason I'd held back since Allie's death, I said, was because I didn't want it reflected back at me that I'd lost three children, and that that's all they *could* reflect back at me. I kept on: the loss of three was different to the loss of one, the loss of one was to ride the ups and downs of one single journey – and that's worse than anyone should have to endure – but the loss of three was to be on three of those journeys separately *and* concurrently, to be looking for (and usually not seeing) the light at the end of three tunnels at the same time. It was also about deeper more complicated processing – beyond telling. I said I thought the sense of isolation was the worst part of grief, I was terrified of feeling it, so I didn't talk about my losses, in order to avoid that aloneness, and so as not to invite others' awkwardness and lack of understanding around me – therefore furthering my sense of isolation. Sobbing early on, I said ever since Allie died, I'd tried hard to accept I was alone in my loss of three now – but that I didn't *want* to see how alone I was.

I spoke of how anticipating Ashley's leaving (he was applying for the Army – didn't get in) brought up feelings of handing over my baby Joseph. Did I tell Ash how I felt? someone asked. No I didn't. It wasn't for him to know; he had enough to deal with. I wanted him to feel the excitement of his life in the outside world as I did when I was about to leave at 18, that I just wanted an easy last few weeks for him, and was spending my time with him in-the-moment.

I'd been frightened of telling the group how alienated I'd felt by their lack of understanding of my circumstances. It took courage. And they were warmer towards me afterwards.

It seems the number of disguises the edging away from *feeling* those deep raw emotions, can take, is infinite. Leaning on my own understanding is fine, my understanding is good – but when it slowly and subtly severs my connections with others – *instead* – it might take courage to see a healthier step for me to take.

I took a healthier step today.

~

14 July 2007

My darling Allie, I was always humbled to be your mum. You were always so very special, so incredibly and deeply beautiful – outside and inside. Thank you for the short twenty years you spent as my daughter. Thank you for all you gave me, and for what the privilege of having been your mum will continue to give me, for the rest of my life. I love you 'very much' too, Allie. I hope you're happy. I miss you.

CHAPTER 8

Reflections From the Valley

Shame hates it when we reach out and tell our story
Brené Brown

During the deeper grief years, a buried voice assured me Simon and Allie's deaths were my fault. The grief leaked in as my psyche could manage, pinning me down in forms of denial until I could consider perspectives I'd been unable to earlier. Had I not intended to share my story, I doubt I'd have dug so deeply into my depths.

Early on, each pain Simon and Allie had suffered during their lives pierced me. Reactions of others challenged me too, as did my relationship with the outside world, and how the losses had changed me. I continued journalling, 'allowing' my grief, attending monthly appointments with Dr David Furrows, whose professional 'voice' started to break through over my critic's, as my research began unveiling hidden truths.

Eventually I could see for myself how I'd internalised a perpetrator of abuse, its roots in patriarchal soil, silently undermining me with the shame-voice of my culture's shadow. Shame was awaiting me in every thorny spectre. Suicide: teenagers – two of them. Grief: why did it take me 'so long'? Anorexia Nervosa: the Tyrant Mother? Domestic Violence: why all this abuse by men?

How did these challenges find their way into my life? What were the names of these magnets on my body and how did they attach themselves to me?

GRIEF

We are healed of a suffering only by experiencing it to the full
Marcel Proust

Living with an array of people's reactions to my children's deaths has partly shaped my relationship with the world. I've had to learn to navigate conversations with new people, weaving in and out of inevitable questions. 'So, how many children do you have?' *I had four babies.* They don't even notice I've switched tenses. *Just the youngest left at home, a millennial – doesn't drive, doesn't cook, you know how it is. What about you?* They don't pick up on the distraction techniques, mostly.

'I couldn't do it – what you went through – I couldn't do it.' *For starters, 'went' through.*

'Why do you think they *did* it?' *Which 'why' do you want?*

On hearing my story, one mother reassures herself to me directly. 'You see, that'd never happen to me – because I *taught* my children to communicate, and they would *tell* me if they were feeling like that.'

Where do I start?

I don't wanna be rude, I'd prefer people *not* see the Grim Reaper when they look at me – such a threatening challenge to their assumptive worlds – but I need to live here too, *and* make room for my children; because I'm not 'cutting ties' or 'letting go'. That's not my experience of grief. The *Continuing Bonds* idea is that just as our relationship with other living people in our life continues when they've left the room and we can no longer see them, so our relationship with our loved ones who've died continues after their deaths.[1] TCF was a place bereaved parents could go where their children were still real, while the outside world now believed they weren't.

I understand the need for people to believe that if they make the right decisions, practice the right spiritual philosophies, or embrace the right parenting methods, then frightening circumstances like mine won't befall them. I don't need them to consider they could, but I do need to not be shamed by their reactions from their unrecognised fears my losses trigger for them.

Like all wounds, the bereaved need their emotions validated. They don't share their pain to be resolved, but to be acknowledged; they're not asking for advice. With appropriate support they're capable of directing themselves. They do need others' courage, to sit with their own fear of death, practice reflective listening, and just 'hold space' for them.

Waking up the morning after my son Joseph died, the first thing I noticed were the busy sounds from the nearby main street – cars and people getting on with their day. *They haven't heard the news yet. Wait till it spreads: the world will stop.* It didn't. The speed at which the world spun without my baby in it was shocking.

I was met with loving compassion from others in the first weeks. With each passing day though, as my grief pulled me inside, seeping insidiously between the cracks, escorting me down its private labyrinth, the chasm between me and my outer world grew. I knew I needed time. But the world didn't stop.

At the beginning of last century, a widow was given a formal mourning period of four years.[2] The bereaved dressed in black, or wore black arm bands, mourning jewellery (a lock of hair enclosed in a brooch or locket), and like Queen Victoria, could remain in black for the rest of their lives if they wanted.[3]

By mid-century, the formal mourning period had reduced to six months.[4]

By the beginning of this century, formal bereavement leave had been established in over 90% of companies as three days.[5] Debate has rippled about including *Grief* in the DSM[6], like an illness, best medicated after six months with antidepressants.

Grief guru, Elisabeth Kübler-Ross said we almost have a 'stamp out depression' campaign, that there's an appropriate sadness that comes with grief that society often considers needs fixing. 'We do not allow the normal depression that comes with grief to have its place.'[7]

Positivity is so important to us that we can feel shamed when we suffer, especially for what our culture decides is 'too long'. Most bereaved parents I've met haven't felt supported in the world with 'adequate' time to grieve for their child. Their presence at TCF, meeting like Christians in the catacombs, to share a taboo subject behind closed doors, was evidence of their unmet need.

March 2011

Perhaps not many would keep a journal as I did after Simon died, with the thought of their future selves going through the experience again. But the details I kept through my grief – even three to four years after Simon's death – have been a great help to me after Allie's. When I have that feeling that I should be doing better by now, I look up the same length of time after Simon's death, and it's so *very* comforting to see I was struggling just as much then. It's not someone else telling me how they were then, or implying how I should be by now; it's the unique me telling me how the unique I was then: *dreadful*. Phew! Doesn't help with the overall meaning-making about the *'bizarre'* life I'm having, but does help my feelings of isolation, of not doing well in my grief, that I 'should' be doing better by this stage, and of not feeling understood.

2 May 2011

I accept the educating role the bereaved themselves have to take on, in addition to their grieving, but am in awe of how almighty the task is, when even those close see grief in terms of 'letting go', 'moving on', 'closure', and 'resolution'.

It's amazing how far-reaching the hurt of little things is – I see a medical scene on telly and have to flip the channel – a young woman... other details I wouldn't think to connect... and I am hurting again without remembering why.

20 January 2014

If I could write for others, I'd pretend I didn't care that I lost my beliefs along with my children, that I'm glad of the strengths I've gained in the Valley, journeying to the edge of the world where the dragons are, peering into their faces, being burnt by the flames, asking 'Where are they? Are they alright? Did I do this to you, my children?' I'd try hard to imply I'm better for what I've seen, that I've picked up invaluable gems in the Valley, that although some part of me believes there's a reason for it all, I don't know what it is, and I'm alright with that. I'd suggest that because I can give it words, it's okay.

But it's not okay. I do care – very much, beyond words. I'd rather have my children back. I'm still lost in it all, and I can still feel the flames.

Attending TCF for eight years, I saw it was common for a parent to suffer about the pains their child experienced, or for their imperfect parenting (is there another kind?). Many parents had excruciating moments in the grief pit when, however their child died, they blamed themselves entirely for not having kept them alive. Sometimes those moments rushed another to mind who could be blamed. Witch hunts and scapegoating after an unexpected death were common into the 1800s.[8] I've seen some spiritualise these panicky moments, accepting that invitation and cutting ties with a person they judged, onto whom they needed – for a time – to project their fears. After each loss, the temptation to blame others came my way; in rare moments, it still does. I've tried hard not to hurt others with my pain, but grief asks deep commitment, to recognise and accept *all* your feelings, to keep working through your grief. I don't believe grief needs 'healing'; I believe if allowed, grief *is* the healing.

Inside Multiple Losses

In the deeper griefs for my children, I experienced similarities and differences.

After each death, I had dreams where my children had died differently than they had.

I wondered what each of them was up to now, determined not to deify them. I wanted them to remain human and close to me. Deifying them gradually happened anyway.

To begin with, I used their names all the time in my journals, then gradually less.

After a long while, I'd come and go from the grieving depths, needing my breaks.

Friendships fell by the way after each loss, although there were differences. After Simon's death, I wanted to be with bereaved parents, but after Allie's, I needed some friendships with others who didn't carry that internal heaviness.

Frequent cemetery visits comforted me after Joseph's death, but happened less with Simon, and less still with Allie. I'd accepted a relationship of *continuing bonds* as the pathway between me and my children.

Apart from journalling, black humour, and chocolate, other coping mechanisms that worked for one loss wouldn't necessarily express grief for the others. Just as we love each child differently, so I needed to grieve each of them differently. And in the grieving, I'd be a slightly different person.

A year after Simon died, I couldn't continue my part-time work; after Allie died, I was grateful for my new part-time position.

I could only grieve one loss at a time, not two or three at once. This was not a choice; it happened naturally. They'd take turns. And as it was in birth, the one who'd died last each time was my baby in spirit. I still sometimes worry about them, occasionally suffering motherguilt if I don't 'adequately' acknowledge them.

From the other side, my children have seemed to want me to know they're together.

I believe that losing several children is not about plumbing the same depth repeatedly, but is a worse psychic pain than the loss of one child. A deeper more complicated psychological journey, especially in a country where multiple losses is uncommon, it's asked more of my sanity, and in additional ways, stretches me further.

Many assume the death of a baby hurts less because 'you didn't get to know them'. For many parents, it *is* like that. It was *because* I didn't get my lifetime with Joseph that I grieved him so much – no less the loss of a son because I'd had him for only two months, not 18 years. The disenfranchisement of a baby's death is a difficult hurt.

No two griefs have been the same, each death is impossible, each brings its own sets of challenges.

Spiritual explanations lost their relevance for me down in the Valley. *'You chose this before you came.' 'You won't be put through more than you can handle.' 'We manifest 100% our own reality.'* The explanations were not the reasons. Most were an irritant to me, an assault on deep suffering.

I've come to see that my deeper grief journey *was* my spirituality. It was all-consuming, all-encompassing. My determination to create a place for myself in the world without having to leave my children behind, has meant bringing all of me, broken, integrated, traumatised, real, with me. Living in a 'healing' relationship with such emotional, psychological, spiritual wounds is a lifelong journey, not a destination – especially when trauma is involved. As much as I didn't want to identify myself by my losses – to be *'that mother'* – these experiences are fundamental to who

I am, have formed and transformed me, and will continue to as I share them with the world. My hope is that we can open helpful gateways for each other's realities – to *'help each other to grieve as well as to grow'*.

ANOREXIA NERVOSA

I didn't say it was your fault, I said I was going to blame you
fridge magnet Allie gave me

As a single mother, I was used to assuming total responsibility. That's why it took me so long to face some of the last contributing factors. Through the lens, Allie's anorexia and suicide intensified a battle inside me after her death. To be blamed for an illness was one thing, but if she'd slipped into that 20% mortality group, then 'causing' a suicide was something else. 'Most of the 20% don't get to starve themselves to death,' Dr Furrows told me. 'Many die from damaged organs' *(like a pericardial effusion)*. 'Eating disorders carry an increased suicide risk – and some suicide.' It took great courage for me to front the AN beast.

As a perfectionist, I held myself to higher standards, self-reproach at 'failure' more severe. I knew the guilt was unhelpful to my mothering – I felt guilty about feeling guilty! Even therapists who disagree about theories and treatments agree that it can be harmful to relationships to be plagued by shame, fear and anxiety.[9] But it wasn't just my perfectionism inviting guilt. As it turned out, my culture's shadow nourished plenty of unquestioned mother myths that kept the shame-fires burning.

An interesting pattern emerged in the research when a condition's cause remained unidentified.

In the 1950s, mothers were blamed for autism in their children – called *'refrigerator mothers.'*[10]

In the 1960s, mothers were blamed for schizophrenia in their children. *Schizophrenogenic mothers.*[11]

In the 1970s, mothers were blamed for homosexuality in their children. *Smothering mothers.*[12]

In the 1980s, mothers were blamed for learning difficulties in their children. *Absent mother.*[13]

In the 1990s, mothers were blamed for stuttering in their children. *Mother speaks too quickly.*[14]

In 2000, mothers were still being blamed for anorexia. *Tyrant mother.* *'Mother speaks for her.'* [15]

These myths spread from field to community, where damage ran rife.

'She's lying there in that hospital bed because of *you*, you know Denny – because *you're* such a bitch.' Unfortunately Rob wasn't the only one who thought so.

The field promoted it.

The GP certainly concurred.

A girlfriend: 'I'll tell you what her anorexia's about. You've gotta let go *control* of her.'

A male friend (not a parent): 'You're not loving her unconditionally. You're supposed to, you know – you're her *mother*. It's *your* love she's starving for.'

Another friend: 'This is here for you, you know. It's here to get *you* to back right off.'

Other "understandings" of anorexia bandied about the community were as deeply 'grasped'.

January 2001

I met a woman at a gathering tonight, and as soon as I said the A-word, she said she was a nurse and knew all about it. They had girls come into the ward with it. 'It's a very selfish sickness.'

'It's not about the weight,' I said.

'No,' she agreed. 'They're actually very manipulative and controlling little girls... They want to *control* everything.'

Such a lack of understanding is one reason I don't discuss it with others. It upsets me, angers me, hurts me – especially on behalf of my beautiful daughter who fits none of these moulds, but lies in hospital bed, sustained by nasogastric lifeline, in the grip of a deadly illness that's not understood even by the field.

In the psychiatric ward, they were looking for an enmeshed mother-daughter relationship, where we were too close, with a fused identity, Allie's anorexia supposedly trying to establish boundaries with her own identity. Or I was the Tyrant Mother from whom she was trying to wangle control with her illness. Years later Dr Furrows showed me that they hadn't seen my strength as the glue that held my family together and kept them safe, but pathologised it according to the model at the time as having caused Allie's illness. 'I don't understand, when anorexia is supposed to have at its core an issue of control – or a *lack* of it – why you treat it by taking all control away from her?' My query to Allie's hospital team was genuine, I desperately needed to discuss it with them, but they weren't used to their treatment being questioned, took it as a criticism of their handling of my daughter, and regarded my 'strength' as dysfunction.

'The thing Allie admired most in you,' David tells me now, 'was your strength of character, and having the courage of your convictions – even if they pissed her off half the time!'

'Anorexia's causes are not a one size fits all explanation,' he continues. 'You have to find out, on a patient by patient basis, what specific internal distress anorexia is expressing – or *concealing* – for each sufferer.' To blame mothers as a group obscures the complex realities of the individual.

David reminds me that all families are 'dysfunctional', but that not all dysfunction is toxic.

When Allie's anorexia emerged, I was angry – that I was powerless to stop this illness, that I was on my own with it, that it had to be this way. I was angry that everyone had been able to drop their pathological contributions into our little family unit, oblivious, and leave me to deal with it.

Anger is an uncomfortable subject for our culture. Regarded forever as an 'unfeminine' trait, women have been socialised to stuff their anger, leaving it to escape in often veiled *'bitchy'* expressions – although an overtly angry woman is also considered a *'bitch'*. Women wary of getting close to each other are often unsure of the relationship the other may have developed with her own assertiveness, and anger.

Amidst domestic violence, it was assumed I'd pick up a placating role with anger, because women are supposed to be 'the relationship maintainers'. As this assumption itself added to my resentment, it became harder to assume that role. In my struggle would be a fight for my right to feel and express my anger too – or any emotion, for that matter.

I attended the Therapy Group for Women Exploring Anger, trying to do my bit to model a healthier path for Allie, to respond usefully to anger, instead of suppressing it, or being manipulated by it, or meditating it away, or doing any one of a hundred things our culture would rather have us do than feel it, and find healthy ways to express it. The internalising of these taboos, nurtured in the shadow, continue to hold patriarchy in place.

6 May 2018

When my marriage ended and I moved away with my children, I read a few books, like *Women Who Love Too Much* that invited a fork in my road. The way my problem-solving process was operating at the time had me blame myself: my marriage failed because I'd 'loved too much'. At how the patriarchy gets women to always assume responsibility, I shake my head.

Women are amazing, we know we are, we recognise it objectively now, but we don't appreciate it fully on the inside yet. As though by reflex, our female problem-solving processes still have us assume overall responsibility. Maree's right when she stresses how very deeply ingrained all this stuff is. Wait, did we just discover another flaw? 'This stuff is very deeply ingrained in us. We haven't exorcised it out of ourselves yet. Well no wonder it still happens!' The patriarchy is alive and well and officiating from the collective unconscious...

We are never finished with shadow work.

This year I see on one of my Facebook groups the term 'Mother Wound' being used to blame mothers. Bethany Webster, who coined the term *Mother Wound*, describes it as 'the pain of being a woman passed down through generations of women in patriarchal cultures. It includes the dysfunctional coping mechanisms that are used to process that pain.'[16] She says, 'The Mother Wound is the core issue at the centre of women's empowerment,' and 'is ultimately not about your mother, but about embracing yourself and your gifts without shame.'[17]

'We all have patriarchy in us to some degree,' says Bethany. 'We've had to ingest it to survive in this culture.'[18]

I sometimes wondered if Allie's anorexia could've been related to the lack of control she felt on my behalf as a woman in violent relationships – as an attempt to somehow address the powerlessness 'a woman' was faced with when confronted by her partner's anger. Was it partly a symbolic battle on behalf of abused women? Or broader, part of the fight the female has always faced throughout history under the patriarchy?

In his latest book *Grounded Spirituality*, Jeff Brown, former criminal lawyer, psychotherapist, and author, writes about 'Patriarchal Spirituality' as 'those ungrounded and inhumane "spiritual" models that have been fostered by emotionally armoured, self-avoidant men.' He speaks in a clear voice, not about 'transcending our humanness – but finding meaning and spirituality within it, right in the heart of our imperfect daily lives.' Jeff Brown offers workshops and men's courses online.[19]

I'd been angry at the fathers, but because I'd internalised my culture's motherblame, father absence was one of the last contributing factors I considered.

'63% of youth suicides come from *fatherless* homes.'[20]

23 May 2016

Now that time's passed, and I'm able to allow the light of logic to shine some reason on the picture, and I've been reading up on motherblame – other parents' stories of their children's anorexia, and normal adolescent individuating – I'm glad to say that I'm a little slower to assume that guilt and blame for Allie's anorexia.

I agree with my friend: anorexia *was* here for me. It was here to challenge me to see that my culture, gender and perfectionism holds me accountable for everything, makes me feel responsible, ashamed, anxious – and finally, after decades of struggle, that I'm *not* automatically to 'blame' for everything.

One way or another, our children bring us growth.

In 2013, Dr Thomas Insel, Director of the US National Institute of Mental Health, referred to Anorexia Nervosa as a 'brain disorder', suggesting the current trend in understanding eating disorders is heading towards a biological basis.[21]

In July 2019, a six-year-long study of 17,000 Anorexia Nervosa cases from around the world identified eight genes associated with an increased risk of developing AN. They also found very strong unexpected links with metabolic function.[22] Hashimoto's, the autoimmune thyroid disease I have, is hereditary. All these years after Allie's illness, the ten pins have almost fallen, as the shame suffered by millions of parents to anorexia sufferers around the world, looks for another host.

To Allie's immense credit, and Dr Furrows' help at depth, she died a fully recovered 'anorexic'. A decade passed before I could accept from him that Allie hadn't officially slipped into that '20% mortality' group from her illness. David doesn't believe Allie's suicide resulted from mental illness. 'To attribute suicide to mental illness is a defence mechanism around a very difficult subject. Plenty of people suicide due to mental illness, but plenty don't. There are layers to a suicide.'

A personality trait anorexia sufferers often share is perfectionism, which David feels did factor in Allie's final night. I felt anorexia piqued her appetite to die for Perfection. I finally realised I could no more have convinced her not to worry about her chemistry results the next day than I could've convinced her she wasn't fat when she had anorexia. It was the perfectionist in charge of perceptions at the time.

An estimated 87% of gifted-and-talented students are perfectionists.[23] I remind myself: *she died a recovered 'anorexic',* and *perfectionism is not an independent precursor for suicide.*[24]

Meanwhile, the incidence of Anorexia Nervosa remains the same. It still has the highest mortality rate of any mental illness.

SUICIDE

It takes darkness to be aware of the light
Treasure Tatum

In one of life's ironies, at age 19, I presented a seminar on *Teen Suicide Letters* in our 'Adolescent Development and Adjustment' course. Who in the room that day would've guessed that several decades hence, I'd hold two such letters from my own teenagers?

In meeting with three other TCF mums bereaved by suicide, I know I'm fortunate to have these letters. Each note was typical of my dear children – Simon's a few sentences, Allie's several pages. Although longer, Allie's 'Reasons' were no more understandable than Simon's. The voice in Allie's note was clearer than those I'd studied, her tone intelligent, mature, resolved – not from a place of emotional ruin. I could hear the relief of her surrender, the lights of home within her sights. She loved Ash, she loved me, trusting we'd accept that she was granting herself this reprieve.

When only 25% of suicides had left a note (15% of teenagers), I was grateful to my children for expressing themselves from that space, and for their loving goodbyes. My son Joseph too wrote his goodbye the only way he could: across the monitor with his last heartbeat.

Living with the suicides has been like living on a merry-go-round; wanting to, but never arriving at 'resolution' about their deaths, I don't get to sit back relaxed and view the whole picture at once, at all the pieces of the puzzle in place, for more than a brief moment. Whether they mean to or not, they take some of the pieces with them, and I just get to hypothesise about the shifting spaces that leaves behind. My observation is that *suicidal* is its own psychological pain, and for each individual's 'Reasons', they're in it. As with Simon's death, the 'Reasons' do their circuit about Allie's death too – although many times I've felt that if Simon was still here, Allie probably would be too. Just as Allie's anorexia impacted on Simon's death, I often think it was *sibling grief* that took Allie's life.

My children were special people, considerate human beings I liked as well as loved, and of whom I was very proud.

Why then do I hesitate to mention their deaths to strangers? That awkwardness around Simon and Allie's that could quickly become shame, or that it's inappropriate to expose others to it?

Stigma: 'mark of disgrace'

At some stage, I realised I was bearing a weight that was not mine to carry. When the word 'suicide' is used, *centuries* of fine print come attached. I remembered it was only within my lifetime that suicide had been decriminalised, but its shocking history explains a lot.

For many centuries, suicide has been regarded a sin by the church, and a crime against the state. In some religions, it is still forbidden; in some countries, still a crime.

For millennia, people who suicided have been deemed unworthy of respect or ordinary remembrance. In medieval times, they were punished post-mortem, their bodies publicly desecrated, 'sometimes in particularly gruesome ways, refused burial rites, their property confiscated. The pain of these harsh sanctions was felt by the surviving family members, who suffered the consequences of the forbidden act, as if by proxy. To protect themselves, they learned to cover up the true cause of death and remain silent.'[25]

In the early 1600s, a legal term came into use to differentiate suicides who had not died due to mental illness, but who'd coolly decided to end their own life: *felo de se* – a felon against the self.[26] The body of a *felo de se* would be dragged through the streets face-down, then hung from the gallows and disfigured.[27] By the 1700s, *felo de se* were buried between 9pm and midnight, outside cemetery grounds, usually at a crossroads in order to confuse them, lest they wander about after death. No priest to preside[28], no music at their funeral[29], no mourners allowed, no grave marker.[30]

At this point, my research became extreme: suicides were treated differently because there was a belief they could become *vampires*.

Belief in vampires was a worldwide phenomenon.[31] In medieval times, both Eastern and Western churches in Europe accepted the reality of vampires.[32] It was believed they caused epidemics, and were blamed for unexplained disease and death.[33] People at risk of becoming vampires were those who were marginalised within their communities, and considered to have a 'discontented soul upon their death'.[34] Suicides were especially feared, often staked to their coffin through the heart or the head[35], a practice that continued in England until the early 19th century.[36] Often a stone was placed over the face[37] or under the chin.[38]

Grave goods were used to turn evil away: *coins* (protective charms so evil spirits wouldn't disturb the body), *poppy seeds* (whose narcotic effect would cause the reanimated corpse to sleep rather than leave the grave), and a *sickle* or *scythe*, meticulously placed over the neck or abdomen to destroy the physical body when the vampire tried to rise from the grave.[39]

If a corpse was considered 'troublesome', it would be exhumed, and 'anti-vampiristic' mortuary customs applied to try to stop its activities.[40] Sometimes a red-hot iron would be thrust into the heart, after which the corpse was scalded with boiling wine.[41] Some were decapitated, their head placed behind the corpse, at its feet or between the thighs, far enough away to stop it reconnecting with the body.[42] Others involved driving iron forks into the heart, eyes and breast, and then reburying the body upside down[43], its coffin nailed shut.[44] Sometimes, the remains were cremated.[45]

It was believed that those who were attacked by vampires became vampires too.[46] If a household was being struck by an illness, the suspect corpse was exhumed, the heart torn out and burnt, sometimes the ashes consumed by remaining family members to cure their affliction, or stem the vampire contagion – a common practice in Eastern Europe.[47]

While belief in flesh-and-blood vampires has declined, fear of the 'undead' remains commonplace in some Slavic countries.[48]

By the late 1800s, treatment of suicides had begun to change, but it was only in 1961 that *felo de se* was abolished as a crime in England.[49]

Until then, people could be jailed for two years, or fined, for surviving a suicide attempt.

I'll just give you a breather to take all that in... maybe have a cuppa...

This disturbing undiscussed history mystifies suicide and helps perpetuate its stigma.

'The legacy of shame, secrecy and silence is still, in large measure, with us.'[50]

At a friend's comment on Simon's photo last year, I shuddered: 'I can see he was a *troubled soul*.'

Words carry weight and power. The words we choose around our taboos contribute to how our culture feels about them, either reinforcing old perceptions and maintaining stigmas, or helping create new inceptions and evolving our consciousness. The term 'commit suicide' is now outdated. The affix '-cide' does mean to kill, and 'sui-' the self.[51] There are over 70 types of '-cides' (herbicide, fungicide, etc); all '-cides' of other people are illegal.[52] Abortion was called *Aborticide* until its legalisation. Although no longer illegal, the word 'suicide' still carries the feeling of the crime. And the word *commit* no longer belongs with it because suicide is no longer a crime to be *'committed'*. 'Ended their own life' says it.

In adding the gruesome history of suicide here, I've felt apologetic to readers, as though the history is mine to apologise for. This is the stigma. As I've felt others' reactions to my losses, I've suspected that suicide's stigma is intensified with more of our unprocessed fears than other types of loss, including our judgement of death – our reluctance to face our own mortality. For most people who've endured unbearable pain in this life, suicide has crossed their mind, yet death is one of our top five taboo dinner topics. Of Australians aged between 25 and 34, conversations about money and death are the number one taboo for almost half this group.[53] Our view that life must be sustained at all costs means we usually treat death as a failure, rather than a natural part of life. We take death away to hospitals in ambulances. While infant mortality has dropped, our expectations of living have increased. Nursing homes care for our elderly. Our loved ones no longer lie-in-state in the bedroom. Death daily on the news, with which we're not personally involved, desensitises us. We've removed death from our everyday lives, have no death rituals anymore, and now have very little *actual* exposure to death.

Suicide's stigma hides Death's shadow.

We push ourselves to be 'successful' at life, and cover up our shame at the times we feel unable to cope and would rather not be here. We don't share that shame feeling with others; we barely recognise it in ourselves. It gets stuffed under, and projected onto places like suicide, and the bereaved. If we owned our dark fascination with the subject of suicide, as individuals, and as a collective, it would help us step closer to accepting our mortality, and lead us to a greater understanding of ourselves.

As a survivor of suicide, 'Suicide Prevention' has translated for me as 'failure to prevent'. Preventing a suicide is not the same as giving a person a 'desire for life'. David Webb, PhD in Suicidology, sees 'psychache' – psychological pain arising from frustrated or thwarted psychological needs – as a much more accurate term for suicidality, which he describes as 'a crisis of the self', its hopelessness arising from an absence of meaningfulness.[54] He feels more attention to the sickness of our society is needed than emphasis on the sickness of the individual. 'Almost every aspect of the human experience is being reduced to our biology alone, with particular emphasis these days on the biochemistry of the brain,' where we become little more than biochemical robots to be managed by drugs… He suggests we need to honour suicidal feelings as important, real, legitimate, 'a sacred part of the human story'.[55] 'We cannot allow science to continue to banish our spirit from this difficult discussion.'[56]

We're discovering a lot about the brain. It might be that reaching our individual capacity for psychic pain sparks a 'self-destruct' mechanism. It might be that this is not a choice, but instinctual.

My aunt, advisor to the Minister for Education, said a lot is done for slow children in the education system, but not as much for the very bright. 'Simon and Allie were so *advanced*, they could've stayed another fifty years and not learnt any more.' She didn't mean just academically. It's a profound relief when someone acknowledges the depth of frustrations my children knew here.

17 June 2009

In the suicidal state, I envy my children being over the struggle of this life. Everything loses its value there – everything. Your perspective narrows incredibly. You grow incapable of considering the broader consequences of it logically. I wouldn't be surprised if blood flow to the brain constricts and narrows capillaries. One thing I'm grateful for when I'm in this state is the insight and understanding it gives me into how suicide can happen, how people who do it feel and think, especially how it's not a selfishness, but an inability to appreciate the *long-term* hurt others would feel from your death.

We look back after the death through the lens. *Where did we go wrong? How could we have prevented this?*

For the one who suicides, in facing their death, looking out through that lens, suicide *is* the answer.

DOMESTIC VIOLENCE

I swore never to be silent whenever and wherever human beings endure suffering and humiliation. We must always take sides. Neutrality helps the oppressor, never the victim. Silence encourages the tormentor, never the tormented.
Elie Wiesel

One of the reasons I left my relationships with my children's fathers was because I didn't want my sons modelling violence or my daughter learning to expect it. As it turns out, that wasn't the only damage of concern.

It was incredible that the connections of domestic violence in Simon and Allie's early lives were the last ones I was considering rather than the first. We blame the mother.[57] And I'm not 'blaming' the fathers – my comment is on how conditioned we are to blaming the mother.

When I recognised the presence of an 'internal perpetrator', I began to research domestic violence. James-the-counsellor from decades before, who'd taught me so much about DV, came to mind. As it happened, he was still counselling part-time; I made an appointment. The week following my first session, James just happened to be giving a presentation on 'The Effects on Children of Living with Domestic Violence'.

The statistics weren't available when my children were small, but they were no surprise to James.

They dropped on me like an A-bomb.

Children who live with Domestic Violence are significantly more likely to develop a mental illness.[58]

> *Children who live with Domestic Violence are six times more likely to commit suicide.*[59]

The shocking facts get inhaled slowly, the implications huge.

'When they live with violence in their own home,' James said, 'children *have* no safe place'. As there's no other room for it at the time, this experience, and all it represents to each child, is often internalised. James suggested suicide was a form of violence. 'Against the self?' I asked. Yes.

Felo de se.

Violence turned inward.

November 2013

Discovering these statistics is excruciating. My poor sensitive, respectful, gifted babies.

'I am my children's legacy' begins to translate as 'I cannot bear anyone having a go at me now.' I have to face everybody firmly so that my children didn't die in vain.

If I'd known... if I'd acted sooner...

Dr Furrows observes my inability to bear even relatively innocuous comments from others as having a cumulative effect. I suspect my shoulder issue includes anger at myself for not having learnt to stand up for myself sooner, modelling more assertive defences for my children, and getting them out of that – as it turns out – extremely toxic environment.

15 January 2014

The trauma revisits. I'm stunned, spun out. My stomach's tight. I feel like I've been hit again today – punched in the stomach – had more abuse perpetrated towards me even today. I feel vulnerable, unsafe, jittery on the inside, like cowering, pulling myself in physically. My body doesn't want to sit back relaxed deep in the chair; it wants to sit on the edge, vigilant, ready.

18 January 2014

I have to look at everything in ways I haven't before. Nothing that happened or eventuated is coincidence anymore. It's all connected. The research says children do not have to directly witness or be involved in violent episodes in order to be affected.[60]

18 December 2014

The effect of learning those DV statistics didn't make me love the men less but rather put things into perspective, as though in my griefs, I was incorporating blame of them too in my anger towards them, and how now it enables me to blame myself less, which in turn makes way for a clearer path for myself and my spiritual wondering.

Domestic violence is a social problem that's endured for a *very* long time. Partner violence happens towards men from women as well, although the adverse effects are generally much greater for women.[61] DV affects every socio-economic stratum across society. Despite the advancements in equality over the decades, the problem remains.

One in four women experiences it…

More than one woman killed a week…

As shifts in awareness increase, as women continue to find their empowerment and fuller equality, and patriarchal systems continue to be dismantled, it's heartening to see men reaching out to each other as women have, to 'hold space' for each other, to support each other towards a more inclusive sense of themselves, of their gender, not based on the rank handed to them by patriarchy, but on a deep appreciation of their inherent value, whatever that means to each one. Shaming men for being male prolongs the conflict; raising awareness, respectfully witnessing their vulnerabilities, welcoming their sensitive strengths – as in men's groups like MKP, Conscious Brotherhood Communities, and online men's courses – helps build our culture in the healthier direction it wants to head. Our wholesome future is not led by 'Males', or by 'Females', but by the integrated humanness of both; yin and yang – together.

CHAPTER 9

Private Ryan

> *I shall meditate upon normality*
> *I shall meditate upon my little son...*
> *I do not will him to be exceptional.*
> *It is the exception that interests the devil.*
> *It is the exception that climbs the sorrowful hill*
> *Or sits in the desert and hurts his mother's heart.*
> *I will him to be common...*
> *And to marry what he wants and where he will.*
> **Sylvia Plath – From 'Three Women'**

My youngest child Ashley, a private person, still lives with me. From the immense respect I have for him, I'll share only a few details.

Ash was the easiest of my children to rear. As it is for parents, I sometimes glimpse my surviving son as a little boy; the expression on his face as he took his first breath, as an incredibly cute toddler, a cheeky four-year-old on his mini escapades from day care/preschool. As a school child – bright, intelligent, clever. As a rebellious teenager – sarcastic quips putting me in my place. Now I share my life with a gentle man, who's easy to live with, who keeps to himself. Every day, I'm immensely grateful to still be a mother.

Ash needs his own space to rejuvenate his energies, drawing the reins on parts of his life as required: socialising, clothes (*great* taste), food, communication. Sometimes I'm caught by how literally he takes my words, and look back laughing at how we'd just held a conversation on two different levels. His texts are a treat: perfect spelling, nothing out of place, to the point, a preference for monosyllables. Why waste three words when you can use two, or two when you can use one – or better still, grunt?

I was scared of parenting Ashley when Allie died, certain I had only one child left because the Universe deemed me an unfit parent. Ash and I continued indulging in black humour, and eating dinner watching *The Simpsons*.

In the days before Allie's funeral, two unrecognisable young men appeared at our front door – the now-grown boys Ash had played with as neighbouring children in our last house. From then on, like guardian angels, the boys kept in constant contact with Ash. The family had four sons, the eldest, Luke, the same age as Simon, the youngest a year older than Ash. Our first weekend without Allie in the world, Ash spent at their house; then every weekend for four years thereafter. The weekends were hard for me without Ash, aged fifteen, suddenly no children left at home, although I acknowledged I desperately needed the time to just grieve. I was especially grateful to the Shaws, to whom Ash referred as his 'weekend family', for scooping him up and loving him as they did. For the first year, Ash, the only surviving sibling, spent his weekend nights sleeping under Luke's bed. For comfort.

Dr Furrows has acquainted me with the increased risk of suicide Ash and I live with for the rest of our lives. Ash and I have each had times when we've crumpled under the weight of the losses. I received several calls from the school that first year, telling me that Ash had come into sick bay in a low space; my anxiety levels would soar, my panicked drives into the school dangerous. *Please be alright Ash, please be alright, oh god...* Ash has always been good at managing himself, especially in such moments; he'd intuitively know to do whatever he could to help himself feel better and distract himself, which was usually stopping at the bakery on the way home; and gaming.

At the prospect of Ash leaving school in Year 11, his music teacher protested, *'But he's gifted-and-talented!'* Ash was musical from the beginning, humming around the house when he was playing, in perfect pitch. He'd make up little tunes with happy melodies, the endings always resolved. Highly intelligent, he came dux of several of his school years without studying, receiving many science and maths awards. In Year 9, of all the students across Australasia (Australia, Singapore, South East Asia, and New Zealand) who'd sat an International Schools Science exam, Ash came in the top 1%.

Ash did his work placement from school at Currumbin Wildlife Sanctuary where Simon worked. He has tremendous compassion for animals, and to this day, ensures animals on our property are handled humanely. Last month he was catching tiny lacewing insects to feed a baby gecko in our kitchen. Last year he contacted Wires (wildlife rescue) to attend an injured wallaby in our yard; it was euthanised on our doorstep. The year before, after helping a baby bat that scratched him, Ash was required to have a tetanus injection at the hospital against the lyssavirus (like 'rabies'). I've seen snakes he's been trying to help, strike out at him, and thankfully miss – one stuck in the garage roller door, another he was helping off the road before it could get hit by a car. Sometimes when I've discovered another snake inside our house late at night, I've assured Ash, 'I tried to get it out myself without waking you! Did you hear me try to muffle my 'snake-in-the-house' scream?' Ash smirks. The second deadliest land snake in the world resides in abundance on our property: Eastern Browns. (Don't take my word for it. Check it out - YouTube channel, meek-and-wild: **Massive Eastern Brown Snakes Fighting at my back door** https://www.youtube.com/watch?v=o2R76j4Gbk8 When uploaded, it was the only footage on YouTube of Eastern Browns in ritual combat.)

Ash has always revived stunned and injured birds that've flown into our windows, cupping them in his hands, feeding them before they could take flight. As a child, he dearly loved the kittens our cat had, and cried when we had to hand them over to the Animal Welfare League. He gathered box, straw, and nesting materials for our rabbit to have her babies, sometimes then typing into the night on his keyboard patting a fluffy baby bunny on his lap.

17 August 2016

I think you're incredible, Ash. I nearly sent you an email last weekend to tell you that I couldn't believe how special you are. I saw that again this morning when I dropped you at work and you got out of the car and crouched down to pat Pearl (the dog). Your affinity with animals shows a lot about you. Pearl knows you love her, she trusts you for taking the time to give her attention. ZeeZee (the cat) knows you love him too and comes looking for your attention and love, knowing he'll always get it from you. Kevin (the peacock) probably would know if he could get down off the roof. Even Zeke (little human) trusts you.

I realise it's not in the words that are used, but in the way they're delivered that makes humour funny. Ash is quick and dry, makes me laugh out loud.

12 September 2008

As we're driving to school this morning, we come up behind a car with a sticker on the back windshield: 'Our Family' – white stick figures of a father, a mother, and two children.

Stopped in traffic, Ash and I, looking straight at the sticker, start snickering aloud.

'We should have one of those,' says Ash.

'Yeah,' say I. 'You, me, a cat, and a rabbit.'

'No,' says Ash. 'You, me, and three headstones.'

Black humour's always been our favourite.

'I had Ash for entertainment's sake,' I'd tell my mum when he was little. He's always been able to hit my funny bone, and have me laugh uncontrollably.

22 July 2009

As Ash was almost ready to leave this morning, his usual, 'Quick, *hurry*' all he had to say to me, I changed a tiny detail of our routine. Sitting at the table, halfway through a cup of tea, I said, 'I'm just finishing my cuppa…' From two metres away, only the two of us left, he replied, '*Mum* – your drinking is *tearing* this family apart.'

When Ash was 12, my friend Joan asked me to babysit her Baby Grand piano. Ash decided *here* was a piano worthy of his attention. With no private lessons, he taught himself to play to a higher level than I'd struggled towards all my life, his sight-reading quicker, tackling and mastering many Nobuo Uematsu pieces from the Final Fantasy gaming series. Sometimes he'd run out the door for the school bus, dumping sheet music on the servery as he passed. 'Here – learn this by the time I get home!' I'd flick through the score, which was always beyond me for a day's practice, and pass it up. One day the piece's standard wasn't as difficult, and I decided to surprise Ash. As he came in the door that afternoon, I started playing, *'To Zanarkand'*, note perfect. Ash smirked for a full five minutes.

My favourite music is the shrieks of high-pitched laughter emanating from Ash's room when he's in the thick of gaming online with friends. Considering how much he plays, he'd have to be brilliant... I have no idea.

Always conscientious wherever he works, my son is a practical asset. As a single mother, I did all sorts of jobs for extra income, including a paper run when Ash was nine. At 2am on a Friday, I'd drive twenty minutes to a storage shed in an industrial estate, survey stacks of unfolded newspapers (at which the name *Rumpelstiltskin* would pop into my head), and fold-and-rubber-band the 500 papers ready for delivery. At dawn, I'd dash home to pick up Ash, and with Anastasia blaring, we'd drive the rounds of the suburb, Ash leaning out the passenger's window, throwing papers onto all the driveways until the job was done. He was a great shot!

At this time in his life, Ash chooses the ordinary. Ten days after leaving school in Year 11, he started a regular job in retail at a local shopping centre, where he stayed for five years.

After a three-month break, he began work with his 'weekend family', as dispatch manager for their car parts imports and distribution business. He worked there for two-and-a-half years, saving his earnings, before taking a belated gap 'year'. Ash spent the time at his computer, gaming. He stayed in touch with the world through a second screen, socialising with friends through his headset.

His latest study has been at a bakery academy on the north end of the Gold Coast. *Weight Watchers, here we come.*

Meanwhile, I want our Private Ryan to do as he wishes. I want him to be happy; I want him to know he's loved, confident that his personal space and choices, whatever they are, will be respected. I'm glad the world still benefits from having one of my children in it, and vastly proud of the beautiful person he is.

CHAPTER 10

Catapulting out of the Valley

*And the day came when the risk to remain tight in a bud
was more painful than the risk it took to blossom*
Anaïs Nin

21 January 2003

'I can feel myself pulling away from the world,' I told Psychologist Alan, the day after Simon died.

'Go with it,' he said. 'Come back to the world in your own time and on your own terms.'

I thought that might be a few months...

Sixteen years later, I'd dearly love to write a happily-ever-after chapter. Although there's no leaving behind losses like mine, I *am* glad to say that a reprieve from spending the rest of my life in the deep dark 'Valley of the Shadow' has been possible. Coming through it was messy, as it snaked a unique trail through one-and-a-half decades of my life.

Soon after Simon and Allie's deaths, physical and psychological conditions began to visit, to accompany my grieving in the Valley.

- Hypothyroid bouts
- Hyperthyroid bouts

- Complex Grief
- Agoraphobia
- Anhedonia
- Generalised Anxiety Disorder
- Social Anxiety Disorder
- Panic Disorder
- Akathisia
- Bruxism
- Complex Post Traumatic Stress Disorder

(See Appendix A for definitions)

As these conditions intensified my journey, I became adept at survival strategies – pulling inside, becoming the 'Hermit' for years on end, in pain most of the time, wanting to be alone, often wishing I wasn't here.

Some of the conditions' visits overlapped, with symptoms in common, which made their diagnosis and treatment difficult. The years 2009–2010 were marked by frequent panic attacks (a panic disorder) as well as vacillating thyroid function (hyperthyroid and hypothyroid bouts). Between blood tests and medication adjustments, the endocrinologist wouldn't discuss possible causes. Towards the end of 2010, both GP and psychiatrist suggested an increase in my anti-anxiety medication. It seemed okay initially, then all three doctors took Christmas leave and were not due back for another month.

And so it was a state called 'Akathisia' that ultimately began my catapult out of the Valley. When you hit rock bottom, there's only one way left to go (*only one for me*): back up again. Of all patients taking the SSRI (anti-anxiety medication) I was on, 1% develop this condition. Akathisia exacerbates the symptoms the medication is trying to treat.

Along with increasing heart palpitations, breathlessness, poor sleep, nightmares, leg and foot cramps, and weight loss, the better-known symptoms of akathisia were far tougher: anxiety, inner restlessness, panic attacks, insomnia, and suicidality. The sleeplessness tired me out, but when I lay down during the day, panic attacks instantly descended. Imprisoned in days that dragged me through December and January, trying to hide under my bed covers, I wondered how I'd survive the next hour.

Unsurprisingly, akathisia drives many to suicide.

8 February 2011

I didn't know how I was going to live through it. It was *horrible* – like grief on top of grief on top of grief. *Insanity*. Severe panic attacks. Every single day I thought I was going to die. Nightmares when I did sleep – that my children were dying, that I was losing another child, and that I didn't know which one. I knew at the time it was big of me to be holding on, day after day, as I was over Christmas and January. I was supposed to increase my dose by another 25mg, but before I saw the doctors again, I'd noted in my anxiety diary, 'I'm not risking that this might be what's making me feel so bad.' Instead of increasing the dose further, I dropped back to the previous dose, and it eventually began to ease.

By the time akathisia was diagnosed in early February, I'd stabilised myself more on my previous dose. (See Appendix B for Akathisia diary)

For the six years I'd been on the anti-anxieties, I'd battled a foggy slow forgetful mind – an exaggerated version of the grief brain. When I'd recovered from the akathisia, and understood it and the medication better, I accepted the suggestion of a medication change-over.

At this time, my girlfriend invited me to her yoga class. Time and again, friends had tried to get me out in the world, but I'd always put them off. Remaining the hermit was easier. As asked, Shanene 'tried again later', and I did join her class. I'd never done yoga before, so it wasn't jaded territory. Perhaps it was the commitment to my own health, but I could feel it was a turning point for me. Weekly yoga has been part of my life ever since.

Medication changeovers can be tough, and I was apprehensive. The akathisia had been horrific. I had no idea I'd have to be off all medications for 14 days before starting the new one. At the end of the fortnight with no medication, I decided to try not to start the new med – my ultimate aim, to come off them altogether.

It'd take six months for the medication to clear out of my system. *Batten down the hatches.*

27 November 2011

At Byron Bay, Aunty Jo, Becky and I visited a crystal shop where I discovered an open Tarot deck for customers to pull a card. I spread them carefully, then pulled one that was dark and scary-looking. It was about my anxiety, and really showed my fear. I made myself see as much as I could – the fear of what I was going through, the medication change, as well as facing this demon – my fear itself. It showed too, my hiding myself from the world, for the world's sake as well as my own. I'm hoping that looking at the scary anxiety card was enough 'coming face-to-face with' it – just *seeing* how I felt about it – for me to experience, and that I don't have to actually do it as tough as I've feared over the coming months.

Medication withdrawal seemed to come in waves.

For six months I hated the world and everyone in it. A *lot* of people irritated me. The yoga did help get me back into my body, but six months later, I wasn't much better. My cousin Ian, who'd eventually come off his antidepressants years before, said it took about two years before he felt like his former self again. This sounded more accurate to me. I took heart in this realism, and ploughed on.

Anhedonia, an inability to experience pleasure, happens via a physiological mechanism in the brain that switches off and says, *'You won't know pleasure now'.* My libido had dropped to zero (*I hated men too*) and music had left my life. I stopped playing the piano, and listening to CDs, or music while driving. Cousin Ian, Bachelor of Music Education, said he couldn't really connect with music when he was on his medication either. *He came through it,* I'd remind myself, but recovery – through multiple losses – looked like a long hellish lifetime away for me.

The only person in the whole world who didn't have the option, metaphorical or literal, of deserting me was me, and I'd lost sight of my light in all that darkness. Heading in a healthier direction seemed automatic; I hoped, but didn't expect, to recover greatly again.

13 March 2012

I thought I'd 'come back to the world' when I felt healed from my griefs, but it's turning out that the process of coming back into the world is healing me. Music's seeping back in, doing its bit. I couldn't connect with it the last few years, stopped playing the piano (so did Ash); music wasn't getting through anyway. It's unfortunately true what people say: the heart can shut down in grief. It obviously needed to.

How I felt about God and spirituality had left me with Complex Post Traumatic Stress Disorder. *What use is it to me if I can choose which clothes I wear for the day if I can't choose whether my children live or die?* A severe type of learned helplessness with an array of difficult overgeneralising symptoms, where I felt like a sitting duck, at the mercy of whatever/whoever decides what happened in my life, C-PTSD was rarer than normal PTSD, harder to recover from, and often stayed the distance. Remnants of it occasionally still hover.

14 March 2012

I've been a child of Israel, wondering around lost in the desert for 40 years. I know I couldn't have been anywhere else, nor done it any differently. I needed to hold people at a distance, people who couldn't see where I was and how hard it was for me, while I was so vulnerable. I don't feel as exposed now, and something's happening to my sight – showing me the goodness in life I used to see, that I haven't been *able* to see for so long, the goodness I thought had just 'gone'. Things I'd given up on are surfacing again for my reappraisal, and I'm feeling surprisingly unconditional towards them. I don't know what's doing this, but it feels right and I'm going with it.

Accepting that anxiety might linger after I'd recovered from the SSRIs, an *Attacking Anxiety* audio course brought concepts for me to consider, like self-talk and positive thinking. Turning up the volume, I was surprised to find my self-talk still quite negative. I needed to learn what gentle self-talk about *anything* felt like, and how to practice it. This is something I continue to do.

But it was the audio on *Positive Thinking* that really stopped me in my tracks. I hadn't liked the invitation of PT to avoid the painful parts asking for my attention, but now it was challenging me as a possible obstacle in my recovery from anxiety. It was speaking to a fundamental part in my thinking, the part that allowed my enquiring mind to go *wherever* it wanted, to 'leave no stone unturned', irrespective of whether or not that landed me in treacherous terrain.

After two years, I conceded that I needed to take responsibility for keeping myself afloat – stable, mentally and emotionally, in a balanced relationship with my inner and outer worlds – alongside whatever had happened to me. Sometimes a *positive approach* manifested as exercising my will in my effort to stay here, and my determination to create a decent life. The popular CBT (Cognitive Behaviour Therapy) is not my therapy of choice, does not address my deeper issues, but I accepted that each approach had its place in my psyche's function. It was helpful to remind myself that the brain is plastic, that change is possible. My emotions need their space, but my mind is not their enemy. Awareness, groundedness, integration, balance – are all important concepts to me.

When my two years off anti-anxiety meds was over, I was very glad to finally have my memory and brain function back again. Another suggestion from the audio course was meditation, something I hadn't practised for years. I added that to the list.

James-the-counsellor who worked with Narrative Therapy, expressed curiosity about 'the alternative story' – the one that's *not* problem-laden, that knows our positive qualities, that usually gets drowned out when life overwhelms us. James' suggestion of 'turning up the volume' on the alternative story is one I still take.

In 2014, I turned a corner. I don't know what was motivating me to push so hard, except that pride and determination can be lifesaving qualities. Minding my boss's business while he was in the US for three months, I started getting up at 6:30 in the mornings and jogging, doing a half-hour meditation before work, and taking weekly piano lessons. I was chuffed that I could get myself this far back to normality. My anxiety had brought on both daytime and night-time bruxism (*teeth-grinding*), which was exacerbated by my anti-anxiety medication (the SSRI) and its increase. In August I flew to Thailand and spent a fortnight getting my teeth crowned.

That 'should've' been it. I 'should've' been back on the straight and narrow. But years in *grief survival* weren't going to surrender their habits without even more concerted effort from me. Getting through a loss short term is different to getting through it long term; different skills are needed. Survival skills had kept me alive, but when I no longer wanted to merely 'survive', remaining shut off as I had in my bubble, to recognise that I could challenge myself forward was another step. These strides are almost as central to my progress as the initial years of deep grief immediately after my children's deaths. I'm still discovering grief survival skills I adopted in the Valley; I challenge myself about them if I feel I need to, on my good days.

30 August 2016
I saw that I'm bringing back some of my selves... as though I'm living myths. This year's brought steps in an interesting direction. To be able

to trust myself in the moment again now is amazing, after so much time in the coma. To walk out of the Valley takes a thousand steps, a different process to being *in* the Valley, an allowing of very different aspects of me.

I've been angry with God/my soul for my children's deaths, for all my pain; I cut myself off in distrust, turned it inward over these years. Stopped following the process. Shrunk my world. Don't move. Don't breathe. Don't interact, or cause a ripple that risks crumbling the house of cards again.

Dr Furrows' words felt like a challenge to me. 'It's good that you've kept yourself safe all this time. You've needed that, and I think you've done a really good job at looking after yourself. I remember that wild person from before Allie died, who was quite hedonistic. I think in some ways it's a pity that all you've been *able* to be is the 'Good Girl' since then. I haven't seen the wild one in many years.' Something about it struck me as sad, like a grief on my own behalf, as though we were reminiscing about an affectionately loved part of me who'd died. In being the *Good Girl*, I was punishing my wildness and individuality as the internalised scapegoat.

Five years after Allie's death, my bright bubbly cousin, a senior flight attendant, would sometimes overnight on the Gold Coast. She'd invite me to stay in her hotel room, insisting I bring my Tarot deck with me. It'd been many years since I'd read for anyone. I was cynical, bereaved, still holding spiritual matters at arm's length, but Bec would remain resolute about swapping Readings.

'My cards are musty…' I told her, unwrapping them from their silk.

'I half expected to see moths flying out of them!' she chuckled.

Doing Readings – 'seeing', tuning-in to, and relaying spiritual truths – connected me to my core, centred me. Several times a year, we'd have these visits, and slowly, relentlessly, Becky's shared spirituality through her love and good will began to rejuvenate my flailing faith in *something*, to encourage me forward with visions of a better future. She was helping return a 'spirituality' to me.

A former-Reader girlfriend implored me to buy a 'spiritual' book. Bibliotherapy had been another support through my griefs, but 'spirituality' remained shady territory. 'But this one's a *bad* boy,' Maree urged.

30 July 2015

'Maree, I can't thank you enough for "Billy Fingers". He returns a space to me I used to live in. I don't know if anyone knows how dead I've been these past years.'

I saw tonight that you have to stretch yourself to believe, 'leap with faith', that faith is a spiritual strengthener, and that you get strength from taking that leap that you wouldn't get if you just acquired the knowledge.

27 March 2018

I'm not as afraid of my psyche as I was before I went into my grief for Simon. There was so much terror at not giving enough room to my grief, fear that my psyche would try to trick me, that it was like a malevolent force – 'the devil' – wanting to see my downfall if I didn't stay awake enough, grieve enough, or grieve 'the right way' – rather than trying to look after me.

I was able to retrieve some of my spiritual beliefs, although knowing absolute truths doesn't seem as vital to me now, my *conviction* about them not as necessary. As I've watched, parenting and aging have probably played their part too.

Turning a corner did not feel possible from inside the Valley. I saw in others at TCF that it's when you stand still and look back that you see you're not in the same place you'd been, that you've made 'progress'.

By late 2016, through sessions with Dr Furrows, I'd asked the bravest questions of myself, excavated as deeply as I'd wanted, and finally felt as though I'd left no stones unturned. Deep inside, something was shifting: grieving was losing its vigour for me. *I was getting sick of it!* I began to feel a great release of energy, and like busting out – celebrating all I'd survived.

As I stepped back and watched, my book began writing me.

Addressing Anhedonia

For many years Readers had tried to tell me I'd have a man in my life again. *What would I do with a man snoring and farting in my bed?* I'd retort. 'Well,' I tried to reason with myself, 'maybe a part of you knows things current Denny doesn't; maybe she's got something lined up for you that'd be good for you?' *Ha! Novel thought indeed!*

I'd hated men. Yet I knew that whatever 'healing' lay ahead for me would be incomplete if I didn't address that hatred. A heavy energy to carry, I acknowledged it didn't contain the whole truth.

So I began, bit by bit, to drip-feed myself against my own cynicism – reluctantly, because it'd been protecting me – but I also believed continued 'healing' was the only direction that'd make sense of all my pain. I *wanted* to be on better terms with the outside world.

It was not about gender. The point was being *able* to experience lightness and pleasure again, to allow myself to accept its nourishment, to value it, and believe that I deserved it. I'd spent so long allowing my grief, it was quite an ask to allow the pleasure, in addition.

Like stepping stones across a monstrous frozen pond, I headed the only way that made sense. As though starting again, I let myself crush on lovely but inaccessible men on the other side of the world; and watched as the surface slowly thawed.

Each year, stories of my US boss's awesome Halloween parties had reached me second-hand. I put together a gothic masked costume and accepted his next invitation. The party *was* awesome! All night long, a vaguely familiar but old experience: a good-looking young man was hitting on me, hard. It left an impression. I used it, *catapulted*, and watched as I started to exit the Valley. *Was the hatred beginning to dissolve?*

From hermit status, my social calendar suddenly filled with parties every weekend, from October till Christmas. More incredible was that I had the energy for them. I *wanted* to celebrate.

A new year, and I was able to look at a dating site. It'd been twenty years since I'd dated; I was shocked at men my age! *I don't look that old?* I kept scrolling profiles, but couldn't make the adjustment. So I uploaded my profile pic, typed overhead in capitals, 'COUGAR (20-35-year-olds only; do NOT message me if you are over 40)' – and underwent a crash course in online dating. Having joined Facebook only five months earlier, the abbreviated form of communication was a challenge. There wasn't much space in those short sentences to sort the wheat from the chaff. I enjoyed mastering the new interactions, squeezing my sarcasm and wit into brief phrases, learning to read people between the words they chose – but what was really heartening was the lack of chauvinism I found amongst the young men. I was 56, and met with only younger men, in person and online from all over the world, ranging in age from 20 to 47.

14 May 2017

The young men are much easier to deal with, and are teaching me a lot, probably because I trust them more, and let them.

I don't know how we managed to keep it as light as we did for as long as we did, with the almost 20-year age difference, except that local BobbyDazzla was a bit older for his years, I was a bit younger by then, and we both did our own thinking. Free spirits who loved the night, we partied up and down the Gold Coast blowing off steam together for nearly two years. Dazzla's spontaneous and obliging company gave me permission to relax and spoil myself. Maintaining a certain distance, which we both needed to handle past wounds, gave us breathing space and kept it fresh. In this casual 'refuge', we made a safe place for us, and didn't damage each other. Dazz was a good man – trustworthy, considerate, with a lot of integrity – just what I needed – and I lightened up and learnt to have fun again. My anhedonia was addressed: tick that box. From his thoughtfulness towards me, I learnt to be thoughtful towards myself, and discovered I was finally capable of living on a lighter level inside myself. A fabulous toyboy, he made me laugh a lot, and I repaired broken trust. We accepted it as temporary, but as a 'transitional arrangement', it was of untold value.

I realise we don't 'finish' grieving the ones we love, but sometimes you hit stretches when you just feel like seeing what other plateaus you can reach, and like growing in other directions as a person. Catapulting out of the Valley *was* possible for me. The moments of sadness for my children that continue to visit are the flipside to loving them. I accept this. When life threatens to overwhelm me, I remember where I've been and what I've survived, and the threat often takes a different perspective, shrinking next to where I've been. In most moments, I thankfully discover I've grieved 'enough'.

Bit by bit I 'come back to the world' in my own time, on my own terms, as the energy avails itself to me – bringing all my children with me. The spirituality awaiting has been interesting, exciting – a lot more awakening going on. It's heartening to me that people are being more real with each other, that finding pockets of belonging is possible, that we can contribute to the world in positive ways, from the inside out, that make a difference.

From my front porch one night recently, I was expressing gratitude into the night for simple details... *Thank you for the beautiful fireplace, the beautiful yard, the clean ceilings I'm looking at today, thank you for this peaceful existence out here in this green valley, thank you Denny, for looking after me...* And I realised that, when we talk about learning to love the human, I think my human needed to love my higher self again, soul, god within, whatever you wanna call it. When I felt that – that the unconditional loving needed to go both ways, from soul to human, *and* human to soul – I felt that loving my soul unconditionally means *accepting its reasons,* whatever they may be, without necessarily knowing what they are. It's been very hard learning to live with my big questions unanswered. But wanting to be at peace with my soul like that – to be able to trust it, not be cynical about it, to come full circle from a childhood of loving an external God, surviving a life like mine, to loving my human, and then my internal god – was encouraging to me.

A year ago, on my PC I began a dialogue between Denny and her Soul. I open the doc when I need to update inside myself. Denny changes; her Soul does too. *'Conversation'* is unrushed, honest, to-the-point, and raw. In writing this book, I felt compelled to come to an amicable conclusion between them, but am glad to report that Denny won't be bullied by an internalised god into 'resolving' her spiritual space about her lifetime of suffering.

Conversation is ongoing.

~

'Learning to grieve well must begin with the self. There are ruins in each of us, a place where 'what once was' lives on like an echo, haunting the landscape of our lives with its weathered foundations. Abandoned, scavenged, and dismantled by time, The Ruin is the holiest place in our heart. It is the ways in which we have been broken that have earned us a place to stand. It is in our life's absences that a wild longing is born. This ruined place is a temple in which to worship, to throw down our grief and our forgetting, and praise what remains. After all, these remains are the evidence of how greatly we have loved, and they should be venerated as the legacy of survival that they are.'

***Excerpt from Belonging: Remembering Ourselves Home
by Toko-pa Turner, Her Own Room Press © 2017***

APPENDIX A

Chapter 10 – *Catapulting Out of the Valley*

Definitions

Hypothyroid bouts – slow metabolism, lethargy, depression (2004–ongoing)

Hyperthyroid bouts – fast metabolism, sleeplessness, anxiety (2004–ongoing)

Complex Grief – grieving for 'too long', more likely with multiple losses (2008–2016)

Agoraphobia – fear of leaving your safe environment (like home) (2003–2016)

Anhedonia – inability to experience pleasure (2010–2017)

Generalised Anxiety Disorder – excessive exaggerated worry, irritability, catastrophising (2005–ongoing)

Social Anxiety Disorder – significant fear in social situations, irritability (2004–ongoing)

Panic Disorder – unexpected repeated panic attacks (2009–2010)

Akathisia – inner restlessness, anxiety, sense of terror, panic attacks, insomnia, suicidality (2010–2011)

Bruxism – teeth grinding (2010–2014)

Complex Post Traumatic Stress Disorder – 'lack of control', learned helplessness through repetitive, prolonged trauma involving sustained abuse in interpersonal relationship/s with an uneven power dynamic (2008–ongoing)

Complex PTSD
Cause: 'Free will', a big concept in my upbringing, lost its value in my losses. I'd felt done-to, expendable, helpless that there was nothing I could do to stop the onslaught of the huge events impacting my life so fully and permanently, that I could not trust God/the Life-force to spare me any more suffering.

Symptom: Learned helplessness, makes me feel I have to put up with situations I don't like.

Symptom: I couldn't be around people. All these years, I've visited my parents of a Sunday afternoon for a game of scrabble. They missed my children too, felt deeply for me, and were relieved to do *something* to support me. They've held a lot of respectful space for me in my grief. The Sunday visits have been a comfort both ways.

Valuing my will is something I'm picking up again in my journey, as the C-PTSD continues being addressed. I appreciate 'will' in my thoughts and intentions, which helps move me forward, helps me pick up momentum again, and observe that choice could become valuable and relevant in my life again.

Anhedonia
According to healthline.com symptom*s* include:
- social withdrawal
- a lack of relationships or withdrawal from previous relationships
- negative feelings toward yourself and others
- reduced emotional abilities, including having less verbal or nonverbal expressions
- difficulty adjusting to social situations
- a tendency toward showing fake emotions, such as pretending you're happy at a wedding
- a loss of libido or a lack of interest in physical intimacy
- persistent physical problems, such as being sick often *(the only one that didn't fit me)*.

Anhedonia may also occur due to a large amount of stress or anxiety in your life.

Other risk factors include:
- a recent traumatic or stressful event. Females are also at an increased risk for anhedonia.

APPENDIX B

Chapter 10 – *Catapulting Out of the Valley*

Akathisia Diary

5 Oct 2010: Started taking an increase in my anti-anxiety medication. Felt better initially...

17 Oct 2010: Have an appointment with the endocrinologist in just over a week, to see if less Thyroxin has sent me into hypothyroid – which I think it has – I'm in its depression.

26 Oct 2010: Thyroid function test levels show thyroid is okay.

22 Nov 2010: Teary, awful brain fog; still agoraphobic.

> *All my doctors are taking a month off over Christmas and will be uncontactable.*

10 Dec 2010: Haven't been sleeping well; a 'simmering desperation' underneath; bruxism (teeth grinding); daily heart palpitations; nightmares about my children dying, trying desperately to resuscitate them.

24 Dec 2010: Feels as though I'm heading into hyperthyroid again, as though I'm starting to get heart palpitations, tightness of breath, my sleep's starting to get broken again; as soon as I wake in the night, my thoughts have sprung to life and my body tenses without me realising it.

30 Dec 2010: Heart palpitations waking me in the night; sleeplessness; poor concentration.

> *Daily heart palpitations for months on end – very distressing.*

6 Jan 2011: Another panic attack today rippled on for four hours.

8 Jan 2011: Breathlessness, heart palpitations, vision disturbances, another panic attack, systemic itching, sleeplessness – all gifts of a thyroid imbalance (diagnosis still a month away) – the best of which is that my much-enjoyed intellect has predeceased me.

11 Jan 2011: Increasing heart palpitations, dreadful sleep, breathlessness, poor concentration, terrible memory, other panicky symptoms. It felt thyroid-related to me. David said before Christmas that he thought it was biochemical, which relieved me greatly to think it's not poor self-management of my anxiety.

17 Jan 2011: Before he left, David suggested I could increase my Luvox to 150mg, but instead, I stopped taking the extra 25mg suggested and reduced it to 100mg again. Having done that for a week, I haven't been dreaming that I've lost another child, and have felt a little better in myself. Too many other variables that could affect this have not been controlled (e.g. thyroid), so who knows? But I'm staying on the 100mg for now.

19 Jan 2011: 'Poor health in itself is demoralising without having anything additional to deal with', my aunt said today.

27 Jan 2011: Feels like a fucking nervous breakdown, and has ever since my thyroid was under question late last year, considering that anxiety, and all the ruminative thinking that comes with it in its extreme state, can precipitate a mental illness. Critic is having a field day.

8 Feb 2011: Diagnosed yesterday with AKATHISIA. All those months I felt so shocking then was not thyroid-related, as it had seemed. David said last night that I seemed calmer and stronger than I had for a while. I told him I'd reduced to my old Luvox dose and it seemed to work more effectively.

Suicides have been attributed to akathisia. I'm not surprised. I didn't know how I was going to live through it.

Bibliography

Chapter 3 – *Breaking the Silence*

References

[1] Domestic Violence Prevention Centre Gold Coast Inc 2019, *Domestic Violence Statistics*, Domestic Violence Prevention Centre, Gold Coast, viewed 26 July 2019, <http://www.domesticviolence.com.au/pages/domestic-violence-statistics.php>.

[2] The National Domestic Violence Hotline 2013, *50 Obstacles to Leaving*, The National Domestic Violence Hotline, Texas, viewed 17 August 2019, <https://www.thehotline.org/2013/06/10/50-obstacles-to-leaving-1-10/>.

[3] Our Watch, *Understanding Violence: Facts and figures*, Our Watch, Melbourne, viewed 17 August 2019, <https://www.ourwatch.org.au/understanding-violence/facts-and-figures>.

[4] Mayo Clinic Staff 2017, *Domestic violence against women: Recognise patterns, seek help*, Mayo Clinic, Arizona, viewed 17 August 2019, <https://www.mayoclinic.org/healthy-lifestyle/adult-health/in-depth/domestic-violence/art-20048397>.

[5a] Gonzalez, JM, Jetelina, KK, Olague, S & Wondrack, JG 2018, 'Violence against women increases cancer diagnoses', *Preventive Medicine,* vol. 114, pp. 168–79, viewed 17 August 2019, <https://www.sciencedirect.com/science/article/pii/S0091743518302159>.

[5b] Soccio, J, Brown, M, Comino, E & Friesen, E 2015, 'Pap smear screening, pap smear abnormalities and psychosocial risk factors among women in a residential alcohol and drug rehabilitation facility', *Journal of Advanced Nursing*, vol.71(12), pp. 2858–66, viewed 17 August 2019, <https://www.ncbi.nlm.nih.gov/pubmed/26279461>.

[6] Cook, J & Bewley, S 2008, 'Acknowledging a persistent truth: domestic violence in pregnancy', *Journal of the Royal Society of Medicine*, vol. 101(7), pp. 358–63, viewed 17 August 2019, <https://www.ncbi.nlm.nih.gov/pmc/articles/PMC2442136/>.

[7a] Mulroney, J 2003, 'Australian Statistics on Domestic Violence', *Australian Domestic and Family Violence Clearinghouse,* viewed 26 July 2019, <http://citeseerx.ist.psu.edu/viewdoc/download?doi=10.1.1.453.1763&rep=rep1&type=pdf>.

[7b] Fernàndez, EB, Ezpeleta, L, Granero, R, de la Osa, N & Domènech, JM, 'Degree of Exposure to Domestic Violence, Psychopathology, and Functional Impairment in Children and Adolescents', *Journal of Interpersonal Violence,* vol. 26, pp. 1215–31, viewed 26 July 2019, <https://journals.sagepub.com/doi/pdf/10.1177/0886260510368155>.

Chapter 8 – *Reflections from the Valley*

References

Grief

[1] Klass, D, Silverman, P, & Nickman, S 1996, *Continuing Bonds: New Understandings of Grief*, Routledge Taylor & Francis, New York.

[2][3] *Mourning*, Wikipedia, viewed 25 July 2019, <https://en.wikipedia.org/wiki/Mourning#cite_note-9>.

[4][5] Kearl, MC, *Personal Impacts of Death*, viewed 25 July 2019, <http://faculty.trinity.edu/mkearl/death-6.html>.

[6] American Psychiatric Association 2013, *Diagnostic and Statistical Manual of Mental Disorders*, (manual used by all registered psychiatrists).

[7] Kübler-Ross, E 2005, *On Grief and Grieving*, Simon and Schuster, UK.

[8a] Betsinger, T & Scott, A 2014, 'Governing from the Grave: Vampire Burials and Social Order in Post-medieval Poland', *Cambridge Archaeological Journal*, vol. 24(3), pp. 472–73, <https://doi.org/10.1017/S0959774314000754>.

[8b] Johnson L, May, J 2019, *A Timeline of Witch Hunts in Europe*, ThoughtCo, viewed 25 July 2019, <https://www.thoughtco.com/european-witch-hunts-timeline-3530786>.

Anorexia Nervosa

[9] Editor-in-Chief Worell J 2002, *Encyclopedia of Women and Gender: Sex Similarities and Differences and the Impact of Society on Gender*, L -Z Volume Two, pp. 792, Academic Press, San Diego, California.

[10] Blakemore, E 2018, *Psychologists Once Blamed 'Refrigerator Moms' for Their Kids' Autism*, History, viewed 25 July 2019, <https://www.history.com/news/autism-theory-refrigerator-mother>.

[11] Symonds, RL 2016, *Schizophrenia and a damaging blame game*, The Guardian, viewed 25 July 2019, <https://www.theguardian.com/society/2016/mar/13/schizophrenia-and-a-damaging-blame-game>.

[12] Brody, JE 1981, *Kinsey Study Finds Homosexuals Show Early Predisposition*, New York Times Archives, viewed 25 July 2019, <https://www.nytimes.com/1981/08/23/us/kinsey-study-finds-homosexuals-show-early-predisposition.html>.

[13] Dembo, MH & Vaughn, W 1989, 'Effects of Mother Presence and Absence on LD Children's and Their Mothers' Causal Attributions for Performance Outcomes', *Learning Disability Quarterly,* vol. 12 (3), pp. 199–207.

[14a] Guitar, B & Marchinkoski, L 2001, 'Influence of Mothers' Slower Speech on Their Children's Speech Rate', *Journal of Speech, Language and Hearing Research*, vol. 44 (4), pp.853–61.

[14b] DeNoon, DJ 2001, *A Biological Basis for Stuttering*, Web MD, viewed 25 July 2019, <https://www.webmd.com/brain/news/20010723/biological-basis-for-stuttering#1>.

[15] Editor-in-Chief Worell J 2002, *Encyclopedia of Women and Gender: Sex Similarities and Differences and the Impact of Society on Gender*, L -Z Volume Two, pp. 789, Academic Press, San Diego, California.

[16][17][18] Webster, B 2014-2018, *Why it's Crucial for Women to Heal the Mother Wound*, Bethany Webster, viewed 25 July 2019, <https://www.womboflight.com/about-the-mother-wound>.

[19] Brown, J 2018, *Grounded Spirituality*, Enrealment Press, Ontario.

[20] Thomas, E 2012, 'President Obama Disproves the "Broken Home Theory"', *Huffpost*, viewed 25 July 2019, <https://www.huffpost.com/entry/single-parent-households_b_1616509>.

[21] Insel, T 2013, 'Toward a new Understanding of Mental Illness', video, *TED*, viewed 25 July 2019, <https://www.ted.com/talks/thomas_insel_toward_a_new_understanding_of_mental_illness/transcript?language=en]>.

[22] Howell, M 2019, 'Genes linked to anorexia nervosa identified in study involving Queensland scientists', *ABC*, viewed 25 July 2019, <https://www.abc.net.au/news/2019-07-16/anorexia-linked-to-metabolism-genetics-qld-researchers-find/11310320>.

[23] Silverman, LK 1999, 'Perfectionism: the Crucible of Giftedness', *Advanced Development*, vol. 8, pp. 47-61, <http://citeseerx.ist.psu.edu/viewdoc/download?doi=10.1.1.699.5032&rep=rep1&type=pdf>.

[24] Shaffer, D & Pfeffer, C 2001, 'Practice Parameters for the Assessment and Treatment of Children and Adolescents with Suicidal Behaviour' *Journal American Academy Child and Adolescent Psychiatry*, vol. 40 (7), pp. 24S–51S.

Suicide

[25][45][50] Alexander, V 1998 *In the Wake of Suicide: Stories of the People Left Behind*, Jossey-Bass Publishers, San Francisco.

[26][28][30][33][49] 2019, 'Felo de se', *Wikipedia*, viewed 25 July 2019, <https://en.wikipedia.org/wiki/Felo_de_se>.

[27] Marks, A 2003 *Handbook of Death & Dying*, chapter 31: Historical Suicide, *Sage Knowledge*, viewed 25 July 2019, <https://sk.sagepub.com/reference/death/n31.xml>.

[29][44] Ingram, AM 1998, 'The Dearly Not-Quite Departed: Funerary Rituals and Beliefs about the Dead in Ukrainian Culture', University of Virginia, Minnesota, pp. 127–32.

[31][34][38][40] Betsinger, T & Scott, A 2014, 'Governing from the Grave: Vampire Burials and Social Order in Post-medieval Poland', Cambridge Archaeological Journal, vol. 24 (3), pp. 468–72, <https://doi.org/10.1017/S0959774314000754>.

[35][41][43][45] Keyworth, GD 2011, 'The undead – an unnatural history of vampires and troublesome corpses in Western Europe from the medieval period to the twentieth century', *ResearchGate*, viewed 25 July 2019,

<https://www.researchgate.net/publication/43495514_The_undead_an_unnatural_history_of_vampires_and_troublesome_corpses_in_Western_Europe_from_the_medieval_period_to_the_twentieth_century>.

[36][37][49] Barry, Hon Sir JV 1965, 'Suicide and the Law', *Melbourne University Law Review*, vol. 5, pp. 6–8, <http://www5.austlii.edu.au/au/journals/MelbULawRw/1965/1.pdf>.

[46-48] Keyworth, GD 2006, 'Was the Vampire of the Eighteenth Century a Unique Type of Undead-corpse?' *Folklore*, vol. 117 (3), pp. 249,254,256.

[51] 2019, 'suicide', *Dictionary.com*, viewed 26 July 2019, <https://www.dictionary.com/browse/suicide>.

[52] 2019, 'List of Types of Killing', *Wikipedia*, viewed 26 July 2019, <https://en.wikipedia.org/wiki/List_of_types_of_killing>.

[53] 2019, 'Discussing Death in Top Three 'Taboo' Subjects', *RiskInfo, viewed 26 July 2019*, <http://riskinfo.com.au/news/2019/05/14/discussing-death-in-top-three-taboo-subjects/>.

[54][56] Webb, D 2002, 'The Many Languages of Suicide', *Suicide Prevention Australia Conference*, viewed 26 July 2019, <http://www.jungcircle.com/DWebb.html>.

[55] Webb, D 2010, 'Suicide Prevention Australia – Newsletter', viewed 15 July 2010.

Domestic Violence

[57] Editor-in-Chief Worell J 2002, *Encyclopedia of Women and Gender: Sex Similarities and Differences and the Impact of Society on Gender*, L -Z Volume Two, pp. 789, Academic Press, San Diego, California.

[58a] Ward, CL Flisher, AJ, Zissis, C, Muller, M, Lombard, C 2019, 'Exposure to violence and its relationship to psychopathology in adolescents', BMJ Publishing Group Ltd, London, <https://injuryprevention.bmj.com/content/7/4/297>.

[58b] 2002, Domestic Violence and its Impact on Children's Development, edited version of presentation delivered at the Department of Community Services' Fourth Domestic Violence Forum held at the NSW Parenting Centre, Old Bidura House Ballroom, Glebe, viewed on 17 August 2019, <https://www.facs.nsw.gov.au/__data/assets/pdf_file/0005/321638/dv_paper.pdf>.

[58c] McDonald, SE, Shin, S, Corona, R, Maternick, A, Graham-Bermann, SA, Ascione, FR, Williams, JH 2016, 'Children Exposed to Intimate Partner Violence: Identifying differential effects of family environment on children's trauma and psychopathology symptoms through regression mixture models', *Child Abuse and Neglect*, vol. 58, pp. 1–11.

[58d] Matthias, J, Mertin, P & Murray, A 1995, 'The psychological functioning of children from backgrounds of domestic violence', *Australian Psychologist*, March 1995, vol. 30 (1), pp. 47–56.

[58e] Bedi, G & Goddard, C 2007, 'Intimate partner violence: What are the impacts on children?', *Australian Psychologist*, vol. 42 (1), pp. 66–77.

[59a] 'How are Different Forms of Violence Interrelated?', Preventing and Reducing School Violence, Fact Sheet #6 – Interrelationships, *Prevention Institute*, viewed on 26 July 2019, <https://www.preventioninstitute.org/sites/default/files/publications/How%20are%20different%20forms%20of%20violence%20interrelated.pdf>.

[59b] Donziger, S 1996, *The Real War on Crime: The Report of the National Criminal Justice Commission*, HarperCollins Publishers, New York.

[60a] Mulroney, J 2003, 'Australian Statistics on Domestic Violence', *Australian Domestic and Family Violence Clearinghouse*, viewed on 26 July 2019, <http://citeseerx.ist.psu.edu/viewdoc/download?doi=10.1.1.453.1763&rep=rep1&type=pdf>.

[60]b Fernàndez, EB, Ezpeleta, L, Granero, R, de la Osa, N, Domènech, JM 2010, 'Degree of Exposure to Domestic Violence, Psychopathology, and Functional Impairment in Children and Adolescents', *Journal of Interpersonal Violence,* vol. 26 (6), pp. 1215–1231.

[61] Strauss, MA 1999, 'Controversy over Domestic Violence by Women: a Methodological, Theoretical and Sociology of Science Analysis', *National Criminal Justice Reference Service,* pp. 32, viewed on 26 July 2019, <http://www.ncjrs.gov/App/publications/abstract.aspx?ID=186243>.

Acknowledgements

Laurel Dumbrell: *Still Standing* would not be here without my aunt, who's published books on the writing process, and tutored writing groups across twenty years in Sydney and its Sutherland Shire. Tears have been cried on this book journey, frustrations voiced, hopes shared, laughter enjoyed. Thank you Aunty Laurel, for being the book's guardian, a loving great aunt to my children through *all your help*, and my personal encourager.

Child & Adolescent Psychiatrist Dr David Furrows: You've been a foundational constant and great stability since the day Allie and I met you. Your direct and indirect input into this book is immeasurable, David. Thank you for facilitating many years more with my daughter, for being a king pin in my life, for helping to keep me on the planet, and for the past two decades of your professional love and utmost care.

Stuart Denman, Ultimate World Publishing: I learnt a good trick in the Valley. Sometimes you can hitch a vital ride with someone else's energy without knowing their beliefs on life. Trusting your intuition is the conduit. I'd tried for over a decade to produce this book on my own, and had no idea how *anyone* could mentor it out of me - but you did, Stu. Congratulations for being great at your job.

Natasa Denman, Ultimate World Publishing: Your Facebook ad intercepted my path in an interconnected moment, offering me exactly what I needed. Driven, hard-working, efficient, the dynamo who drew me in, you run an invaluable business, Nat. By creating the key to unlock the publishing door, you help so many more authors' messages reach the world to benefit the masses.

DISCLAIMER

While this is a book of memories, I've done my best to impart my life's stories truthfully. In writing to help educate, I've changed some names to respect the privacy of those whose recollections may differ. As many accounts have been reconstructed from documentation in my journals, the perspectives shared in this memoir are mine. If reading them triggers painful memories or creates distress, please seek support from a trusted friend, professional, group or helpline.

www.ingramcontent.com/pod-product-compliance
Lightning Source LLC
Chambersburg PA
CBHW021143080526
44588CB00008B/192